PROPHETS IN THE LOCAL CHURCH

By the same author:

Come, Holy Spirit
Does God Speak Today?
Some Said It Thundered

PROPHECY IN THE LOCAL CHURCH

A Practical Handbook
and
Historical Overview

David Pytches

HODDER AND STOUGHTON
LONDON SYDNEY AUCKLAND

British Library Cataloguing in Publication Data
A catalogue record for this book
is available from the British Library.

ISBN 0-340-59566-3

Published by Hodder and Stoughton,
a division of Hodder and Stoughton Ltd,
Mill Road, Dunton Green, Sevenoaks, Kent TN13 2YA
Editorial Office: 47 Bedford Square, London WC1B 3DP

Typeset by Hewer Text Composition Services, Edinburgh
Printed in Great Britain by Cox & Wyman Ltd, Reading.

DEDICATION

This book is dedicated to Bishop Brian Skinner, my long-standing friend of two continents and over twenty years of working together.

His constant cheerfulness and sense of humour through serious crises together, not excluding earthquakes, revolutions and his failing eyesight; his gift for articulating my point of view with far greater clarity and charity than I could ever do myself and his simultaneous presentation of the views of others who might disagree with equal clarity and charity, has made him a most valued counsellor.

His ingenuity, which I first observed in his raising of a fine herd of pedigree pigs from a poorly marked sow going cheap, has made him a very creative co-worker.

His ability to face my impossibles and prove that they were still possible after all – admirably demonstrated by his stripping down and reassembling a Land-Rover diesel engine in his own backyard in Chile (after three garages had failed to find the fault without failing to charge a fortune) – has made him a wonderful neighbour.

His vision and skill in getting on computer just about everything at St Andrew's, Chorleywood, that could be programmed; his patience, tirelessness and compassion for people pastorally, and above all his resolute faith, his absolute integrity, along with his utter humility and commitment to Jesus Christ, has made for a relationship which I have enjoyed immensely and treasured richly.

I thank God for you, Brian.

ACKNOWLEDGMENTS

I would like to thank the staff of St Andrew's for encouraging me to write this little book. I am also grateful to Bishop Graham Dow, Mrs Prue Bedwell, Mrs Hilary Sogovsky, Mr Michael Pilavachi, Canon John Gunstone, the Rev. Barry Kissell, the Rev. David Parker, the Rev. Robert Hope, the Rev. Dr Mark Stibbe, the Rev. Dr Max Turner, the Rev. Dr Christopher Cocksworth, the Rev. Dr Peter Pytches, and lastly but by no means least, to Mary, my wife. They have all read parts of the manuscript and furnished me with their constructive suggestions and criticisms. This has been greatly appreciated. None of them has read the whole manuscript and none can therefore be held responsible for any of the views expressed in this book. That responsibility has to be mine alone. I must also acknowledge a debt of gratitude to Miss Carolyn Armitage, the religious editor, and Mrs Bryony Bénier, editorial assistant of religious books, both at Hodder and Stoughton, for their wisdom and encouragement in the preparation of this book.

There are many sources referred to in this book, though often the original material has been paraphrased to leave the reader with the essential idea. Some of those cited apparently have well-recognised gifting in prophecy. The fact that these sources are acknowledged in no way implies that the author necessarily identifies with everything else which may have been written or (has been reported as being) said by them.

CONTENTS

Introduction 1

PART 1: PROPHECY TODAY

1 Is there a biblical case for prophecy today? 7

2 What do we mean by prophecy and prophets? 10

3 What kind of a person is a prophet? 28

4 How can we learn to be prophets? 31

5 How is prophetic gifting initiated? 45

6 How is prophecy received from God? 51

7 How is prophecy analysed? 76

8 How is prophecy relayed? 83

9 How is prophecy evaluated? 95

10 How is prophecy managed in the local church? 102

11 Practicalities for public worship 110

12 What about church order? 117

13 Towards a better theology 127

PART 2: PROPHECY YESTERDAY

14 Prophecy in the early Church 149

15 Prophecy during the Dark Ages 162

16 The French prophets   169
17 The German prophets   176
18 The Ranters   183
19 The Quakers   197
20 The classic case of Edward Irving   213
21 Revelation and mysticism   223
22 Prophecy and ecstasy   240
23 Religious experience validated   252
24 What about second sight?   266
25 Do non-Christians receive revelation from God?   274
26 Forbidden fruit for prophets   279

Conclusion   293
Appendix: Revelation and the human brain   295
Notes   303
Bibliography   317

INTRODUCTION

The gentle sarcasm of Charles Dickens as he introduces his *A Tale of Two Cities*[1] is beguiling indeed:

> It was the year of Our Lord one thousand seven hundred and seventy-five. Spiritual revelations were conceded to England at that favoured period, as at this. Mrs Southcott had recently attained her five-and-twentieth blessed birthday of whom a prophetic private in the Life Guards had heralded the sublime appearance by announcing that arrangements were made for the swallowing up of London and Westminster.

One of the obvious concerns for those wishing to promote the practice of prophecy in the Church is the naiveté and gullibility of certain church members. They take everything, including themselves, so seriously. In a healthy church people do need to have a good laugh at themselves sometimes. The task ahead is a serious one, and the Lord must always be taken seriously, but Solomon was so right when he said that 'a merry heart doeth good like a medicine'. A church will never grow in prophetic gifting where there is no space for some humour when mistakes occur, as they inevitably will. No man or woman is infallible – certainly not a prophet. We have met a number who have been greatly used of God in prophecy, but we do not know of one who has not been wrong about a prophecy at one time or another.

False prophets are always fair game for scorn and

a proper focus for scrutiny. Reflecting on the tragic happenings in the Branch Davidian cult in Waco, Texas, Bishop Michael Marshall makes a comment in the *Church of England Newspaper* for March 19th, 1993. He writes: 'All we know is that David Koresh [their wounded leader] believes that God tells him what to do and how to do it, down to the last detail. Yes, that little phrase "The Lord told me" lies at the heart of the most bizarre and dangerous distortions of all religion.' We cannot deny the dangers of prophecy, any more than we can deny the dangers of electricity. Pretence at having a divine revelation in order to acquire some significance among one's fellow beings is just as serious a fault as the dial-a-prophet syndrome in the lazy Christian who seeks the blessings of the Christian life without the discipline of a living relationship with God.

But while there are dangers of false revelations, there are the more serious dangers of no revelation at all. This is all the more tragic once it is understood that God really does want to communicate with us. Paul prayed earnestly for the church that the brethren might have the Spirit of revelation (Eph. 1:17). John addressed the same church (and gave the same charge to six other churches) saying, 'He who has an ear, let him hear what the Spirit says to the churches' (Rev. 2:7).

Ninety years ago, just after his return from India where he had been the Metropolitan Bishop, J. E. C. Welldon made an observation, in his book *The Revelation of the Holy Spirit*, which is very pertinent for our churches today. He wrote:

In all the Christian Church, and in the Roman Catholic Church as much as elsewhere, truth has ascended from the lower regions to the higher; it has sprung up in some humble cell or distant valley; it has been despised and eschewed, and even persecuted; it has fought its way to credit and honour; and only at last, after many days, has it received the stamp of official consecration.[2]

As with truth so with life. It moves from the grass-roots upward rather than from the brass-hats downward. Change in the Church begins at the local church level. Prophets are the major agents for change. We must train them, release them and listen to them.

John Zizioulas has said that 'the Church was instituted by Christ in the past but it needs to be constituted by the Spirit in the present.' The Moscow statement of the 1977 Anglican Orthodox Dialogue also made the point that 'the Church lives by the continual invocation of the Holy Spirit.'

How long can we go on saying and hearing the right things without doing anything about it? Our congregations certainly need a dynamic communication from God today, for knowing and doing his will. The prophetic voice of the Lord is available to those God knows will listen and obey. No local church can be doing everything. No church can and no church is meant to. But each church can seek to find out what the will of the Lord is for it in its own locality and beyond. As we all, individually and corporately, seek to hear and to do what the Spirit is telling us, then the Lord's glorious purposes will be accomplished on earth as they are in heaven.

Today we live in a climate of much ignorance and prejudice about prophecy. Hopefully the material in this book will be enough to convince the reader from Scripture that, in spite of a myriad abuses, God still does speak in this way. Hopefully the reader will be encouraged to seek, and experience, the gift of prophecy.

The first part of the book, 'Prophecy Today', is a kind of handbook in teaching how to listen, how to discern, how to receive and how to use the gift of prophecy. The material here should help those leaders who, hitherto, may have felt rather out of their depth in a scenario where mistakes are unavoidable since they are an inevitable part of the learning process.

The second half of this book, 'Prophecy Yesterday',

looks back to see how the gift has been used and misused by prophetic people in history. Some may wonder why such strange material has been included but there are many good lessons to learn from that hard school of church history.

Who would willingly choose to ignore those useful lessons from the past when, otherwise, we will have to learn them through the painful process of personal experience? Any good leader developing a prophetic ministry in his church should be au fait with the failures of the past. That makes us wary, but it does not make us want to give up on prophecy altogether. How could we when we are so convinced from Scripture, and from our beneficial experience of prophecy itself, that prophecy is for today?

What has not been included here is a history of revelations in revivals which would be a very rewarding study and require a separate book. Most histories of revivals have been edited up to make them 'respectable' and, according to the special interest of the particular publishing house, have often been offered to the public as a one-sided account.

In *Prophecy Yesterday* we see a little of how the Church has so re-ordered affairs in the Body of Christ that prophecy has been suppressed as inconvenient and irrational. In doing this, however, it has cut off a vital means of communication. What army could risk that? The Church today may not be shooting itself in the foot but there is grave danger that it may be doing just that to its ear and its tongue, as the wind of the Spirit blows again and God is beginning to stir once more with his prophetic gifting.

PART ONE

PROPHECY TODAY

1

IS THERE A BIBLICAL CASE
FOR PROPHECY TODAY?

Prophecy is in the air today. Christian bookshops are plen-
tifully supplied by Christian publishers on the subject. The
secular world has its New Age prophets. We are meeting
'prophets' in the flesh who appear to have supernatural
gifting. The serious Christian cannot dodge the issue. It
is on today's agenda. Since it would seem to be a gift the
Lord intended for the Church, and many 'Bible-believing'
Christians are seeking to prophesy, we shall do well first to
look at the New Testament evidence for its justification in
the Church today. The reader can look up the references
in their biblical context and make up his or her own mind
on what to think about it all.

What Jesus said about prophecy
1 Jesus encouraged the Church to be receptive to
prophets – 'Anyone who receives a prophet because he
is a prophet will receive a prophet's reward' (Matt. 10:41)
(cf. Shunammite woman in 2 Kgs 4:8–37).

2 Jesus promised to send prophets (Matt. 23:34) (cf.
Eph. 4:11, 12).

3 Jesus warned against false prophets (Matt. 7:15) (cf.
1 John 4:1).

4 Jesus said: 'False prophets will appear to deceive the
elect' (Matt. 24:24) (cf. 2 Thess. 2:1–3).
'The presence of the counterfeit is positive evidence that
the real thing must be around.'[1]

The ascended Christ endowed the Church with prophets

1 'It was who he gave some to be apostles, some to be *prophets*', etc. (Eph. 4:11–12).

2 God has appointed *in the Church* first apostles, second *prophets*, etc. (1 Cor. 12:28).

Prophecy was a gift to be released for the last days (Acts 2:17). Prophecy is listed among the spiritual gifts (1 Cor. 12:10). Paul urged the Corinthians to seek to prophesy (1 Cor. 14:1, 39).

Paul warned the Thessalonian church not to despise prophecy (1 Thess. 5:20–1).

Active prophets are mentioned in the New Testament

1 A number of prophets are mentioned (Acts 13).

2 Agabus warns of a famine to come (Acts 11:28).

3 Judas and Silas are referred to as prophets (Acts 15:32).

4 Paul says that 'in every city the Holy Spirit warns me' (Acts 20:23).

5 Agabus warns Paul (Acts 21:10–11).

6 Philip's four daughters were prophesying (Acts 21:9).

7 A false prophet, Bar-Jesus, is dealt with (Acts 13:6–11).

8 Paul had prophecies made over him by Ananias (Acts 9:17); by other prophets (Acts 13:1–2); by other prophets (Acts 20); by Agabus (Acts 21:10, 11).

9 Paul himself received many revelations from God and exercised a prophetic ministry (Acts 27: 10, 23, 31).

10 Paul also wrote to Timothy, saying: 'Do not neglect your gift, which was given you through *a prophetic message* when the body of elders *laid their hands on you*' (1 Tim. 4:14).

11 Prophets are identified in the fall of 'Babylon', which

reflected the approaching end of the age. Babylon's ruin will be the cause for rejoicing by the prophets, who will presumably be living witnesses of that event (Rev. 18:20). The blood of prophets (presumably these are latter-day ones) within the city will also testify to their wickedness (Rev. 18:24).

Summarising the case for prophecy today

The role of the prophet and the gift of prophecy in the New Testament was promised by Christ, preached by the Apostles and practised by his disciples. Prophecy was widespread in the New Testament, involving contrasting personalities such as the cultured Silas and the rough diamond Agabus; the mystic John and the intellectual Paul. There were not only men but women too (1 Cor. 11:5), such as Philip's four daughters (Acts 21:9). We find prophets at Jerusalem, Antioch and in the churches of Asia Minor, as well as Corinth, Thessalonica and Rome.

'The near ubiquity of prophecy . . . is impressive. No matter how much a given New Testament document may attack false prophecy or seek to regulate the charisms, there is not a single instance in which the widespread phenomenon of the prophetic gifts is condemned or even questioned. It is regarded as part of the normal life.'[2]

2

WHAT DO WE MEAN BY PROPHECY AND PROPHETS?

What is prophecy?
It is an oracle (message) from God through an individual;
God's direct response to the human situation. Prophecy
is one of several 'charisms', or gifts of the Holy Spirit,
mentioned by Paul in his first letter to the Corinthians
(12:10) and elsewhere. The purpose of prophecy is to
reveal God's word and will, his truth and his purposes
to his people. This could have a wide range of meaning
since everyone is challenged to speak as it were oracles of
God (1 Pet. 4:11).

Prophecy has generally been understood to cover the
following main categories:

1 Preaching the gospel of the Kingdom of God. 'Preaching is teaching God's revealed truth with application; such
teaching with application is prophecy, [and] always was.'[1]
An example here would be the ministry of John the
Baptist.

2 'The opening and interpreting of the Word of God by
a proper gift of the Spirit for the work.'[2] Examples of this
could be the preaching of George Whitefield or Charles
Spurgeon.

3 Being a critic of the times. James Houston commends
Os Guinness: 'He is a prophetic critic of our times and
exemplifies the rigour of thought needed to critique
whether we have Christian minds in our society.'[3]

4 Speaking into social conditions. For a biblical example
see Pharaoh Neco, 2 Chr. 35:21–2. For contemporary

examples see Kenneth Slack's *Martin Luther King*[4] and David Edwards' review of *Partners in Protest* by Diana Collins, a story of life with Canon John Collins, the founder of Christian Action and the Campaign for Nuclear Disarmament. Provost Edwards concludes: 'It is not every day that God gives us a prophet, let alone two.'[5]

5 The study of the end times: comparing contemporary world happenings with Scripture.

6 Prophecy is praise: 'To praise and to know God is prophetic.'[6] See examples from Exod. 15:20–1, 1 Chr. 25:1, the Psalms of David and Acts 2:11 where Joel's words were fulfilled when he said that they 'spoke the wonderful works of God' (Joel 2:26).

A further example from church history would be Caedmon (c. 650), the Jarrow 'saint' who was regarded as the earliest English poet to receive the gift (in a vision) for praising God – through rhyme. He composed a hymn in a dream which appears in the Moore MS (8th c.) of Bede.

7 Supernatural revelation of God's will and purposes for the 'strengthening, encouragement and comfort' of God's people (cf. Amos 3:7 and 1 Cor. 14:3 – see also my book *Some Said It Thundered*).[7]

8 An oracle spontaneously inspired by the Holy Spirit and spoken in a specific situation.

It is categories (7) and (8) which primarily concern us within these pages although, as always, when trying to tidy the Holy Spirit into neat divisions, there may at times appear to be some overlapping.

What is a prophet?

1 A prophet is a person who is God's servant and his mouthpiece. Moses said, 'I am slow of speech and tongue.' The Lord said, 'Who gave man his mouth? . . . Is it not I, the Lord? Now go; I will help you speak and will teach you what to say' (Exod. 4:10–12). The Lord said, '[Aaron] will speak to the people for you, and it will be as if he were your mouth and as if you were God to him' (Exod. 4:16).

'Thus the person who prophesies is not the inventor of the words to be spoken. That person is rather the conveyor of the message. Aaron spoke what Moses told him to speak and no more. The message was Moses' message though the precise words used to convey it were Aaron's.'[8]

2 There would appear to be a difference in the New Testament between those with gifts of prophecy and those who exercise the office of a prophet. Paul seems to make the point in 1 Cor. 12:27–30, 1 Cor. 14:31, 36–8, 39, and it is exemplified in Acts 21:9–10.

But the demarcation line between the two is admittedly indistinct. A comment of Edmund Burke is applicable here: 'No man has ever been able to say exactly when twilight begins or ends, though all men can distinguish between night and day.' This is one of the realities of life that we have easily learned to live with, and we simply have to live with it concerning the prophetic ministry. We shall attempt to develop this distinction more fully below with the help of Scripture.

Differentiation in prophecy

We have made a distinction above between the prophets mentioned in the New Testament and those with simply a gift of prophecy. Not all who prophesy are called prophets in the New Testament; that is the first difference to note. We now make a further distinction, though again the precise differentiation is difficult to define. Some of the prophets mentioned in the Bible were inspired to give us the Scripture (2 Tim. 3:16) but there were others, who are called prophets, whose words were either never recorded or never considered to be of equal value to those included in the canon of Scripture.

It is possible that those prophets who did have their pronouncements incorporated in the canon may also have had other prophecies which were not. (This might solve the little problem of Mark 1:2–3 where Isaiah is cited for what is not recorded in the canon as actually coming from him!

Perhaps Isaiah said it first and this, with his other sayings, was preserved in some other Jewish collection of text relating to the Messiah that was never included in the Old Testament canon.) Some prophecy has been more highly valued than other prophecy. There seems to have been a selection process taking place, either deliberately and consciously or even unintentionally and unconsciously. Two levels could well be reflected in Scripture – one more valued, the other less valued, the latter because possibly it was not so clear: they prophesied 'in part'; they only saw 'through a glass darkly' (1 Cor. 13:9, 12 KJV). We must not overstress this 'indistinctness', however, as Paul may have understood it to apply to all prophecy.

While a two-level category of prophecy may be suggested here we should never insist upon such clear-cut distinctions. The Holy Spirit eludes systemisation. Who can say where the wind is coming from or where it is going (John 3:8)?

Some others would see the differentiation of prophecy in terms of the context in which the words were given, rather than in terms of high-level and low-level prophecy.[9]

And yet others would see a graduated authority spectrum of the prophetic ministry. Max Turner claims that Paul shows an awareness of 'rather full "authority of general content" (i.e. it has a true propositional structure)', but nowhere does Paul suggest that he is claiming 'divine authority of actual words'.[10] He suggests that the 'rather full "authority of general content"' puts the apostles at one end of an 'authority spectrum', which has at the other the 'vague and barely profitable attempts at oracular speech such as brought "prophecy" as a whole into question at Thessalonica . . . A prophet's speech might fall anywhere on the spectrum.'[11]

However we may choose to differentiate, we tentatively follow those scholars who are suggesting that in both the Old and the New Testament two prophetic levels are evident[12] and, without being bound by such a thesis, it is useful to observe its possible delineations.

High-level prophecy

Moses saw himself as a prophet. He told the people of Israel, 'The Lord your God will raise up for you a prophet like me from among your own brothers. You must listen to him' (Deut. 18:15). This of course was ultimately fulfilled in Jesus as we see in the New Testament (John 1:21; Acts 3:21–2; 7:37).

Moses' particular calling to prophecy was to be reproduced in a succession of prophets who would continue to bring God's word to his people. Moses surely believed that God was speaking through him when he said, 'I will raise up for them a prophet like you [Moses] from among their brothers; I will put my words in his mouth, and he will tell them everything I command him. If anyone does not listen to my words that the prophet speaks in my name, I myself will call him to account' (Deut. 18:18–19).

Moses viewed his own kind of prophetic ministry as bringing the actual words of God to the people, so that to ignore his prophetic message amounted to ignoring God himself. No one could lightly claim such authority for a message and the penalty of death was threatened to anyone who falsely claimed it (Deut. 18:20). Having said all this, it has to be admitted that the other canonical prophets do not necessarily fit the Moses description (Deut. 18:15).

Low-level prophecy

While the phenomenon of prophecy in the Old Testament is most often characterised by the claim to absolute authority, there are some occasions where a different type of prophecy is described as a dramatic sign of God's presence among his people. A notable example of this is found in Numbers 11:24–30, where, after the seventy elders have been appointed by Moses to help govern the people, we are told that they all prophesied together.

The primary purpose of this may not have been so much to communicate a message from God (though we do not deny that they may have done just that) but more as a sign that the Spirit of God was among them (Num. 11:25). Those who prophesied that day apparently did not do so again.[13]

But those who know the story will remember that two of the elders were not with the others in the Tent of Meeting at the time and the Spirit of God fell upon them also. They too prophesied even outside in the camp (Num. 11:26). Joshua tried to put a stop to this, thinking it some kind of a threat to Moses' authority, but Moses made the humble reply: 'Are you jealous for my sake? I wish that all the Lord's people were prophets and that the Lord would put his Spirit on them!' (Num. 11:29).

There would appear to be some similarity between the Numbers 11 episode and the 1 Samuel 10 (vv. 9–12) and 1 Samuel 19 (vv. 20–4) episodes where each time Saul prophesied, this secondary kind of prophetic anointing seemed to be operating.

When Joel predicted that prophecy would become the experience shared by God's people generally, it may well be that he was referring to this secondary type. His prophecy, quoted by Peter at Pentecost, said: 'And afterwards, I will pour out my Spirit on all people. Your sons and daughters will prophesy' (Joel 2:28–9).

Absolute authority of high-level prophecy

The episode of Moses encouraging prophetic gifting for all God's people appears to go against his earlier warning about being presumptuous (Deut. 18:20), unless it is understood that there is a difference in the kind, the context or some graduated authority spectrum in the prophetic ministry.

The main thrust of the prophetic tradition in the Old

Testament is characterised by a claim to the absolute authority of the message given – that which was eventually incorporated into the canon of Scripture exemplified by Moses, Elijah and the major and minor prophets.

But the same Spirit of God moves his people to speak for God in an edifying way seemingly using a secondary kind so that its divine origin is or becomes clear. Such words then become signs of God's power. It is in this situation that the sinner, realising that the secrets of his heart are laid bare, falls down and worships God, saying, 'God is really among you!' (1 Cor. 14:25).

There are clearly some prophets mentioned in the Old Testament of whose words the Holy Spirit has seen fit to preserve only a few; men such as Iddo the seer (2 Chr. 9:29), Uriah, the son of Shemaiah, from Kiriath Jearim (Jer. 26:20), an anonymous old prophet living in Bethel (1 Kgs 13:11), Ahijah (1 Kgs 14:4–16), another anonymous prophet speaking to the king of Israel (1 Kgs 20:35) and the many unnamed prophets in the different prophetic schools. These were all called prophets and we can justly assume that they gave a number of prophecies to merit their title. Such prophecies, however, have been considered in some sense secondary and left unpreserved, or not considered of such worth as those included in the canon of Scripture.

If the categorisation of prophecy into two tiers is valid, then these latter examples would fall into the low-level category.

The purpose of the high-level prophecy seems to have been something on the grand scale:

1 To challenge the people and their rulers when the covenant and its law were being broken and to remind them of what the terrible consequences would be.

2 To help the rulers of Israel where necessary. In a sense the government of God, since the time of Saul, was exercised through the monarchy and the divine revelation brought by the prophet (cf. 2 Kgs 6:8–23), even to the

pronouncing of judgment oracles against foreign powers (Amos 1).

3 To prepare Israel, and the world, for the coming of the Messiah.

4 The Old Testament prophets were God's spokespeople for addressing the concerns of the Old Testament (i.e. Old Covenant).

5 To ensure an inspired record for the future.

The 'cessation theory' of inter-testamental prophecy
The Jewish rabbis taught that prophecy had ceased since the destruction of the First Temple. 'Rab Samuel bar Inia said, in the name of Rab Aha that "the Second Temple lacked five things, which the first Temple possessed, namely, the fire, the ark, the Urim and the Thummim, the oil of anointing and the Holy Spirit [of prophecy]."

'Rabbi Abdimi of Haifa said, "Since the day when the Temple was destroyed, prophecy has been taken from the prophets and given to the wise" and Rabbi Johanan said, "Since the Temple was destroyed, prophecy has been taken from the prophets and given to fools and children."'[14] These last two, we notice, did not actually say that prophecy had ceased but only that recognised prophets were no longer prophesying.

To this should be added the testimony of 1 Maccabees 4:46 (from the Apocrypha) – 'They laid up the stones [of the altar, after the Gentiles had defiled it] in the mountain of the house in a convenient place until there should come a prophet to give answer concerning them'; also that of 1 Maccabees 9:27 – 'And there was great tribulation in Israel, such as was not since the time that no prophet appeared unto them'; and finally 1 Maccabees 14:41 – 'The Jews and the priests were well pleased that Simon should be their leader and high priest forever, until there should arise a faithful prophet.'[15] These texts are often cited to show that prophecy had ceased, but again we suggest that it was the office of prophet which was no longer operational.

Besides this we have a quote from the Jewish historian Josephus who writes: 'From Artaxerxes down to our time, the complete history has been written, but has not been deemed worthy of like trust with the earlier records, because of *the failure of the exact succession of the prophets*.'[16] This is an interesting comment indeed, coming from the pen of a man who himself had prophesied. The young Josephus, born of a priestly family which traced its pedigree back to the Hasmonaeans, had been the governor of Galilee when he was taken prisoner by the Romans commanded by Vespasian. There were clamours for his execution as he was brought before Vespasian, who ordered that Josephus be kept in the closest custody, intending to send him as soon as possible back to the Emperor Nero.

Josephus somehow persuaded Vespasian to allow him to say a word to him in private. Once on their own Josephus began:

> You suppose, sir, that in capturing me you have merely secured a prisoner, but I come as a messenger of the greatness that awaits you. Had I not been sent by God himself, I knew the law and how a general ought to die. Are you sending me to Nero? How so? Will Nero and those who succeed him before your turn comes remain on the throne? You, Vespasian, are Caesar and Emperor, you and your son [Titus] here. So load me with your heaviest chains and keep me for yourself; for you are master not only of me, Caesar, but of land and sea and all the human race; and I ask to be kept in closer confinement as my penalty, if I am taking the name of God in vain.[17]

Vespasian was unwilling to take his prophecy too seriously, believing that Josephus could simply be lying to save his skin. Josephus was asked why he had not warned the defenders of Jotapata, where he was taken prisoner, that the town would fall and had not foreseen his own captivity. He replied that he had, in fact, prophesied to the people of Jotapata that the town would fall after forty-seven days and that he himself would be taken alive by the Romans.

After questioning the other prisoners on their own, Vespasian found this was true and began to take his predictions seriously. He did not release Josephus but treated him with kindness and consideration at all times.[18] History reveals that the prophecy about Vespasian becoming the emperor was to be exactly fulfilled.

Josephus was not the only Jew to predict that Vespasian would become the Roman Emperor. The famous Rabbi Yohanan ben Zakkai, who supposedly escaped a besieged Jerusalem by pretending to be a corpse borne out in a coffin by his disciples, is reported to have said to Vespasian, 'Behold you are about to be appointed king.'

The question has to be asked, 'What was really meant, at that time, by prophets and prophecy?' There were none holding the office of a prophet during the inter-testamental period as far as we know, with the possible exception of Anna the prophetess whose 'office' is simply mentioned without explanation (Lk 2:36). This lack of explanation may imply that prophecy at the lower level was more prevalent than we realise or that we have read too much into the cessation theory of prophecy.

Prophetic phenomena still operative
There certainly does not appear to have been anything like the high-level kind of prophecy that we have in the accepted Old Testament canon during the inter-testamental period but there is no doubt that people continued to have low-level revelations from God. Many rabbis who accepted the cessation principle, however, also 'believed that prophetic phenomena were still operative in the inter-testamental period and in sub-apostolic times'.[19]

Wayne Grudem, whom we have just quoted, cites some other interesting cases from sub-apostolic times in his learned study on 1 Corinthians. One simple example is that of Rabbi Meir (AD 140–64) who is recorded as recognising a woman, previously unknown to him, as soon as he saw her, 'by means of the Holy Spirit', and he also knew the substance of a quarrel which a woman had just had with her husband.

Another similar example is that of Rabbi Gamaliel II (AD 80–120). He was going along the road when he saw a loaf of cheap bread on the ground. He told Tebi, his slave, to pick it up. A little later he saw a Gentile and said to him, 'Mabegai, take this loaf!' His amazed servant asked the Gentile his name. 'Mabegai,' he replied. The servant could not understand how the rabbi knew who he was speaking to. 'Have you ever met the rabbi before?' he questioned further. The Gentile replied, 'No!' The rabbi believed the name had been revealed to him by the Holy Spirit.

Rabbi Hanina ben Dosa (AD 20–120) would pray over the sick and would be able to predict whether they would recover. He also predicted on his own death-bed, the sudden death of another rabbi. Roger Beckwith cites the example of a mysterious 'voice' which informed John Hyrcanus of the victory of his sons; another 'voice' which informed Simon the Just[20] of the death of the emperor Caligula and an end to his threatened desecration of the Temple.

The Jewish thinker and exegete Philo of Alexandria (c. 20 BC to c. AD 50) is another example, though a very different one. He never claimed to be a prophet but had 'recollections'. When 'under the influence of the divine possession I have been filled with corybantic frenzy', he said.[21]

Other people also continued to prophesy *before* the coming of John the Baptist (Luke 7:26) who according to Christ was 'the prophet Elijah' referred to in Malachi (Mal. 4:5). The prophetess Anna (Luke 2:36) was prophesying then as some prophets do now. Roger Beckwith[22] cites a half dozen or more examples of this in his learned study *The Old Testament Canon of the New Testament Church* and recommends Ludwig Blau's article 'Bat Kol' in the *Jewish Encyclopedia* for a wider range of examples.

'Daughter of a voice'

The prophecies of this period have not been given much attention since they do not come into the same category as those which are included in the Old Testament canon. However, the fact that God continued to communicate in this way is significant. The rabbis called these revelations 'bat kol' – literally the 'daughter of a voice'.

The Jewish Talmuds regarded the 'bat kol' as 'a chance snatch of speech overheard' and interestingly enough some of those who exercise a prophetic ministry today have said that that is exactly how their 'words' seem to come to them.

It is obvious that Jewish religious leaders would not hold this kind of revelation in high esteem because they would see in it a different quality or purpose from that which is included in the Old Testament canon. Possibly they felt it necessary to down-play prophecy till the messenger should come (Mal. 3:1). The messenger was to be John the Baptist (Luke 7:27) though many Jewish leaders did not in fact believe it when John appeared.

Actually the Gospels mention a remarkable number of revelations given to individuals such as Zechariah, Elizabeth, Mary, Joseph, the Wise Men, the Shepherds, Simeon and Anna the prophetess before ever John the Baptist began his prophetic ministry.

God was still speaking

Like the messages of some of the prophets (such as Iddo the seer) mentioned in the Old Testament, 'bat kol' revelations were generally too insignificant to include among the records of Holy Writ (with the possible exceptions of Gen. 22:11f, 15–18 and Dan. 4:31f). Nevertheless, as we would expect, there is enough evidence to show that God was still speaking directly to his people in this way. Even the Pharisees did not deny the reports that such were still heard now and again; they simply treated such reports with reserve.[23]

While the prophetic office seems generally to have ceased during the inter-testamental period, the ministry of prophecy itself, i.e. God communicating directly with his people through another human mouthpiece, seems to have continued.

Another example, if we are allowed a projection forward, of this kind of prophecy may be seen in the case of Caiaphas, who as high priest prophesied: '"You do not realise that it is better for you that one man die for the people than that the whole nation perish."' He did not say this on his own, but as high priest that year he prophesied that Jesus would die for the Jewish nation, and not only for that nation but also for the scattered children of God, to bring them together and make them one' (John 11:50–1).

It is not necessary to assume that the Hebrew and/or Aramaic terminology describing the prophetic phenomena always implies a claim to absolute authority.

Prophecy from the New Testament onwards

The Christian prophets of the New Testament (Covenant) must include all those who have been or will have been appointed by Christ to this office or ministry until his Second Coming. They are God's spokespeople for today. They address the concerns of the New Covenant which embrace the affairs and the life style of all the New Covenant people – both Jew and Gentile. In spite of the differences between the two discernible levels of prophecy, there are a number of definite similarities in the modes of receiving divine revelation (both in the New Testament and Church history since) so some illustrations and examples from the Old Testament in the course of this book are not irrelevant. These similarities, however, must not be understood to imply an authority and character equal to the high-level prophecy.

The New Testament evidence would seem to confirm the existence of the same kind of grading or differentiation for prophecy as in the Old Testament. It appears that (at least) two levels of prophecy are discernible there.

Paul makes a distinction

Paul encourages prophecy: 'Be eager to prophesy' (1 Cor. 14:1, 39). He does this in a way he would never have done if he had understood prophecy only in high-level terms of absolute verbal authority.

Graham Houston writes:

> The prophet who communicated the very words of God to the church was not able to hold back the message, as we have seen from the examples of Jeremiah and the apostles in Acts. Such prophets demanded to be heard, and their message could be received or they could be rejected as imposters. As in Thessalonica (1 Thess. 5:19–21) so in Corinth prophecy was to be evaluated: 'the others should *weigh carefully* what is said' (1 Cor. 14:29).[24]

'This form of prophecy', to quote John Stott, 'was not considered to be a message which brought the very words of God to the people. It was rather a timely word of instruction, encouragement or rebuke which brought the general thrust of God's guidance to the Church in each particular situation.'[25] This was very different from the kind of prophetic utterances Paul himself made when he claimed that his own statements to the churches were absolutely authoritative. We see this in his challenge to those who claimed to be spiritually gifted and to have insights into what God was saying:

'Did the word of God originate with you? Or are you the only people it has reached? If anybody thinks he is a *prophet* or spiritually gifted, let him acknowledge that what I am writing to you is the Lord's command. If he ignores this, he himself will be ignored' (1 Cor. 14:36–8).

Paul is claiming here to be as authoritative as the canonical prophets of the Old Testament. Just as Moses had done (Deut. 18:18–19), so Paul could claim that God was speaking directly through him (1 Cor. 14:36–8). Like Moses again (Num. 11:24–30) who wished that all the Lord's people were prophets and that the Lord would put his Spirit on them, so Paul urged the Christian brothers in Corinth to 'be eager to prophesy' (1 Cor. 14:39).

Graham Houston, whose book *Prophecy Now* has been a useful resource for this chapter, makes out a similar case for Peter, John and Jude. It seems they also could be said to present a two-tier view of prophecy.

Scholars make the distinction

In the Middle Ages, Thomas Aquinas, one of the most influential Catholic theologians, wrote: 'In every period there have always been some who have the spirit of prophecy, not to set forth new teaching of the faith, but to give direction to human activities.'[26]

In our own day we find a sympathetic and apt comment in John Stott's recent book *The Contemporary Christian*. While he believes that God still speaks today he qualifies this by saying: 'We should certainly reject any claim that there are prophets today comparable to biblical prophets.' He goes on, 'There may well, however, be a prophetic gift of a secondary kind, as when God gives some people special insight into his word and his will, but we should not ascribe infallibility to such communications.'[27]

Michael Green endorses the last point and adds some succinct clarification which could apply to a low-level prophecy: 'Prophecy is not the equivalent of Scripture. Prophecy is a particular word for a particular congregation [or person] at a particular time through a particular person. Scripture is for all Christians in all places at all times.'[28]

Likewise David Pawson shares helpful insight on the subject: 'Scripture only gives *general* guidance – how to live but not where, how to marry but not who to marry, how to do our job but not what job to do. We need the help of the Spirit to apply the general to the *particular*. The sons of God are those who are led by the Spirit of God (Rom. 8:14) as well as those who live by the Scriptures.'[29]

It is clear from the New Testament, David Pawson writes, that the Church is guaranteed 'dual revelation of the general and particular throughout this present age, through His past and present words.'[30]

Paul Cain, a modern 'prophet', living in the USA, who would in no way claim to be a scholar, expresses a similar view when he says: 'Prophecy is not to bring new revelation of new truths but fresh revelation on old truths.'[31] His own prophetic ministry involves the application of Scripture truth to the human situation, individually or corporately, today.

Low-level prophecy is not only about understanding and insight into old truth, though that may often be part of it, but more the application of old truth to a new situation in such a significant way that those who understand what has been said and receive the benefit of it, recognise that it could not have come in any other way but by revelation from God.

The role of the Christian prophet and the concern of Christian prophecy is clearly spelt out by the apostle Paul:

to strengthen, to encourage and to comfort (1 Cor. 14:3),

to convince, to instruct (1 Cor. 14:24, 31), and by the example of Paul's life,

to direct (Acts 13:2) and to predict (Acts 27:10, 23–4).

Today's prophecy is for the purpose of edification and not the laying down of doctrinal foundations for the Church, for these have already been laid down in the canon of Scripture.

The spirit of Christian prophecy

John describes how to discern this: 'For the testimony of Jesus is the spirit of prophecy' (Rev. 19:10, cf. 1 John 4:1–2, 1 John 5:1 and 1 Cor. 12:3). If a prophecy draws attention to the one who speaks it, there is something wrong with the prophecy. 'It is not an ego trip for the person concerned.'[32] If a prophecy detracts from the orthodox teaching regarding the person and work of Jesus Christ, then the prophecy must be false.

Prophecy in the last days

The Apostle Peter stated clearly that the outpouring of the Holy Spirit at the first Pentecost was the fulfilment of the prophecy of Joel when he cited the prophet's words to the curious onlookers around him and said: 'I will pour out my Spirit on all people. Your sons and daughters will prophesy, your old men will dream dreams, your young men will see visions. Even on my servants, both men and women, I will pour out my Spirit in those days. I will show wonders in the heavens and on the earth, blood and fire and billows of smoke. The sun will be turned to darkness and the moon to blood before the coming of the great and dreadful day of the Lord. And everyone who calls on the name of the Lord will be saved' (Joel 2:28–32, Acts 2:17–21).

The availability of the gift of prophecy to the Church has been present ever since that first Pentecost. Sadly it has been largely suppressed: 'for most of church history it was felt safer to neglect or redefine prophecy rather than risk the infiltrating of false doctrine'.[33]

The prophetic gift in the Old Testament, though frequent (and possibly continuous), became particularly associated with periods of socio-political crisis. There has apparently been a similar pattern during the 2000 years of Church history: prophecy, though always potentially available, has been most evident during times of spiritual revival which, so often, have also been associated with periods of socio-political crisis. Joel (2:28–31) clearly indicates that prophecy will be intensified during the period immediately preceding the Second Coming of Christ, predictably a time of such crisis with wars and rumours of wars (Matt. 24:6–8).

Though we have been living in the last days ever since the first coming of Christ, 'God's last "Word" to man' (cf. Heb. 1:2), we must certainly be nearer to the last day now than when Peter quoted Joel at the first Pentecost. That being the case, we should be prepared for a tremendous surge of prophecy. Some have interpreted the coming of Elijah before the 'great and dreadful day of the Lord' mentioned in Malachi (4:5) as the manifestation of the whole Church as a prophetic people – the 'corporate Elijah'.[34] Whatever the correct interpretation may be, there must surely be a fuller realisation of Joel's prophecy before the Second Coming and Final Judgment which could well be within our own lifetimes.

3

WHAT KIND OF A PERSON
IS A PROPHET?

It is helpful to discover what kind of people God has
called into the prophetic ministry. We look briefly at three
particular areas: the prophet's spirituality, personality and
psychology.

The spirituality of the prophet
Receiving revelation from God normally requires openness to him; time spent in his presence standing 'in the
council of the Lord' (Jer. 23:18); a right relationship with
him in obedience and a sincere desire for purity (Isa.
6:6–8). We should note well the paralleling by Jesus of
the prophet with the righteous man (Matt. 10:41).

But it is also necessary to point out that the receiving of
'revelation' from God is no guarantee of greater spirituality or holiness. Julian of Norwich wrote: 'The Revelation
itself does not make me good. I am only good if as a result
I love God more . . . it is of more value to you than to
me . . . I know for certain that there are many who have
not had any revelations or visions outside the ordinary
teaching of the Holy Church and yet who love God better
than I do.'[1]

'It is noteworthy', writes Jim Packer, 'that most speakers
and books on holiness say little about ministry, while most
speakers and books on ministry say little on holiness. It has
been this way for over a century. But to treat holiness and
ministry as separate themes is an error. God has linked
them, and what God joins man must not put asunder.'[2]

What Jim Packer says about ministry in general applies equally to prophecy in particular.

It is important to make this point but we should not overlook John Wimber's world-wide conferences promoting prophecy, at the beginning of this decade, entitled 'Holiness unto the Lord' with their call for sanctification. Certainly prophets have greatly erred through neglect of these things (Jer. 23:21–32) and too often backslidden (Isa. 28:7). Prophets should exhibit a holy awe of God (Exod. 3:5, 6). His word must be their joy and delight (Jer. 15:16), their touchstone (2 Tim. 3:16) and sword (Heb. 4:12).

They should have a mind set to gain understanding and a heart to walk in humility (Dan. 10:12). It is their secret history with God which prepares them for the prophetic ministry (Matt. 6:1–24).

With the hindsight of maturity, John Paul Jackson, a man with a recognised prophetic gifting, says: 'We tend to be known more for being characters than for having character. The sad result is that the church distrusts what God entrusts us with.'

The personality of the prophet

Many prophets have had the reputation of being 'enfants terribles'. They showed little fear of mankind (1 Kgs 18 and Amos 7:12–17). Biblical prophets seemed strongly independent, often eccentric; some may have appeared unpopular and not easy to receive (Matt. 10:41). Nowadays, where those with prophetic gifting are not received they tend to become withdrawn, individualistic and nomadic Christians. These people greatly need encouragement. Left on their own they may easily go off at a tangent through lack of proper checks and balances. Of course if they refuse to submit to authority in the local church (or because of some personality quirk they self-reject) they will have only themselves to blame for feeling left out in the cold.

John Paul Jackson observes that 'many revelatory

people are allowing their entire identity to lie in their gifting. Thus, when their gift is questioned or rejected it becomes a direct assault on their personal identity.'[3]

The psychology of the prophet

They sometimes appeared mad (Hos. 9:7), naked (Isa. 20:2, 3), unhygienic (Ezek. 4:12, 13), unpredictable (1 Kgs 21:20), preposterous (1 Kgs 20:35–43), lonely (Jer. 15:17), depressed (1 Sam. 8:7) and rejected (1 Kgs 19:10). Many we know who exercise a fruitful prophetic ministry today seem to have suffered from early relational problems and often have a strong sense of rejection. We conjecture that this may have contributed positively to the development of their spiritual gifting. Just as a blind man, being denied the blessings of sight, unconsciously develops some compensatory gift in hearing and touching, etc., so some having been deprived of the normal wholesome parental and sibling relationships in childhood may unconsciously compensate by developing a more mystical sensitivity towards things supernatural.

In discussing either the psychology or the personality of many of those called to be prophetic people it would be quite wrong to suggest that all those called of God to this ministry are likely to manifest all these particular traits in their personalities. But it is only right to say that some may well display some of them and there is biblical precedent for this. It is needful to know this may be the case so that we do not unconsciously reject a prophetic person's ministry on account of some difficulty in that area. Because of these specific characteristics prophetic people may often appear particularly reticent about admitting when they have been wrong about a prophecy.

4

HOW CAN WE LEARN
TO BE PROPHETS?

The whole subject of prophecy is so elusive when it comes to trying to explain the 'mechanics' of it, so subjective regarding the experience of it and so sovereign regarding God's gifting for it, that it is difficult to be as instructive as we would like. These things are caught rather than taught. We say this without in any way backtracking on anything that has been said so far. But there are some valuable clues which are not to be despised because of their obvious nature nor their transparent simplicity.

1 Learning by seeking the Lord in prayer
If Elijah is our model for prophecy, the aspiring prophet must discover the effectiveness of prayer. 'Elijah was a man just like us. He prayed earnestly' (Jas 5:17). Jeremiah knew that prayer should be a characteristic of a genuine prophet when he said, 'If they are prophets and have the word of the Lord, let them plead with the Lord Almighty' (Jer. 27:18). Prophets are not manipulators, nor political stringpullers behind the scenes. They are rather those who fight in secret against the real stringpullers: the devil, and the hidden forces of society and of their own flesh. They do this by means of their intercessions. They will inevitably pray too for increasing revelation: 'How much more will your Father in heaven give good gifts to those who ask him!' (Matt. 7:11, see also Jas 1:17, 1 Cor. 14:1). Having received they will need to keep coming back to 'seek his face' (Ps. 27:8, see also Zeph. 1:6, 2:3 and Phil. 4:8).

2 Learning by seeking the Lord in Scripture

Where the Bible is readily available, as it is to us in the West, we (and especially those who would prophesy) need to soak ourselves in the word of God. 'Let the word of Christ dwell in you richly' (Col. 3:16, see also Ezek. 2:8–3:4). There are many valuable lessons from the lives and ministry of the prophets recorded there and the fullest revelation of God is to be found in the gospel of Jesus and the teachings of the apostles in the New Testament.

3 Learning by being alone

Many Old Testament prophets, certainly Moses and also New Testament prophets like John the Baptist (Matt. 31:4) and the Apostle Paul (Gal. 1:16) could be said to have been trained in the silence of the wilderness – even Jesus himself (Lk 4:1). They all passed through deep trials and temptations alone there in the desert. Many have followed in the same way since, thinking of the hermit Antony (c. 521–356) in the Arabian desert to our modern day Carlo Carretto. From his famous *Letters from the Desert* we learn that he used to spend six months of the year in the Sahara to prepare himself for work among the city poor. He has since written *The Desert in the City*[1] to show that one does not literally have to go to the Sahara to be alone and to be silent. He now stays permanently in the Umbrian Hills in Italy where he lives the life of a hermit.

Donald Whitney strongly commends the discipline of silence. He calls it

> the voluntary and temporary abstention from speaking so that certain spiritual goals might be sought. Sometimes silence is observed in order to read, write, pray, and so on. Though there is no 'outward speaking', there are several internal dialogues with self and with God. This can be called outward silence. At other times silence is maintained not only outwardly but

also inwardly so that God's voice might be heard more
clearly.[2]

4 Learning by relationship with others
Others seem to have learned or enhanced their gifting by
belonging to a school for prophets or a community (1
Sam. 19:20). John Wimber tells how in his early years he
often visited a horse farm in Illinois where his grandfather
worked. He trained walking horses.

Tennessee walkers have a remarkably high-strutting
gait, different from any other horse in the world. One
day John was with his grandfather while he worked on
a horse with a problem gait. His solution was to hitch a
pacer – a horse with the correct gait – to the horse with
the problem and let them walk together. After a few days,
the problem horse's gait became consistent, just like the
pacer's. His grandfather used to explain that when a horse
cannot do its job, if you connect it to one who can, soon
both will be doing the job correctly.

Wimber goes on to say that he has been training men
and women for thirty-two years. During this period he
has learned that the secret for success with people is the
same as with horses: hitch a person who cannot do a job
with one who can, and soon both will know. This is how
Christ trained the Twelve: they lived with him and began
to live and work like him.[3] Some Christians have found it
most helpful to join with others who already prophesy or
who are learning together.

Bishop Graham Dow tells, in a letter to the author,
how, being convinced from the Bible that prophecy was
for today, he began to listen with others in an afternoon
prayer group, sitting round in a circle. This was followed by
sharing. People were encouraged to contribute any words
(however few) or a picture and told not to worry as, if they
had got it wrong, it would simply fall to the ground.

In this way people may learn from each other both how
tenuous and how simple revelation and prophecy can be.

'As iron sharpens iron, so one man sharpens another'
(Prov. 27:17).

5 Learning by experience of life

David Parker, an American theologian and teacher living
until recently in Chorleywood who also has an effective
prophetic ministry, tells how he was once lamenting that
he, and others like him, did not have a spiritual father to
teach them how to move into the things of the Spirit. He
was praying about this and as he did so he saw himself
in an old study scanning cobwebbed bookshelves for
something which might help him to learn how to minister
in the Spirit.

At last his glance fell upon a musty old tome entitled
The Ways of the Spirit, which he took down eagerly, only to
find it was not what he thought at all – it was a scrap-book!
On the first page was a tear-stained handkerchief; on the
second a bandage with dried blood on it from a child's
skinned knee, and so on. As he stared at it he sensed
the Lord was telling him that some things one can learn
about prophecy come only by experience.

6 Learning by listening

Two books which I have found most helpful are Joyce
Huggett's very popular *Listening to God*[4] and Klaus
Bockmuehl's not so well-known but profound book *Listening to the God who Speaks*,[5] full of clear biblical
teaching and published just before he died. Joyce Huggett
has a gentle but timely warning for charismatics who, she
says, have 'a certain head start and severe limitations'
over the question of listening. 'We charismatics need no
persuading that God is at work today, changing people's
lives in a supernatural way. We have seen it for ourselves.
We rejoice. We want to be open to everything God wants
us to do and to say.' But she goes on to point out that
the charismatics' 'very enthusiasm can be their greatest
handicap'.[6]

Preoccupation with God's works of power can so easily cause us to miss 'the still small voice' of God. Spontaneity can sometimes be counterproductive in trying to listen to God. We need to shut up and be still but this kind of discipline is as rare as hen's teeth in some charismatic circles! What is quite clear is that if we do not listen we shall not hear. But there is no methodology for listening. We only hear God because and when he chooses to speak to us. No system of meditation or other learned practice can conjure up a word from God. There is no methodology but there are certain principles. Obviously the prophet must take time to listen. This is not easy.

Some sixteen years ago Barry Kissell, a colleague on the staff at St Andrew's, was greatly influenced by a book called *The Russian Mystics*.[7] Barry was reminded of his need for silence in order to listen to God. 'He leads me beside quiet waters, he restores my soul' (Ps. 23). It was not dead silence but living stillness that Barry was now looking for.

In his book called *Walking on Water* he tells how he went to The Grail, a centre in Pinner which belonged to the Catholic Church, and explained that he needed a place for one day each week where he could be alone to seek God.

The leader took him out into the beautiful grounds and showed him a 'poustinia' – a garden cabin with a bare table and chair and a bed along the wall. There was a candle in a bottle and an empty bowl for water. Barry was delighted and booked up for the next Thursday. When the day arrived Barry entered his designated poustinia at 8.30 a.m. A whole eight hours stretched before him in which to give the Lord all his time and attention. He placed his Jerusalem Bible on the table for his devotional reading. Beside that he laid out a notebook and two pens of different colours. This all seemed so important in a room so devoid of furniture. He settled down and glanced at his watch again. It was 8.35 a.m.

Shutting his eyes he began to pray to the Lord in tongues which was a gift he had exercised daily for nearly eighteen years. He prayed prayers of thanksgiving and interceded for his friends, family and church; he prayed also for some of his material needs.

He was thinking of a Faith Sharing Mission he would be leading the following week. He prayed for the vicar and his wife, the church leaders at the church he was going to, the team he would be taking and the travel arrangements. He prayed for those he knew who were sick. He found he was struggling to keep his prayers going, so he prayed the Lord's prayer. He looked at his watch. It was 9.15 a.m.

Barry Kissell continues:

> I opened my Bible at the Psalms and read one, then I turned to Proverbs before finding my place in St John's Gospel, at the Scripture Union reading for the day . . .
> Looking at my watch again I could see it was 9.45 – I had been in this poustinia for an hour and a quarter . . . there were six and three quarter hours to go!

Leaving his garden cell he went to the main house to collect some left-over coffee and then returned to his seclusion.

> I began to wonder what I was going to do for the rest of the day . . . I drank the coffee and thought of Carlo Carretto – a little brother belonging to the Community of Charles de Fourcauld. Carlo spent six months of his year in a cave in the Sahara desert and the rest of the year working in a slum in one of the world's major cities. His writing gives the impression that in the quietness of the desert God was with him in powerful ways. It was there that he heard God, who gave him the inner strength he needed to help the poor and downtrodden, and also the inspiration for his many books.
> By now the sun was streaming through my window

– I sat back in my hard wooden chair and relaxed. It was exactly eleven o'clock when I awoke!

To clear his head he went for a walk.

I had faithfully done all the things which I had been taught to do, and now at 11.15 I was beginning to feel quite fed up. As I approached the woods I sensed the Lord saying to me: 'Barry, when are you going to be still and look to Me?'

Wandering back to my poustinia I sat down again. Immediately I found myself fighting the temptation to say something, or turn up a favourite passage of Scripture, or go for another walk, or have a second cup of coffee. It was then that I decided, come what may, I was going to sit still for an hour. If God wanted to speak, I was ready to listen.

At this point the battle really began. My mind started to rotate like a merry-go-round, filled with thoughts of impending commitments and responsibilities. I tried as best I could to put the brakes on and bring every thought to Christ. Slowly, ever so slowly, my mind slowed down and began to reflect the quietness of the surroundings.

Having begun to master my own thoughts, something more sinister started to happen. I suddenly felt fearful and wanted to leave the poustinia . . . I began to think that I had probably got the whole business out of proportion.

Fortunately I had decided to stay put for an hour and reluctantly I sat still and resisted the fear. It occurred to me that while Jesus was alone in the wilderness for forty days He also had a devilish visitation. Satan tried to undermine the relationship which Jesus had with the Father.

Barry recognised this attack of fear as one of the 'fiery darts of the evil one'. He wrote:

At last I was able to maintain the silence and waited patiently for the Lord to speak to me. I was intrigued about how this might actually happen . . .

It was now 2 p.m. – the hour was up – and yet God still had not spoken. I thought I would give him another half hour and then go home . . . I listened but no audible words were spoken . . . my high expectations of the morning were unfulfilled and I was seriously doubting the authenticity of those spiritual writers from the desert. I went home.

The next morning I sat down to try to analyse what had happened and to see if this retreat business was worth pursuing. I began to see that beside the negatives, there were in fact some little encouragements. During that last half hour I had once or twice entered into a deep silence as if I was in God and he somehow was in me . . . I decided to try the retreat again.

When I am not travelling, Thursday [still] finds me either in the poustinia or The Grail garden or, in the extreme cold of winter, in a room in the main house . . . I sit quietly and seek the Lord, and I find that He comes to me in non-verbal ways. It is as if His Spirit touches my spirit and at times I sing or dance for joy. After such moments the Scriptures really come alive and many new thoughts begin to come to delight my soul.[8]

Barry has been given a prophetic ministry which, if it did not come to him out of his times in the poustinia, has certainly been greatly enhanced by them.

James Ryle, a ministerial friend from Boulder, Colorado, who has a well-developed prophetic ministry, has written a book about the subject. In it there is a chapter on learning to listen,[9] in which he spells out three necessary prerequisites for hearing God. They are a pure heart, a hearing ear and a responsive life.

John and Paula Sandford talk about the need to listen to God in their book *The Elijah Task*[10] and refer to the words of Jesus (Luke 8:18), 'Take heed therefore how you hear'. Their comment on this is, 'The longer we are with Jesus, the more our minds are prepared to hear according to his true nature.' This can be illustrated by a story from Joyce Huggett who talks about knowing 'the Father-heart of God'. She told how a friend had phoned one night to talk to her husband, David, who was out. 'Oh well,' said the friend, 'you'll do. I was going to ask whether he would be interested in a new job. I'd like to put his name forward if I may.' 'Well,' replied Joyce, 'I'm ninety-nine per cent certain that David would say that at the moment he feels God is asking us to stay in Nottingham.'

When David came home Joyce put to him the question: 'If someone asked you if he could put your name forward for a new job what would you say?' David repeated almost the same words which Joyce had used earlier. She explained in her book, 'I live with David. We have spent years working at the art of communication. I know his mind. I know his personality. I know his plans. I talk to him and listen to him.'[11] Joyce could not have put it better. Let us hear God according to his nature.

7 Learning by obedient response to revelation already received

Another prophet, Bob Jones, explained how he began. It was after an experience of being filled with the Spirit and he was alone in his truck when he felt the Lord telling him to prophesy against abortion.

'How do I do that, Lord?' he asked. 'Just raise your voice and speak it out,' the Lord seemed to be telling him. So he did just that and began to prophesy. He suddenly saw pictures of the slaughter of the innocents under Pharaoh and Herod as he listened to the mothers and babies screaming. Sickened by the awful horror of it he heard himself conclude with the words, 'As you destroy the first-born and the fruit of the womb so shall you be destroyed.'

He began to find himself 'knowing' things that were going to happen which he had no real interest in and then he would hear these things reported in the media, happening just as he had known 'in the Spirit' that they would do.

8 Learning by becoming aware

A little while ago I was talking to a lady in the north of England for whom I had great respect. She told me of an experience which had greatly puzzled her. She had been in York Minster one day admiring the famous stained-glass rose window. As she was facing the window the words 'In three days I will destroy this temple' came vividly to mind.

She thought she was just recalling Scripture. But the words continued to plague her. Suddenly she realised it was not actually Scripture at all. What Jesus had said was, 'Destroy this temple, and I will raise it again in three days' (John 2:19). She was greatly perplexed. Was it all a lot of rubbish then? It so happened that three days after her visit that part of the minster was destroyed by fire.

She could not make out what purpose there could be in her hearing those words. It was too late to do anything about it now. I felt the Lord was beginning to trust her with revelations and that she should jot them down. Once she could see that she was getting a number of genuine revelations she should feel encouraged to begin sharing them with the church leadership (Gal. 2:1, 2) who would then be more open to anything else the Lord might be showing her.

Even looking directly at the contents of a microscope slide through a microscope, children are notoriously unable to see anything at first, except vague mush. Only after a teacher guides their awareness do they become able to discriminate the cells, nuclei and so on which are apparent to the trained biologist. Young student nurses and doctors, after being given lectures on the signs and symptoms of various conditions, are known to sit on buses observing examples of the disease in the people around them. Physical data which has always been there becomes available to them for the first time.[12]

So it is often the case that God has revealed things to his people which have never been noticed before through lack of awareness.

9 Learning by correction

Bob Jones (who has himself since had to learn from the correction and discipline of the Church) has told how the tragic downfall of televangelist Jimmy Swaggart, which was made public on February 17th, 1988, had previously been revealed to him by the Lord – even to the exact date. Bob had shared this strange revelation with friends some time before the news broke. When that sad day finally came and it was made public, Bob became very excited. 'We got it!' said Bob. 'We were right on target! Jimmy Swaggart has fallen!'

During the days following there was a tremendous outcry and evangelical Christians were portrayed generally as a bunch of hypocrites. The Lord's name was widely reviled and scorned. Bob went on to tell how after a while, still boasting of the accuracy of the prophecy, the Lord got him on one side and rebuked him. 'That is one of my sons you are talking about – a son I love has fallen and you seem to be rejoicing at it! How would you feel if one of your sons had fallen from grace and people went around talking about it and causing you great shame? You should have mourned and not rejoiced!'[13]

10 Learning by teaching and training

God clearly has his own ways of training. Some church leaders are beginning to teach on the subject of prophecy and some to train. It is probably best to follow up teaching by forming a few small groups where there can be open sharing about what it is believed the Lord may be saying to individuals. The leader of each group can then report back to the parish priest or church minister who may in time discern a significant pattern in what they are hearing concerning the mind of the Lord.

Alternatively three or four people may be asked to stand before the congregation who, after prayer, could be invited to speak out any words they sense the Lord may be giving them. Those at the front can then be asked to say how they themselves witness to any of these words in their own spirit so that the congregation can get some useful feedback. The wise leader should then be able to build some positive teaching into the exercise.

11 Learning by taking the risk
David Parker tells how the greatest thing for him in getting started was when people with mature prophetic gifting prayed for him and then asked him what he was hearing or seeing. He had really to try to listen and even then what he thought he heard seemed very faint and tenuous. They urged him to speak out what he thought he was seeing – in faith (Rom. 12:6).[14] For him it was necessary to learn to take the risk of getting the message wrong.

12 Learning by asking questions
Ask your leaders and your friends from time to time how they think you are getting on. Don't put them on the spot by being too direct or urgent with them. They may either be too encouraging or too discouraging if you do not give them time to think it over first. Even if they do not have a particular prophetic ministry themselves they sense what edifies and may still have some very helpful comments to make.

Also if you have the opportunity to approach one, ask a visiting prophet questions that you need help over. Besides debriefing with leaders and other friends, get feedback from individuals to whom you have given prophecies. This is a sure way of learning even if the answer implies you still have a very long way to go.

13 Learning by service and submission

'But Jehoshaphat asked, "Is there no prophet of the Lord here, that we may enquire of the Lord through him?" An officer of the king of Israel answered, "Elisha son of Shaphat is here. He used to pour water on the hands of Elijah"' (2 Kgs 3:11).

People ate with their fingers in that part of the world. Servants (usually women) then brought washing bowls. One bowl was set under the eater's hands and then water was poured over them. Soon afterwards the servant would take a towel which was over his arm to dry the hands. It was considered a very menial task. 'An older prophet trained a younger prophet by humiliating him, crushing . . . his pride, revealing his smallness and incapability before God. Test after test was put upon the neophyte. The test was only a success if he *failed* to pass it.'[15]

> Prophets in training make fools of themselves more times than they make sense. The Lord characteristically gives a young prophet two or three true visions, and the prophet in turn speaks the warnings to the congregation. And it works! About that time the tyro prophet begins to take 'his stand on visions, puffed up without reason by his sensuous mind, and not holding fast to the Head' (Col. 2:18b–19a RSV). He becomes strongly deluded and next thing you know, he is utterly abased and humiliated before his fellow parishioners. God arranged it that way and, even if the prophet has abundant common sense, he cannot escape the process of humiliation essential to his training.[16]

The Church is waiting for mature, broken, prophetic

people whose heart is for the well-being of the Body of Christ rather than on the well-being of their gift.

14 Learning over a period of time

We are thinking of a marathon, not a sprint. John Paul Jackson from Illinois describes his own personal reaction when he learned that there was no instant training for a prophet. While reading *The Elijah Task* by John and Paula Sandford, he came across the words: 'It . . . probably takes no less than a dozen years to make a man [prophet] of God.' When he read that, he said, 'I became so angry that I threw the book across the room. My thinking was that I had been engaged in so many supernatural experiences that surely I was a "prophet of God". That was twelve years ago. Today I strongly suspect it may actually take a lifetime.'[17] He goes on to say that he sees three stages in the maturing of the prophetic. The first is the call which may come quickly. The third is the commissioning which is glorious. The second stage is long and arduous. It is this second stage which is so easily overlooked by those with revelatory gifts.

Conclusion

We have spelt out fourteen major elements in the learning process towards becoming a prophet. They are all vital. Taking all these steps, however, will not make one a prophet. The call to prophesy and the releasing into this ministry is a sovereign work of God. In the next chapter we underline the various ways by which God appears in the Bible to have initiated this revelatory gifting.

5

HOW IS PROPHETIC GIFTING INITIATED?

There seem to be at least four possible means shown to us in Scripture by which the gift may be received. These are by impartation, manifestation, inheritance or faith. Under each of these headings we give the appropriate biblical examples.

Imparted gift

The normal mode for imparting was through the laying on of hands: 'I long to see you so that I may *impart* to you some spiritual gift to make you strong' (Rom. 1:11).

Laying on of hands

'Now Joshua . . . was filled with the spirit of wisdom because Moses had *laid his hands on him*' (Deut. 34:9).

'Fan into flame the gift of God, which is in you *through the laying on of my hands*' (2 Tim. 1:6).

'Do not neglect your gift, which was given you through a prophetic message when *the body of elders laid their hands on you*' (1 Tim. 4:14).

Having said this it is important that we do not rush round seeking to impart the gift in this way. Paul's warning about hurried ordinations, where he says 'Do not be hasty in the laying on of hands' (1 Tim. 5:22), also has some relevance here.

Bill Hamon, a North American church leader and author of a number of books on the subject of prophecy, who is evidently being used widely as a prophet, and is personally responsible for activating hundreds of others through the impartation of this gift, is a strong advocate of the impartation through the laying on of hands *by the elders*.

John Sandford, who laid hands on Agnes Sanford wrote:

> Agnes had been a healer and then a teacher for many years prepared through much discipline and experience to be a prophet. Her training had been accomplished already before her call. Thus she stepped naturally and easily in the prophetic office.
>
> She was anointed to be a prophet through the laying on of hands by another prophet. Neither she nor I had thought of any such thing before the prayer. It was purely an act of the Holy Spirit. Nevertheless, it would have been invalidated without the confirming signs . . . Her call included her job description, yet only sketched in outline. The Lord gave her the major strokes of the brush after she was in place.[1]

1 Mantle prophets

The gift could also be imparted, apparently, by being in close contact with someone else who exercised the gift:

For example, the prophet and his servant:

'[Elisha] picked up the cloak that had fallen from Elijah . . . [and] the prophets from Jericho, who were watching, said: "The spirit of Elijah is resting on Elisha . . ."' (2 Kgs 2:13–15). There is a parallel to this in the experience of Moses where 'The Lord . . . took of the Spirit that was on [Moses] and put the Spirit on the seventy elders' (Num. 11:25). Theodoret has a felicitous comment on this: 'Just as a person who kindles a thousand flames from one does not lessen the first while he communicates light to others so God did not diminish the grace imparted to Moses by the fact that he communicated it to the seventy.'

George Fox, the founder of the Society of Friends,[2] had

the gift of prophecy. He tells how the prophetic ministry came to him. 'There was one Brown, who had great prophecies and sights upon his death bed of me. And he spoke openly of what I should be made instrumental by the Lord to bring forth. And he spake of others that they should come to nothing . . .

'And when this man was buried, a great work fell upon me' (probably he means here that he fell to the ground and lay perfectly still, as has often been observed at certain charismatic/pentecostal meetings) 'to the admiration of many, who thought I had been dead, and many came to see me, for about fourteen days' time. For I was very much altered in countenance and person as if my body had been new moulded or changed.

'And while I was in that condition, I had a sense and discerning given me by the Lord, through which I saw plainly . . . and the same eternal power of God, which brought me through these things, was that which afterwards shook the nations, priests' – any paid minister of the Christian religion – 'professors' – any who called themselves Christians – 'and people' – those who professed no Christian faith at all. 'And a report went abroad of me that I was a young man that had a discerning spirit; whereupon many came to me from far and near.'[3]

Schools, guilds or communities of prophets
We notice that a *procession of prophets* met Samuel (1 Sam. 10:10) and a *company of the prophets* was meeting with Elisha (2 Kgs 4:38). The master-prophets were given the title 'Father' (1 Sam. 10:2, 2 Kgs 2:12, 6:21, 13:14).

The Huguenots experimented with a school for prophets at Cevennes in Southern France in the 1680s. This was led by Pierre Jurieu.

It seems that if one keeps company with a prophet for long enough, something of the prophetic gift may eventually 'wear off' on oneself!

Manifested gift

The anointing for prophecy may occur during the assembling together of God's people, but it is not limited to such times. Worship with music seems to enhance the atmosphere for a manifestation of the prophetic gift.

In the congregation

Paul refers to this when he deals with the nine gifts of the Spirit spelt out in 1 Corinthians 12: 'Now to each one the manifestation of the Spirit is given' (1 Cor. 12:7). Here the gift does not seem to be permanently invested; rather there is a spontaneous sovereign anointing by God which is given for that moment in that particular situation.

The gifts are given when the congregation comes together (for the Lord's Supper). Where members are open to receive gifts and willing to step out and use them by faith for the common good those persons may well be entrusted by God again with the same gift.

Where this happens increasingly, others in the Body of Christ will begin to discern that certain members are developing a ministry out of a particular gift. Those persons are becoming good at using a gift from God when he sends it. This does not mean that the rest of the congregation should not be open and seeking the same gift for themselves. They are all encouraged to use whatever gift God gives them, as we have already seen: 'Now to *each one* the manifestation of the Spirit is given for the common good' (1 Cor. 12:7).

Paul goes one step further and refers to 'a kind of working' – an office. God sees which of his servants have developed a ministry and creates an office out of it. This is quite simple. The others in the congregation recognise the ministry given and exercised and the person who prophesied is now known as a prophet. The whole process begins with what Paul calls 'manifestations'.

These manifestations are outward signs but cannot be taken as automatic or absolute proof of any inward grace.

As with Holy Spirit anointings there is not always any evidence of outward manifestations either. We are talking about bodily sensations of burning, tingling, heaviness of limbs, trembling or even falling down under the power of the Holy Spirit.

An example of how this gift is distributed comes from our own experience with Elspeth Cole, a former missionary from Rwanda partly supported by St Andrew's, Chorleywood. She shared with us a vision (received in prayer) of an angel on the roof of St Andrew's dispensing gifts during a service of worship through a hole in the roof.

As the angel shovelled what looked like gold leaf on to the people worshipping, Elspeth asked: 'What does this mean?' 'These are the gifts that I am giving to my people but no one is picking them up,' came the angel's reply. This vision was a real challenge to us. We recognised the truth of it in our particular situation at that particular time and it would still be true for us today. We just do not 'pick up' or use a hundredth part of the gifting God has given us for his service.

In isolation

The manifestation of the anointing may not be limited to when the church is assembled together for worship. This is a story of the revered Desert Father Moses going to consult one of his younger disciples named Zachary: 'Tell me what I must do?' he enquired of Zachary. The latter threw himself down at the old man's feet and said, 'Are you asking that from me, Father?' The old man answered him: 'Believe me, Zachary, my son, I saw the Holy Spirit come down upon you, and so I must consult you.'[4] Father Moses had discerned an anointing upon Zachary for prophecy.

The sounds of music

An anointing for prophecy may also be stirred up through the sounds of music. For example we read: 'While the harpist was playing, the hand of the Lord came upon

Elisha' (2 Kgs 3:15 – also 1 Sam. 19:18ff and 1 Chr.
25:1). David would have been moved to compose some
of his prophetic psalms while playing the harp.

Inherited gift

The Bible would seem to give examples of prophets who
have been born with the gift.

Some such as Jeremiah (Jer. 1:4–5) or John the Baptist
(Luke 1:15, 16) are born with it. Heman (1 Chr. 25:1) the
singing prophet was Samuel's grandson[5] and therefore he
may have inherited the gift.

It is interesting to contrast this with Amos' comment
about himself: 'I was neither a prophet nor a prophet's
son' (Amos 7:14). It would seem that he believed that
some could be trained for the prophetic ministry and
others were recognised for having inherited the gift. He
disclaims either for himself but still believes he has a word
from the Lord.

An inherited gift might also be understood from Paul's
letter to the Romans (12:6) where prophesying is included
among a list of very functional gifts which belong to those
who could have easily been born with them. A recent study
seems to confirm this view.[6]

A gift received by faith

Scripture clearly teaches that gifts may be asked for
and can be received by faith. Jesus himself encouraged
believers to ask for things: 'Ask and it will be given to
you' (Matt. 7:7). He refers to the fact that earthly parents
give good gifts to their children. If that is the case, he says,
'How much more will your Father in heaven give good gifts
to those who ask him!'

The gift of prophecy, then, may be sought, received and
exercised by faith. This last area of faith has already been
briefly touched upon in the previous chapter under the
heading of 'Learning by taking the risk'.

6

HOW IS PROPHECY
RECEIVED FROM GOD?

The charismatic bishop Cyprian claimed that he was directed into hiding by the Lord at a time of general persecution
around AD 252.[1] During a later period of persecution (AD
257) Cyprian received another revelation, that allegedly
foretold his martyrdom, thereby enabling him to set
his house in order. On at least four occasions Bishop
Cyprian appealed to prophetic claims[2] when he exhorted
the churches in his care to unity at a time of deep conflict.
How do people receive such revelations from God?

The Bible provides much light in answer to this question.
'For God does speak – now one way, now another – though
man may not perceive it. In a dream, in a vision of the
night . . . he may speak in their ears' (Job 33:14–16). This
passage is one of many which spell out the different ways, it
would seem, that people in the Bible received their revelations, and that is what we shall be looking at in this chapter.
We shall discuss the impulses for revelation, find examples
of this in the Christian Church and take note that certain
phenomena may accompany prophetic anointings.

The impulses for revelation
The secret of prophetic consciousness eludes scientific
investigation and the process of spiritual inspiration resists
exact definition. It is clear, however, that the prophetic
inspiration was not confined to any one mode of illumination but was manifold – 'at many times and in various
ways' (Heb. 1:1).

The Hebrew word 'nabi' is translated 'prophet' in the Old Testament. The term 'prophet' describes the more gregarious characters who came from prophetic communities and local holy places. 'Abram travelled . . . [to] the site of the great tree of Moreh at Shechem . . . The Lord appeared to Abram' (Gen. 12:6). Abram became Abraham and was acknowledged by God to be a prophet. (Gen. 20:7).

There were others, mainly the loners it seems, who were also called prophets (1 Sam. 3:20) but were known as 'seers' (1 Sam. 9:9, 18–19) – from two different Hebrew words, 'roeh' and 'hozeh' – because their gifting came mainly through 'seeing', although the other senses were not excluded.

Isaiah was a *seeing* prophet (Isa. 1:1).
Jeremiah was a *hearing* prophet (Jer. 1:4–9).
Ezekiel was a *seeing* prophet (Ezek. 1:1).
Hosea was a *hearing* prophet (Hos. 1:1).
Amos was a *seeing* prophet (Amos 1:1).[3]

Comments on 'seeing' and 'hearing'
The seeing and hearing may sometimes seem to be an 'inner eye' or 'inner ear' with neither the sight nor sound seen or heard by others present: 'visions that passed through my mind' (Dan. 7:15); 'I, Daniel, was the only one who saw the vision; the men with me did not see it' (Dan. 10:7); 'My companions saw the light, but they did not understand the voice of him who was speaking to me' (Acts 22:9).

Teresa of Avila made an interesting observation after 'hearing' the Lord speaking to her. 'The words were very clearly formed and unmistakable, though not heard with the bodily ear.' 'They are quite unlike the words framed by the imagination which are muffled (cosa sorda).' Again she comments on a vision where the Lord stood beside her while she was in prayer and she both heard and saw him 'though not with the eyes of the body nor of the soul!'[4]

Agnes Sanford spoke of her first hearing God in her teens: 'God spoke to me, though I did not know at the time that it was He, for He did not speak in any way that one would expect . . . Only now, looking back, do I realize that it was God who met my spirit when my spirit met Him in faraway places quite alone.'⁵

At other times it is an external sight or sound clearly seen or heard by witnesses (Dan. 5:5–8; John 12:29).

A practical teaching outline

For the purpose of providing a teaching outline in this first section we shall first identify the various ways revelations in the Bible have apparently been received along with some biblical references. We shall then take these one by one and supply a more modern illustration of their practical out-working with occasional comments, so that readers are not left to assume that such experiences were limited to Bible characters only. In our third section we shall observe that certain phenomena may accompany an anointing from God.

Identification of modes from the Bible

1 Face to face. The Lord speaking 'face to face' to Moses (Num. 12:8). This was seemingly a form of revelation which was granted only to Moses and Christ himself (John 1:18).

2 Dreams (Deut. 13:1 RSV, Joel 2:28).

3 Visions and picture impressions (Dan. 7:15, Acts 7:55–6 and 16:9, 10).

4 Voices (1 Sam. 3:4, Acts 9:4).

5 Trances (Gen. 15:12, Dan. 8:18, Acts 10:10 and 22:17).

6 Supernatural visitations (Dan. 9:21, Luke 1:11).

7 Transportations to the third heaven, rapture or other out-of-the-body experiences (Ezek. 8:2–3, 2 Cor. 12:2, etc.).

8 Nature (Num. 22:28, Ps. 19:1–4).

9 Situations (1 Sam. 15:28) and circumstances (Amos 8:1).

10 Subjective impressions (Jer. 23:9).

11 Riddles (Num. 12:6, 7).

12 Allegories or parables (Ezek. 17:2).

13 Puns (Jer. 1:12, Amos 8:1–2).

Illustrations from more recent history

1 *Face to Face* – the Lord speaking face to face to Moses (Num. 12:8) and to Jesus (John 1:18)

This was seemingly a form of revelation which was granted only to Moses (Num. 12:8) and Christ himself (John 1:18) so further illustrations are obviously unavailable.

2 *Dreams* (Deut. 13:1 RSV, Judg. 7:13–15, Joel 2:28)

Most of us at some time have had a significant dream. We also know that God has spoken to some of the best known Bible characters in dreams. In his Confessions, St Patrick tells how, aged twenty-two, he escaped from slavery in Ireland in obedience to a vision. Once free he had a dream in which he was called to return and convert the pagan Irish. He did not actually undertake this mission until AD 431 when he was over forty.

Dreams happen during sleep. All of us 'sleep' through some four or five dreams a night which occur regularly at roughly one-and-a-half hourly intervals. After a series of in-depth tests, Dr William Demant, research fellow in psychiatry at Mount Sinai Hospital, New York City, concluded his talk to the American Psychiatric Association in 1960 with the following words: 'We believe that if anybody were deprived of dreams long enough, it might result in some sort of catastrophic breakdown.'[6] In other words, if we did not dream we would probably go mad.

Dreams are primarily about the dreamer's own personality and usually not about external matters; they present a picture of the inner situation. We note the words of the wise 'Teacher' who said 'a dream comes when there are many cares' and 'much dreaming and many words are meaningless' (Eccles. 5:3, 7).

It would be a great mistake to believe that God was speaking to us in every dream, though every dream serves the purpose that God has intended. But now and again the dreamer may awake with a strong impression that a certain dream was significant. It is well to think about all those dreams and even to write them down. If nothing is immediately discernible things may become clearer after the recurrence of similar dreams.

'Before I conversed with his lordship, God was pleased to give me previous notice of it,' wrote the young George Whitefield about his first interview with his bishop.

Long ere I had at least prospect of being called before the bishop [Dr Benson], I dreamed one night, I was talking with him in his palace, and that he gave me some gold, which seemed to sound again in my hand. Afterwards this dream would come often into my mind; and whenever I saw the bishop at church, a strong persuasion would arise in my mind that I should very shortly go to him. I always checked it, and prayed to God to preserve me from ever desiring that honour which cometh from man.

One afternoon it happened that the bishop took a solitary walk, as I was told afterwards, to Lady Selwyn's, near Gloucester, who not long before, had made me a present of a piece of gold. She, I found, recommended me to the bishop; and a few days after, as I was coming from the cathedral prayers, thinking of no such thing, one of the vergers called after me, and said, the bishop desired to speak with me. I, forgetful at that time of my dream immediately turned back, considering within myself what I had done to deserve his lordship's displeasure.

When I came to the top of the palace stairs, the bishop took me by the hand, told me he was glad to see me, and bid me wait a little till he had put off his habit, and he would return to me again. This gave me the opportunity of praying to God for His assistance, and adoring Him for His providence over me.

At his coming again into the room, the bishop told me he had heard of my character, liked my behaviour at church, and enquired my age. 'Notwithstanding,' said he, 'I have declared I would not ordain anyone under three-and-twenty, yet I shall think it my duty to ordain you whenever you come for Holy Orders.' He then made me a present of five guineas to buy me a book, which, sounding again in my hand, put me in mind of my dream, whereupon my heart was filled with a sense of God's love.[7]

3 *Visions and Picture Impressions* (Dan. 7:15, Acts 7:55–6 and 16:9,10)

John Finney reports the case of a 34-year-old hospital worker who had taken an overdose: 'I lay in hospital with everyone running around me and I felt this real calmness and saw a vision. A "being" came to me and said, "I'm not ready for you yet – I'll call you when it's time."'[8]

Joyce Huggett observes: 'The vision seemed to be a favourite means of communication' and reflected that as a teacher of deaf children by profession, it would never have occurred to her 'to try to teach them anything without some form of visual aid'. 'Communication experts assure us that we remember what we see far more permanently than we recall the words we hear. In the light of this, I was fascinated to find God transmitting very ordinary messages to his people by means of a method which we pride ourselves is "modern".'[9]

A missionary had written from Kenya to an elderly lady in Scotland who supported her in prayer. She asked her especially to pray for the children in the baby-home where she worked. Returning to Scotland for leave she even wondered if the old lady would recognise her.

Not only did she recognise me, she also recognised my pictures in my photograph album.

'Ah, there's Chepkemoi and there's Kendu – and dear little Kiprotich,' she murmured happily. 'But how can you tell?' I marvelled. It was the first time I had brought this set of prints to Scotland and there were no names in the album. She looked at me with the matter-of-fact simplicity of those who, in the tradition of Brother Lawrence, continually practise the presence of God: 'He showed me their faces as I prayed,' she said.[10]

4 *Voices* (1 Sam. 3:4, Acts 9:4)

Personally I do not think that I have ever heard the audible voice of God though I have been very aware that God has spoken to me many times. However, a few years ago, we were running a conference at Swanwick for church leaders, when my colleague, Barry Kissell, asked how many present believed that at some time in their lives they had heard the audible voice of God. By a show of hands some 20 per cent of those in that full assembly (350 people were present) believed that had been their experience.

Let it be assumed that 10 per cent present were mental sufferers (which we have no reason to believe but there is always the possibility of some in any large company), this would still leave the other 10 per cent – some thirty-five people in that group who believed that at some point or points in their lives they had heard the voice of God!

We are aware that under certain mental conditions people do hear frequent voices which are definitely not from God. In testing out individuals the frequency would be one of the major factors to make us wary; the content of the messages would be another. Those voices are signs of sickness when they are frequent and generally negative, unclean, destructive, self-exalting or blasphemous.

A wholesome example comes from John Finney, already

cited above, who reports the experience of a 38-year-old unemployed Anglican who said:

> I was on the common and the wind was gently blowing. I was all alone with just the cattle and the horses. Suddenly I felt a warm feeling come over me. I distinctly heard my name. I looked round. No one was there. Again I heard my name. Before I knew what had happened I was down on my knees praying. I felt that everything was going to be OK. When people saw me they said that my face was shining. I felt strong and alive. I knew that that day God had spoken to me. From that day on, I have followed Christ.

When the Spirit Comes with Power

In his book *When the Spirit Comes with Power* John White tells the story of 'Sandy: The Voice on the Stereo', describing the experience of Sandy Solomon. She was a single 37-year-old woman. Her family was middle class, black and upwardly mobile.

She had been raised a Methodist and baptised as an infant but she had never understood what grace and the new birth were. Dr White described her as a self-effacing, balanced woman with a healthy sense of humour. She was intelligent, perceptive and determined to succeed. She had become an assistant vice-president of a major national bank with duties as a regional financial controller/planner.

On December 26th, 1983 when Sandy was at home enjoying a record on her stereo equipment she suddenly noticed what seemed like static drowning out the music. She could not make this out at all and thought it might perhaps have been interference from the radio although she had never noticed anything like it before. Then with the music completely drowned out the static suddenly stopped and in the silence she heard a man's voice saying quite simply and clearly, 'Surrender to Jesus!' Just as suddenly the static returned and faded until the music came on again!

The whole incident lasted less than a minute, she thought. She was frightened as she puzzled over how this could have got onto the recording. She replayed the record a number of times but never again did she hear that voice. Slowly she realised the time had come for her to resolve her relationship with God but she still delayed this for a number of days until, prompted again by an evangelistic programme on TV, she made her way across Los Angeles to the Vineyard Fellowship at Anaheim where she 'accepted the Lord'.

For Sandy that was only the beginning of many strange encounters with God. In spite of some of the usual setbacks and suffering that Christians encounter, when John White last met Sandy, she was still serving the Lord in the power of the Holy Spirit.[11]

5 *Trances* (Gen. 15:12, Dan. 8:18, Acts 10:10 and 22:17)

David Aune distinguishes between 'possession' trances and 'vision' trances. In 'possession' trances he suggests that an external supernatural being or power has taken control of a person while in the 'vision' trances it is thought that the soul leaves the body, or that it is subject to visions and hallucinations of various kinds. In the Old Testament revelations appear to have been received in both forms. There are so many possible varieties of this experience that it is difficult to select a typical example, so we make do with a significant one.

In her well-known book *Something More*, Catherine Marshall (widow of Peter Marshall, one-time chaplain to the US Senate) tells a story which involved her friend Virginia and Mr Wolff, her 63-year-old father. Mr Wolff had been admitted to Tampa Tuberculosis Sanatorium seven months previously, after an X-ray had revealed three cavities about the size of silver dollars in the top of his left lung. He was not responding to treatment and his health was in serious decline.

The hospital was treating him with INH (Isoniazid). This was considered a miracle drug, but it was doing nothing for Mr Wolff. The three cavities had enlarged into what looked like the figure of eight. The physician did not dare prescribe the drug for longer than another six weeks. There seemed little hope.

One day, some three weeks later, Virginia was reclining across her bed after meditating on her Bible and turned her head to one side to take a nap. Her eye was attracted towards a patch of sunlight on the wall.

She was still following the train of her meditation when she was interrupted by the vision of an X-ray picture of lungs, three times larger than life, which was coming into focus in the middle of the sunlight patch. She was convinced that this was an enlarged replica of her father's X-ray. She had studied these same shadows and scar tissues so often on the hospital X-rays that she recognised the unusual figure-of-eight cavity and the single dollar-sized one at the top of the left lung.

Still puzzling over whatever the vision could mean, she saw a white line about three inches wide move slowly up the wall. As the white line passed the lower tissues of the lung, it left behind healthy lungs with the scar tissue gone. It continued moving over the diseased parts and she observed now that there were no more cavities and all the tissues were healed.

Virginia stared at the vision, not knowing what to make of it. She had not been thinking of her father, much less praying for him. Then, to her amazement, she saw a replay of the whole scene on the wall – exactly as before, leaving behind two perfect lungs. 'Then Dad's well,' she whispered to herself. She immediately phoned her mother to tell her the news: 'Mother, Dad's healed,' she insisted. Her mother tried to calm her down, feeling sure that Virginia was out of her mind.

A few days later fresh X-rays were taken as part of the normal procedure. Virginia now had very special reasons for wanting to know the results, but they were slow in coming as the hospital reported that there had been a mix-up. They claimed that they had been sent X-ray pictures of someone who had clearly never had TB.

As by now the reader can imagine, the next X-rays not only revealed no sign of TB at all but the sputum and culture tests were negative also. 'How do you explain that?' Virginia asked the doctor. 'I haven't any explanation,' he admitted. Then Virginia went with the doctor to see her father and they were able to hear his side of the story . . .

'It happened one day at my nap time. I was just lying here,' he said, 'when all at once there was the strangest feeling – like something draining from my body and out of my feet – a surge of well-being then filled my whole body. I felt warm and cared for and loved – loved – that's it. Loved! Never felt so well in my life! No reason to be here now! I'm going home.' On comparing notes, it turned out that Mr Wolff's healing came at the same time that Virginia was receiving that revelation of the picture in the sunlight patch.[12]

6 *Supernatural Visitations* (Dan. 9:21, Luke 1:11)
It may come as a surprise to some Christians to learn that angelic visitations are not only included in biblical experience but also are the occasional experience of many Christians. The scene was a pastor's house in Kansas City. The fellowship had been meeting to pray every single night for five or six months. It was a Wednesday night – April 13th, 1983 – when the Lord spoke directly to Mike Bickle, not audibly this time but 'internally'. He was sure that God was telling him to 'call the people together for a solemn assembly. Call the people together to fast and pray for twenty-one days! This people in the heart of the nation will be like Daniel who, when the children of Israel were

in captivity in Babylon, went on a twenty-one day fast' (Dan. 10:2).

Mike Bickle understood that this was the key to the release of the children of Israel (the Church). The words continued: 'There will be 500 people in this city. They will stand before God as Daniel did because there are promises for this nation as there were for the children of Israel. This nation is in bondage just like the children of Israel. And God wants to free this nation just as he did the children of Israel.'

The Lord said: 'I am going to raise up a Daniel from the heart of this nation as I did from the children of Israel. Read on from Daniel chapter nine! Five hundred people will come together and they will fast for twenty-one days and they will seek my face and that will be the beginning of my purposes in a new dimension in this nation!'

Mike was trembling – scared to the bone! However could he get up and say that? He was only a very young and new minister in town. He could imagine the charges of presumptuousness which would be levelled against him if he ever dared to do such a thing through a city-wide summons.

He told his wife Diane and shared his fears with her. She was dumbfounded! 'Darling,' he said, 'God has just told me through the angel Gabriel to call a solemn assembly from this city to fast and pray.' The Kansas City Fellowship was having regular Sunday meetings for from 300 to 400 people by that time and God had said there would be 500 who would respond to this call. Mike finished by repeating what God had told him: 'You lift up your voice and I will move the people! Do it because you have no choice. This is a command!'

Diane found it hard to make any suggestions that would help him. 'All I know,' she said, by way of consolation, 'is that if things go wrong I'm sure we can go back to St Louis.' Mike was surprised to sense in his spirit that he was becoming a little more resolved on the matter: 'I'm

going to give it a shot,' he murmured as if to test out his
own reaction. 'If we are done in this city we are done
but I know I've got to do it if this is really God. I'll call
Bob Jones [who had the reputation of a prophet] in the
morning.'

It was April 14th. He called Bob. 'Bob, I have not
known you for long but I know you are a prophet of
the Lord. I have had a very scarey word from the Lord
that you don't know about.'

'Yeah, I already know about it!' came Bob's calm
drawling reply. 'Amazed' was hardly the word for it –
this was all just too bizarre for words to Mike!

Bob had said he'd already 'seen' it and pressed Mike to
go over right away.

Mike grabbed a couple of witnesses to take with him
and they jumped into his automobile. When they reached
Bob's home he came out to greet them all and then
sat them down as Mike launched into what was on
his mind. 'Bob, I really need a word from the Lord
right now!'

Bob replied: 'I have the word from the Lord already.'

'What do you have?' asked Mike.

'I saw him,' said Bob.

'Who did you see?'

He said: 'You know who I saw!'

Mike replied: 'Bob, I did not see anyone. That's not
how God spoke to me! Who did you see?' Mike was
feeling a little peeved and impatient with this cat and
mouse approach. Each of them believed he had had
a revelation from God but each was using the other's
revelation to confirm his own. It seemed important for
each not to give too much away while hoping that the other
would corroborate his experience through the recounting
of his own revelation – hence this frustrating enigmatic
step-by-step dialogue.

Bob said: 'I saw the angel Gabriel.'

'What did the angel Gabriel say?' asked Mike.

'He said: Give the young man Daniel chapter 9 and he will understand!'

That's incredible, thought Mike to himself. We really have got to do this thing after all – we've really got to summon a twenty-one day fast. Aloud he enquired: 'Will anyone respond to the call?'

And Bob replied: 'He said there would be 500 people!' The same number exactly that the Lord had said to Mike – it was truly the word of the Lord!

So Mike made a city-wide call for a solemn fast to begin on May 7th. Just as he had feared there was opposition: the pastor of a leading church in town publicly condemned the unknown young upstart for his audacity and called upon the Christian public to mark his words concerning Mike Bickle: 'Five years to the day that young man's name will be a vilification in the church,' he announced.

Mike found that kind of attack particularly difficult. Criticism from the world was predictable. Condemnation from leading men of God was totally unexpected. A gentle tut-tut in private from an older, more experienced Christian – yes, maybe, but not a public curse from a leading churchman! The first night 700 came. Sometimes up to a thousand were present. They prayed non-stop from 6 a.m. to midnight right through the three weeks.[13]

7 *Transportations/Raptures* – transportations to the third heaven, raptures or other out-of-the-body experiences (Ezek. 8:2–3, 1 Kgs 22: 19–23, 2 Cor. 12:2)

Ezekiel was taken from exile to Jerusalem, Micaiah ben Imlah became involved in the deliberations of a heavenly council, and Paul (whether in the body or out of the body) was caught up to paradise where he heard inexpressible things that a man is not permitted to tell.

Those who are cynical or suspicious about the very possibility of such experiences may rarely discover truly Christian people who have such experiences. Any who have had such occasional experiences are often unwilling to own up to them, even to those who are sympathetic, either because they do not have permission to share them or they want to avoid any hint of pride.

But those who believe that the possibility exists will probably meet Christians now and again who have had a transportation or rapture at some time in life – often associated with a near death or death experience. Some Christians genuinely believe that at some point in time they have felt themselves step or slip out of their bodies, leaving their sensory apparatus behind, and have still 'seen' things that are going on among those they have just left or even in other places. People who have received such experiences cover a wide range of personalities, from the founder of the Jesuits, St Ignatius of the castle of Loyola and son of nobility, to the hill-billy prophet Bob Jones, son of a cotton picker in Kentucky – both incidentally ex-soldiers.

Bob Jones has described his first 'out-of-the-body' experiences.[14] He was taken, it seemed, out of his body and brought before the throne of God. The glory, the piercing light that went right through him and showed up in detail everything that he saw there, so terrified him that it took him about three months to recover – he shook so much. He thought that to see what he had seen he should have died and only the presence of an angel standing in front of him protecting his eyes enabled him to survive.

When he came back into his body he was still hurting from a burning feeling within his very bones; the fear of the Lord was so awesome to him that his main desire was to get as far away from it all as he possibly could.

He knew that what he had seen was the real thing but he still did not realise that it was God's call upon his life – or rather he still did not want to realise it. Later in the same book[15] there is an account of what seems like a 'death' experience which with hindsight was obviously a 'blessing' to him and certainly enhanced his prophetic ministry.

J. Cameron Peddie writes of his experience (which turned out to be an anointing for the ministry of healing) in

his book called *The Forgotten Talent*. On a particular day
he was alone and was preparing lunch. 'What happened
might have been expected in the sanctuary, a cathedral
or some piece of holy ground. But it happened as I stood
at the sink in the kitchen, paring potatoes, a knife in
one hand and a potato in the other. What my thoughts
were I cannot remember but I have no doubt that being
alone I was talking to the (heavenly) Father about the
work I wished to do. Whatever thoughts engaged my
attention, suddenly I felt myself gripped by a strange
benevolent power that filled me with an unspeakable
sense of happiness. I seemed to be drawn up out of the
body and did not know where I was, whether "in the body
or out of it".'[16]

Agnes Sanford wrote of a similar experience:

Before I left the camp, a young woman was inspired
to pray for the opening in me of what she called the
spiritual eye, or a quickening of the gift of discernment
. . . I did not feel anything at that time. Sometimes one
feels waves of heavenly heat or holy joy; sometimes
one does not. One must trust, not on one's feelings
but on God!

Two days later amazing things happened to me . . . I
don't know where I was in body when my spirit took this
strange adventure . . . I am sure that I was not asleep.
This was no dream. My body may have been in my
study waiting for me to come back from a meditation
. . . I myself was somewhere very far away . . . nor was
it heaven . . . I saw no living thing until Jesus walked
down the valley past the folded hills, and as He came,
every fold filled up with light. I saw him with the eyes
of the spirit, but not in bodily form. Then he spoke to
me, though not in words, only in thought . . . I am
not expounding any theory. I am only stating what
happened to me, as truthfully as I can.

But I point out a very significant thing: I was not in

a body. Many people have flashes of memory of places never seen in this life, or of something that could not have happened in their lifetime, and assume that this proves reincarnation – that is being reborn in body after body upon this earth. I do not believe in this dreadful theory. I do believe in immortality, and my experience when the consciousness was blanked out in this life and I entered into the timelessness of heaven gives me a bit of comprehension into immortality.[17]

8 *Nature* – revelation may also come through nature (cf. Ps. 8:3–4, Ps. 19:1–4, Ps. 143:5, Matt. 2:1–12, Rom. 1:20)
Moses heard God from a burning bush. David heard God (Ps. 18:6) in the earthquake (v. 7), volcano (v. 8), lightning (vv. 9, 14), dark clouds (vv. 9–11) and thunder (v. 13). Jesus clearly saw the hand of God in nature when he found a barren fig tree (Mark 11:13–21). He told his disciples to consider the birds of the air and the lilies of the field (Matt. 6:26–9). The wise men followed a star (Matt. 2:2).

God may also teach a lesson through nature, as the discouraged Robert the Bruce of Scotland found to his advantage. When hiding from his enemies in a hollowed oak he observed a spider try again and again to spin a web by hitching his threads to a distant point, till at last the spider succeeded. Robert felt inspired by that example of persistence in nature to fight another day.

In the desert the hermit St Antony was once visited by a wise man. He was surprised that Antony could endure to live in such a place deprived as he was of the consolation of books. Antony replied: 'My book, philosopher, is the nature of created things, and I can read in it the works of God whenever I wish.'[18]

9 *Situations and Circumstances* – sometimes God speaks through certain situations (1 Sam. 15:28) or circumstances (Amos 8:1)
Some, it seems, receive revelations when at prayer or at

a special trysting place with God; some alone meditating on the Bible or worshipping in a meeting; many get them in bed when asleep or waking, others when out walking in a busy street or a country lane, yet others at a cocktail party or in a train looking out of the window or reading a newspaper (a headline shouts out a message from God), while yet others may get them at work. Some get them when simply glancing at a person – often the first thing they notice causes them to take a second look. It could be anywhere at any time – morning, noon or night.

Some would say they are prompted to listen or look by a prod or thump in a certain part of the body. Perhaps this was what Ezekiel was referring to when he said, 'The hand of the Lord was upon [me] . . . I looked . . .' (Ezek. 1:3,4). Similar experiences which are repeated also seem to be signals to alert some prophesying people to get ready:

'Suddenly I felt an invisible person had given me a thump in the stomach,' wrote Christine Huggett. 'I opened my eyes wide in alarm. Thump! There it was again! Then it was coming at regular intervals. And something else was happening too; my tongue was moving uncontrollably in my mouth. It was as though I should be speaking but did not know what to say.'[19]

Some feel a pressure or a presence (the Lord or his angel). Others have sensed sudden feelings of being dissociated from everyone else for a few seconds or minutes, as though a kind of glass separated them from the throb of natural life around them.

Some prophecy seems to derive *subjectively from a circumstantial impression* of words (often biblical), scenes, pictures (Amos 8:1, 2). Certain people report simply 'knowing' without words or pictures. Others recognise a problem through the pain felt in specific parts of the body or by touch.

In other cases a revelation from God may come through a vision or trance which seems to be intrinsic to being in a certain place at a certain time. In her moving book

William's Story,[20] Rosemary Attlee tells of her anguish as she wrestled with the fact that her seventeen-year-old son William was dying of leukaemia. While her family were off shopping she went into the quiet, little used (and soon to be closed) St Peter's Church in Sandwich. There she desperately implored God to let her know the time-span of William's illness. 'In an instant there seemed to be an agreement,' she writes.

'If I happened to be standing on a memorial stone, I could read that as a sign.' Slowly she looked down to a nineteenth-century inscription at her feet. The stone commemorated a man who had died aged twenty plus a few weeks. Rosemary took that to be God's answer. And so it turned out to be. William died aged twenty plus a few weeks. When she later revisited the same church with her husband to look at the stone once again, they searched the whole floor, *but there was no stone* (cf. Dan. 5:25).

'Mind the Gap!' Recently, instead of a church house party away, because of the problems of cost and accommodation we had a church 'At Home' weekend with David Parker, an American, addressing us. Few will ever forget an example he gave of how God had recently spoken to him over the p.a. system of the London underground with words very familiar to commuters – 'Mind the Gap!' Hearing those words David Parker had sensed God challenging him to mind the gaps in his own life. He also challenged us as individuals to mind the gap between where we were in our spiritual pilgrimages and where God wanted us to be. In the same way he challenged us as a church to think where we were and where God wanted the church to be!

That simple word had a profound impact on us as it has had on others elsewhere who have heard that message. We all sensed that God had spoken prophetically and powerfully that day. Quite simply God speaks in many different ways. The important point to recognise is that, unlike the pagan idols, our living, loving God is wanting a relationship which involves a two-way communication:

sometimes man speaking to God and sometimes God speaking to man. 'For God does speak – now one way, now another – though man may not perceive it. In a dream, in a vision of the night . . . he may speak in their ears' (Job 33:14–16).

10 *Ecstasy*

Some people tell of an ecstatic sensation of bubbling up inside! This almost brings us back full circle to where we started this chapter. But it is significant to mention it again here if we are to make it relevant. The Hebrew word translated as 'prophet' is *nabi* and has the root *nb* meaning 'to bubble forth'.[21] In one of his many books on prophecy Bill Hamon struggles to describe the way he receives prophecies from God:

> I must admit that I cannot find words to explain in detail how it works any more than I can explain in natural logic how I was born again and became a new creature in Christ Jesus . . . When I laid hands on the first person, the spirit of prophecy began to stir and boil within my spirit. Prophetic words began to fill my mind for the person . . . the same thing happened when I laid hands on the next two. When I laid hands on the fourth one, there was such a strong bubbling forth of the prophetic anointing and such a flow of prophetic thought for the person that I began to debate with God in my mind concerning what was happening. I told him I had not asked for this, and I asked whether it was his sovereign move. Was I supposed to release this prophetic flow to the people? He spoke clearly and told me to allow the prophetic flow to go out to the people as long as it kept bubbling forth. So I did . . .
>
> When I prophesy to numerous people one right after the other, I do not minister by visions, dreams or other knowledge previously received . . . I receive words directly from my divinely enabled spirit just as I do when I speak in tongues (1 Cor. 14:14, 15). I see

the thoughts about to be expressed in words only micro-seconds before they are spoken – just enough time to decide whether I have faith to speak it, whether I am using proper phrasing, and whether it would be wise to speak what I am perceiving (1 Cor. 14:32; Rom. 12:6).

Personally, I rarely receive much revelation knowledge about a person before I lay hands on that person and begin to prophesy. My natural mind has no way of knowing whether or not the things being prophesied are accurate.[22]

Obviously such a person would need to have a well-tested history of prophetic ministry before s/he was allowed to minister in church fellowships and conferences as Bill Hamon apparently does!

The subject of ecstasy in prophecy is developed later in this book (chapter 22).

11 *Riddles* (Num. 12:6, 7)
Riddles, parables and puns seem to be spontaneously communicated to the senses and such 'words' are often 'dark sayings' (Ps. 78:2 KJV) – very enigmatic. Paul says that 'we see in a mirror darkly' (1 Cor. 13:12 RV) – 'a poor reflection' (NIV).

Soon after Vice-President George Bush was nominated for the US presidency in 1988 by the Republican Party, one of my prophetic friends had an enigmatic word concerning Bush which no one could understand. Bush was reported in the press to be out hunting on his vacation and this was what this friend said about it: 'Bush is out hunting quail and the quail is behind the bush!' It was not until a few weeks later that Bush announced that Dan Quayle was his choice for vice-presidential candidate in the forthcoming election. This news came as a complete surprise to just about everyone.

It might well be asked for what purpose was this riddle. What good result did this accomplish? It created an awareness in one person who was hitherto unaware that God would speak to him in this way. From that time on he realised that he needed to be alert to the fact that God was showing him how he might intend to communicate with him on a more long term basis. God was revealing the code!

12 *Allegories or Parables* (Ezek. 17:2)
These are often the substance of dreams, but they may suddenly occur to someone in prayer or anywhere at any time while simply musing, but in a way which makes it clear that God is communicating something significant.

13 *Puns* (Jer. 1:12, Amos 8:1–2)
A friend on a recent faith-sharing mission in Finland was asking God to reveal particular details to identify people God wanted him to minister to at that meeting. The picture of a saw (for cutting wood) suddenly came into his mind's eye. He found himself focusing on the teeth of the saw. He pondered on it prayerfully for a second or two. Suddenly he realised the puzzle played on a pun. He announced that he felt there was someone present with 'sore teeth' who needed prayer. A pastor came forward with a condition which seemed to be exactly described by that 'word' and was duly prayed for!

Possible accompanying phenomena
Seemingly certain effects can accompany the anointing, such as fallings under the power of God, bodily sensations and tremblings (Ezek. 3:23, Isa. 21:3, Jer. 23:9, Dan. 10:10).

W.R. Inge uses his own words to describe how Teresa of Avila was affected with 'a kind of catalepsy with muscular rigidity and cessation of the pulses'.[23]

Reported modern-day feedback suggests various kinds of stirring within. One who professed to have prophetic gifting described a strong surge from the pit of the stomach: 'I had to just open my mouth and say whatever came out. It kept spilling out and then just faded.'

A recent TV programme on the healing of Mrs Jennifer Rees Larcombe who had been crippled for eight years told how she went to various healing meetings and had visited healing centres in the hope of being cured. But no healing came and she had written a book on facing life without being healed.

She was often asked to speak at meetings on suffering which she would occasionally manage to do, wheelchair permitting. One day she went to speak at a meeting in Haslemere, Surrey and during the question time after her talk a fairly new Christian present, a South African lady, spoke up very quietly and said she was sorry to interrupt, and she had never done anything like this before, but she had to say that Jesus was going to heal Jennifer. After they had gathered round her to pray Jennifer was indeed healed.

Wendy, the South African lady, said later that while listening to Jennifer she felt the Lord quite strongly saying that he was going to heal her but she did not dare to say anything. Later, during the question time, she opened her mouth to say something. From the video interview one got the impression she meant to say something else but out came those words.

There were two little asides in the interview which may also be significant. One was that Wendy had gone to the meeting fasting. The other was that for the first time in her life she felt valuable to God after having been involved in this miracle. She had been brought up in South Africa and, being of mixed race, had always had the feeling of being rejected. (This feeling may have been a factor in her prophetic gifting – see chapter 3.)

Another person reports a similar spontaneous stirring about prophesying: 'Something stirs within me. Something starts to come from within – stirring within that rises up within me – it is something intuitive, not intellectual. I was shaking. I was clasping my hands. It was awful! (see Dan 8:17, 27).'[24]

Yet another reports 'the weight [burden of it] was so heavy I thought I was going to die and I was forced to speak it out'. A recent account concerning revelation which led to the healing of a serious elbow injury gives the same kind of imperative: 'The physical feeling [that accompanied a very detailed description by Francie Lygo] was like thousands of volts going through me and I just felt I had to say something.'[25]

We could add other phenomena to the list: tingling lips or mouth area, burning in some part of the body or a feeling of fire in the belly, palpitations, a sense of heavy weight or burden that crushes until the prophecy is given out, almost squeezed out. These are not proofs of genuine anointing. We simply observe that these phenomena have often accompanied genuine anointings. Some are led to sing what God has put on their hearts or in their mouths either in prose or poetry.

Some are led simply to write the words down, maybe in prose or poetry (Jer. 36:2, Hab. 2:2). The kind of uncontrolled frenzy (1 Sam. 19:23–4) that is reported in the Old Testament would, however, be unacceptable in a church setting (1 Cor. 14:40). It would be 'unfitting'.

David Aune distinguishes between 'controlled' and 'uncontrolled' possession which was sometimes the condition for receiving trances. Saul's experience (1 Sam. 19:23–4 referred to above) is a classic example of 'uncontrolled possession' though we do not know whether he received any kind of trance experience in the process. Aune believes that although the initial experiences of the revelatory trance (like the initial power anointings from the Holy Spirit) are often involuntary, uncontrolled and unpredictable, nevertheless, with practice, those subject to such experiences can subsequently learn to control them.[26] 'The spirits of the prophets subject to the control of the prophets' (1 Cor. 14:32).

Psycho-sociological influence

We are aware of the complex area of psycho-sociological influence and group expectation that can create a powerful climate for suggesting certain behaviour. Response to this does not necessarily invalidate any revelation produced under those circumstances.

We recognise that there is a deep desire in most of us to be accepted in our own group. It is not difficult, consciously or unconsciously, to adopt the appropriate behaviour to be accepted or to aspire to whatever end is expected.

David Aune highlights the fact that the external phenomena surrounding some spiritual happenings exhibit a behavioural and experiential structure. This is socially communicated and therefore may be 'learned' by those who have such spontaneous experiences.[27] This would doubtless have been a major factor in those Old Testament schools of prophets under Samuel and Elisha.

Neither are we unaware of the possibility for projecting personal desires and feelings on to God. These are admittedly areas of concern and it is no good pretending that they do not exist. But then they must always have existed as long as men have been prophesying in the world. We must not rule out the possibility that God may well choose to work through these complexities rather than apart from them. Good theology and psychology need not be mutually exclusive frames of reference.

7

HOW IS PROPHECY ANALYSED?

Introduction
The New Testament Greek words used for 'revelation' and 'reveal' describe insights which are of divine origin and which enable Christians to know something from the perspective of the Kingdom of God.

It is a foretaste of the full unveiling of God's secrets which will take place on the day of Christ's return. Yet revelation is not limited to knowledge about that eschatological event, or even in a more general way to knowledge about things to come. Revelation takes place when a believer comes to see himself, the church and the world from a Kingdom [of God] perspective.[1]

Differing stages of prophetic revelation
There would seem to be three clear stages or levels in the prophetic process:

the revelation itself
the interpretation of the revelation
the application of the interpretation

Mishandling may occur at any level, but mistakes do not invalidate the original revelation.

The following example illustrates the importance of this. On a visit to the Kansas City Fellowship some five years ago we learned a significant lesson about the revelation behind prophecy. (Incidentally we never actually heard anyone there refer to himself as a prophet nor to the church as having prophets. The church had, however, been built up on the prophetic ministry and if some of those people were not prophets we are forced to wonder whoever could be considered such!)

One 'prophet' had a vision in which he plainly recognised another member of the fellowship whom he later confronted as being involved in some kind of fraud. The accused brother hotly denied any such thing. The matter was taken to the leadership – where it should have been taken in the first place – and the leader began to question the 'prophet' closely. 'I swear I recognised him in my vision,' said the 'prophet'.

'And what else did you see that made you think he was involved in some kind of a fraud?' asked the leader.

'I saw his head in a cloud and there were dollar signs all over the cloud,' replied the 'prophet'. Who would not have assumed some shady dealing there?

Eventually it turned out that the reason the man's head was 'in the clouds' was because something was going on that he knew nothing about. The 'accused' brother called for a full investigation of the books at his office which revealed that one of his partners was in fact embezzling the funds of their business.

But for the careful intervention by the leader the true interpretation might never have come to light. Neither would it, of course, had the 'prophet' not taken the risk of acting on the revelation he had received. The embarrassment over the original confrontation was soon transformed into profound gratitude for the revelation which saved the man from ruin before it was too late.[2]

The revelation itself

We are not discussing here *how* revelation is received but *what* is received.

The motivation and the source

All knowledge is not necessarily good for us to know. There is forbidden knowledge, which neither man nor woman may tap. There are secret things which belong only to the Lord but the things that are revealed belong to us and to our children for ever (Deut. 29:29). We therefore need to know how we should tell whether the knowledge revealed to us is given from a right motivation and comes from a good source or not. To help us God has put into the Body of Christ some who have a specific gift for this.

There is a *gift for discerning motivation and the source*: this is the distinguishing of spirits (1 Cor. 12:10). This gift is not for interpreting the prophecy or deciding if it is true or directing the church on how or when to apply it, but for identifying the source of the prophecy and the motivation behind it.

For example, after Paul was released from prison at Philippi, his party was met by a slave girl who followed them around, shouting: 'These men are servants of the Most High God, who are telling you the way to be saved' (Acts 16:17). What this girl said was absolutely true, but the way she said it troubled Paul. Once he had determined what the Lord wanted him to do about it, because we are not called to go around casting out every spirit, Paul cast this spirit out of the girl.

The motivation had been to harass Paul in his ministry, and the source was clearly demonic, even though she had spoken the truth. The one who knows how 'to separate the precious from the worthless will be God's spokesman' (Jer. 15:19 New American Standard Bible).

The interpretation of the revelation

Interpretations also belong to God: Joseph said, 'I cannot do it, but God will give . . . the answer he desires' (Gen. 41:16).

So much will depend upon interpretation and the interpretation will depend upon so much. This whole area, however, is not simply concerned with interpreting dreams and visions but solving riddles and explaining enigmas (Dan. 5:12). Revelation may not necessarily be understood literally; it takes decoding to know the whole meaning.

Some have a gift for interpretation. This is something which needs to be developed with prayer and experience.

The first interpretation may not necessarily be the true or only one; it may even be wrong and the right interpretation may only come later. For example, the word 'Nicodemus' impressed itself strongly on a pastor as he spotted a newcomer in the church. He presumed the Lord must be telling him that the man had potential for leadership: in fact it turned out that he needed to be born again!

There are a few further points about who should do the interpreting.

1 The one who receives a revelation may also interpret it. But not all who receive revelation can interpret it. Clearly the butler and the baker (Gen. 40), Pharaoh (Gen. 41) and Nebuchadnezzar (Dan. 2) were unable to interpret their prophetic dreams.

2 Others may interpret someone else's revelation out of their gifting, like Joseph (Gen. 40:8) and Daniel (Dan. 2:24).

3 Still others may interpret out of their office (the leaders of the Church), not necessarily out of their anointing but out of their appointing.

Those who become involved in interpretation soon discover that certain elements are significant: symbols, colours and numbers, for example. As experience grows it becomes possible to recognise meaning in symbols (Rev. 12:9), colours (Rev. 7:9, 19:8 cf. Isa. 1:18) and numbers (Gen. 40:12) where they are contained in the revelation itself, though these are not to be taken as constant since the meaning of symbols may vary from person to person and interpreter to interpreter. For example, 'chains' may mean bondage in sin to Satan for one person but bondage in love to Christ to another; 'a lion' in one person's dream could be Christ 'the Lion of Judah' and in another the devil who is described as 'a roaring lion looking for someone to devour' (1 Pet. 5:8). Pictures of birth may not refer to a new baby coming but to something new beginning; likewise a death may not signify that someone is to die (though it did with Abraham Lincoln concerning his own assassination (Job 33:16)) but may be some trait in the old nature that is to be put to death. Pictures of children may be speaking of our own inner child and people of the opposite sex may represent the other side of our real self.

This mystical area of symbolism needs great care indeed. Though knowing something about these symbols may be very helpful to some, we must never develop our perceptions into fixed formulae for general application. What symbolises something meaningful in the situation of one person may be most misleading in the situation of another.

We discover the meaning of our own symbols by trial and error and should always keep in mind the wise words of Solomon: 'Much dreaming and many words are meaningless. Therefore stand in awe of God' (Eccles. 5:7).

The application of the revelation

1 *Who, what, how, when and where*

It may be that the one who gives a prophecy also has the correct interpretation. The outcome may still be counterproductive, however, if he misfires with the application. There is a who, when, how and where about communicating a revelation.

There are also similar questions for the application, such as 'What am I expected to do about it?' 'When should I act on it?' 'Who should be told?' As with prophecy in the Scripture, there could also be more than one application.

2 *The fulfilment*

It is possible to have a predictive revelation, properly

interpreted and applied but unfulfilled within the immediate future. God's ways are not our ways and in the case of both Joseph and David they had to wait *a long time* and endure rejection and suffering before the time of fulfilment arrived. Though visions seem very immediate it would be wrong to assume the fulfilment was necessarily to be so.

3 *Are the predicted results inevitable*?

The answer to this question must be a qualified 'no!' if we check up on this in the Bible. There are three clear examples or statements to show that under certain conditions, following certain responses from man, God will readily change what has been declared. We think how Hezekiah's death was predicted (2 Kgs 20:1 and 5) but through an appropriate response Hezekiah's life was spared. Nineveh's judgment was foretold by God through Jonah but when the citizens repented God changed his mind, much to Jonah's disgust (Jonah 3:4, 10; see also Amos 7:3). So much will depend upon man's response to God's pronouncements (Jer. 18:8–10).

Having said all this, however, it must also be stated that should there not be the appropriate response from us, after what the Lord deems sufficient reminders, then the prophecy will be executed. Then it will be too late; the time has come, the target has been selected, computer bearings have been taken, the button has been pressed and the missile is already on its way – then, as with Jeremiah, we hear God saying: 'Do not pray for this people nor offer any plea or petition for them; do not plead with me, for I will not listen to you' (Jer. 7:16, 11:14).

Biblical example of these three stages

We consider the case of Paul and Agabus (Acts 21) and discern the three stages of this prophecy.

Revelation: It seems Agabus saw Paul in Jerusalem bound in the hands of the Gentiles, where he would be held prisoner surrounded by hostile Jews (Acts 21:11).

Interpretation: Agabus seems to have assumed the Jews

would bind Paul and hand him over to the Romans (Acts 21:10–11). He was mistaken in his interpretation over who would do the binding (Acts 21:33).

Application: Agabus and his friends seem to have been mistaken in their application. They took it as a warning to Paul not to go to Jerusalem. Because of independent revelation (Acts 20:22) Paul was sure that he was meant to go and that this was simply confirmation, including a warning of what he should expect there (Acts 21:31).[3]

8

HOW IS PROPHECY RELAYED?

For our starting point we need to remind ourselves of how
Jesus appears to have operated in the prophetic ministry.
We set this out as simply and clearly as possible, as far as
we can understand it, from Scripture.

The example of Jesus himself

1 Jesus only said and did *what* he heard and saw the
Father doing (John 5:19).

2 Jesus only said what the Father said, and only said it
how the Father wanted him to say it (John 12:49). There
are counter-productive ways of saying what we sense God
is saying. Paul, on the other hand, talks about 'speaking
the truth in love' (Eph. 4:15). My wife, Mary, was once
praying for a woman who came forward, among others,
for prayer following a Sunday morning service. As they
waited together upon the Lord, Mary suddenly got the
distinct impression that this woman's problems arose from
an incestuous relationship with her father as a teenager. To
confront the woman with this could prove to be traumatic,
and in any case, as with all the gifts of the Spirit, it is
important always to bear in mind that one could be
wrong. Mary prayed and the Lord put it in her mind
to ask the woman if it would be all right to pray about
her relationship with her father as a teenager. The woman
agreed and no sooner had Mary started praying than the
woman began to weep profusely and out came the whole
story. God had shown my wife the right way to use the
insight he had given her.

3 Jesus only did things *when* the Father told him, and not before (John 16:12). Even though Mary was his mother, Jesus resisted her urgent appeal to intervene when the wine ran out at the wedding in Cana of Galilee (John 2:3–4) and delayed markedly following the emotional pleas of his two friends Mary and Martha at the time of Lazarus' apparently terminal illness (John 11:3–6) because the time was not right.

4 Sometimes it seems that Jesus was shown things that he did not feel it was right to tell the people concerned at the time (John 16:12). Some revelations may never need to be shared but simply serve as a spur to prayer or a star to guide us in our pastoral care for others.

Practical lessons from experience

It is appropriate and useful to provide a few practical helps for those who want to prophesy. Having created a small 'corpus of wisdom' from those who have experience in prophecy and those who lead churches where the gift is exercised we offer the following guidelines point by point:

1 For prophesying we use the same vocal organs, the same mouth, lips, larynx and accent as in normal speech. But the message may be written down in prose or poetry. It may seem right to communicate it in some kind of drama. If the prophecy is sung (1 Chr. 25:1, Zeph. 3:17, Col. 3:16) it should bless the ear as well as the heart – in other words, don't try singing publicly if you do not have a reasonable voice to sing with! Other people are usually the better judge of this! King David, who was inspired from his early days to articulate many prophecies in the Psalms, became known as 'the sweet singer of Israel'.

2 Prophecy uttered in church (if we follow Paul) ought to be given standing up (1 Cor. 14:30). Paul does not explain why but we may assume there were obvious reasons. Possibly it was to ensure that the person was fully in control of him/herself – the spirits of prophets

being subject to the control of the prophets (1 Cor. 14:32). Standing up also facilitates visibility in a meeting. The leader can see who is speaking or singing. It usually enhances audibility also. Do your best to speak or sing clearly. Do not move forward to do this unless requested by the leadership. Simply 'offer' your 'word' standing where you are.

3 Those who want to be heard in church should beware of nervous movements. One young lady shared a good word in church which went almost unheard because of the way she was continually shuffling her feet. All eyes were focused on her trainers.

4 A person prophesying will gain a more responsive audience if s/he avoids prefixing the prophecy with such words as 'Thus saith the Lord' as such a blunt declaration would seem to challenge the right of any hearers to weigh the words themselves. It is much easier for the hearers to receive prophecy if it is offered with a preface such as 'I believe the Lord may be saying', etc.

5 There is no need to give the prophecy in a strange voice – give it naturally. Those who earnestly desire to prophesy will certainly need to soak their hearts in Scripture: 'Let the word of Christ dwell in you richly' (Col. 3:16). If the version you use is the KJV the words may well come out in Elizabethan English, but this should not become a model for others to copy nor be adopted in order to give prophecy greater authentication.

6 No one should be surprised if the prophecy is couched in biblical language or full of Scripture. The Book of Revelation is prophecy (Rev. 1:3) and contains over 400 citations from Old Testament Scriptures.

7 Neither should anyone be surprised if it is not given in biblical language or biblical imagery or texts of pure Scripture.

8 Sometimes a prophecy may be accompanied by some dramatic act (1 Kgs 11:30) or a mime (Ezek. 4:4) or a significant personal commitment (Hos. 1:2, Jer. 32:8) or

it may come through the interpretation of a 'tongue' (1 Cor. 14:5,6).

9 Revelation itself may not always be as edifying as it ought to be because of the insensitive way it is given (John 12:49). Paul writes about the vital importance of 'speaking the truth in love' (Eph. 4:15). Joseph's dreams were rejected because they were tactlessly communicated (Gen. 37:10).

10 Seek the Lord about the right time for giving the prophecy (John 16:12).

11 It would be better not to call yourself a prophet even if you become one. Marie Stopes once addressed the bishops at a Lambeth Conference. Reportedly her opening words were: 'You are the priests; I am a prophet.' The danger with that kind of claim is that it leaves the hearer wanting to investigate her claim to be a prophet rather than being focused on the helpful things she had to say about marriage, sex and birth control. The same thing happened recently when a Christian chief constable reportedly claimed that he spoke as a prophet when he attacked the moral state of the country. The attention was drawn to the man and whether he could really be a prophet while people forgot the message, which was an important one. There is admittedly another factor with these two cases, which is that society does not tend to accept any prophets too readily.

12 Not all who have the gift of prophecy are prophets. Agabus was a prophet while Philip's four daughters simply had the gift of prophecy (Acts 21:8ff). (See also chapter 2.)

13 Never boast of your gifting or insist that you have any gift.

14 Never try to manipulate things to prove you are right. In particular, do not circulate your prophecy concerning a specific individual in the local church to other church members! Remember, if you are wrong this may amount to slander – one thing that Paul frequently and

particularly warned his readers against. (See 2 Cor. 12:20, Eph. 4:31, Col. 3:8, Titus 3:2 This would soon bring the prophetic ministry into serious disrepute.

15 Never insist that you are right. Lack of signs of genuine humility in the prophetically gifted is something which sets the ministry back in the local church. If you are right then you can trust God to see that his word will not return to him empty but will accomplish what he desires (Isa. 55:11). The Preacher said, 'Cast your bread upon the waters, for after many days you will find it again' (Eccles. 11:1). It may seem unsatisfactory at the time but those who minister in the prophetic must learn simply to cast their message 'upon the waters' and leave it there.

16 The Christian needs to remember that in the exercise of any of the gifts of the Spirit one could sometimes be wrong. No one is infallible. Leaders do not have to serve long in the church before they come across lovely spiritual and sincere people who have been sincerely but seriously wrong. Be assured that many leaders have already had tragic experiences of this kind of situation.

17 Try to avoid being emotional in speaking out even if you feel it intensely, and never rant. (Only twice in twenty years have I ever had to take action behind the scenes on this one. One man apologised when I gently tackled him about it but left soon after to look for a more 'spiritual' church.)

18 Try to keep the 'word' brief. Many begin in the spirit but in their nervousness continue in the flesh.

19 If you are sharing a revelation that has been given you previously it can be edited beforehand so that it comes out more clearly. Daniel (7:1) wrote down 'the substance' (NIV) or 'the main facts' (RAV).

20 Don't be surprised, however, if the word God gives you is brief. Haggai once had a very brief word: 'I am with you'! (Hagg. 1:13). A lady was singing in a group at St Andrew's when a friend sensed God saying of her, 'She has chosen the better part.' It seemed such a trivial

word that she would have forgotten it had she not bumped into the lady afterwards by the door so she shared what she thought the Lord had said. It was surprisingly apt and significant because the lady concerned had felt God telling her to drop a number of things and devote more time to prayer, which she was trying to do, but she was feeling almost guilty about the things she was giving up.

21 Other words that are not known beforehand simply 'burst forth' under the anointing. Paul is probably referring to this when he says that he who prophesies should do it 'according to his faith' (Rom. 12:6). The first words are like taking a stopper off the bottle. In his book *It Hurts to Heal* John Huggett likens it to taking paper tissues out of a box. Once the first is out the second follows. 'I receive a few words in my mind and as I speak them out I'm given a few more, and so on, until it suddenly stops.'[1]

22 Don't be surprised, if you are being given a lot of significant revelation, that you suffer fierce opposition (2 Cor. 12:7). The Lord allows this to keep us humble and to remind us that our prophetic 'power is made perfect in weakness' (2 Cor. 12:9). His 'grace is sufficient'.

23 S/he who receives a prophecy may give it outside the church gathering to the individual concerned in the appropriate way (via the leadership if it involves correction or direction). The recipient should never act on it, but await confirmation, unless the prophecy itself is a confirmation, coming completely independently concerning something God has already been speaking to the individual about in other ways and at other times: e.g. Gideon overhearing a Midianite soldier recounting his dream and the fellow soldier's interpretation (Judg. 7:13–15).

24 Once the person who has the prophecy has given it to the church or the leadership, then s/he has discharged his/her responsibility. Leaders will not necessarily act upon it immediately. They may simply ponder it, as Mary did (Luke 2:19), or not act upon it at all! That is their responsibility and no longer that of the prophetic person.

25 Never give a date for the Second Coming of Christ, the Day of Judgment or the end of the world. It is not for us to know (Matt. 24:36, Acts 1:7). As has been so well said: 'God's *time* terminology differs considerably from ours. He never seems to be in a hurry. He often seems to take longer than we think he should.'[2] Nearly 2,000 years ago the Lord himself said, 'I am coming soon' (Rev. 22:20). Abraham's impatience resulted in Ishmael (Gen. 16). Saul's impatience lost him his anointing (1 Sam. 13:13). God has his own time and season for things (Eccles 3:1–8).

We think that 'now' and 'this day' must be immediately. Between the 'now' when Samuel said Saul's kingdom would not continue and the time he actually lost it were thirty-eight years (1 Sam. 13:1–14) and between the announcement: 'The Lord has torn the kingdom of Israel from you today and has given it to one of your neighbours – to one better than you' (1 Sam. 15:28) and the time when this actually happened were some twenty-four years.

God talks about things that are not now as though they are: Abraham 'believed . . . God who . . . calls things *that are not as though they were*' (Rom. 4:17). It is sometimes difficult to determine whether a personal prophecy is speaking of things past, present or future.

26 Never give prophecies for correction or direction to individuals in the local church without first consulting the leadership.

27 Novices who aspire to a prophetic ministry are very tempted to go for an 'easy' target using general denunciations or calling the church to repentance. As there will never be a church in the land that does not need to repent of something, this kind of blanket approach would seem to be a 'can't lose' situation. Actually we will lose a great deal if we are not discerning. The blanket is simply a 'wet' one. We could all too easily lose the prophetic ministry completely if we have not first lost half the congregation.

There is no doubt that one aspect of the Holy Spirit's

work is the conviction of sin (John 16:8) but Satan is also the accuser of the brethren (Rev. 12:10). Therefore very special care should be taken about calling the church publicly and directly to repentance. The Holy Spirit is actively working in this way, of course, but his way of doing it brings faith, true repentance and encouragement.

Over the years we have talked with others in local church leadership who have confirmed the view that public prophecies of this kind have nearly always seemed of the flesh and counterproductive. If the speaker has been hearing God speaking of repentance while worshipping the Lord in a public meeting s/he should beware that God is more likely, in the circumstances, to be first calling him or her to repentance personally.

A little practical common sense should indicate that using prophecy in any crude, shaming or insensitive way is bound to bring the whole prophetic ministry into disrepute. What we have found is that when God really wants to use revelation publicly to bring people to repentance it is usually so subtle, loving and tender that no one else would realise it except the person concerned and this way one feels almost wooed into repentance.

28 It is best to avoid resorting to prophecy in any way for resolving church disputes, especially where it concerns one of the leaders, if the person who gives the prophecy is directly or indirectly, personally or emotionally, involved. Such use can easily sour a situation and quickly bring the prophetic ministry into disrepute. Of course if a complete outsider, who is genuinely ignorant of what is going on, has a prophecy, this may well be a healing 'word' from the Lord.

29 We would give the same advice about ministering to the sick and dying. We are mindful of the prophecies sent through the post to David Watson when he was dying of cancer. Many were so wrong and made one ashamed to be identified with the restoration of prophecy to the Church if it was going to come to this. But we trust the whole

Church has learnt from it. It is just too easy, when one is emotionally involved, to let wishful thinking override. God is sovereign and can certainly use prophecy if he wants to. We have the example of Jesus in the case of Lazarus (John 11:14) and also that of Isaiah in the case of Hezekiah (2 Kgs 20:1). In the former case the word could be utterly trusted because of Jesus' perfect relationship with God the Father. In the latter case a sign was requested of Isaiah to confirm the prophecy and the sign was clearly given. It is a very serious thing to assume divine authority for a false promise – especially where it concerns a life or death situation.

Even those coming from outside who give prophecies to the dying, where there is no prior knowledge that the person concerned is seriously ill, should not be heeded unless the prophecy comes with the promise of a clear sign which should be demonstrably confirmed before being believed. If this is not given and the sign not fulfilled then the 'prophecy' should be completely discounted.

No one wants to throw doubt on a prophecy to a dying person which promises restoration of health, so it is nigh on impossible to get proper discernment in such a situation. What is in fact a serious deception may be allowed to go unchecked. Too often a discerning friend, who thinks a 'prophecy' given by a well-wisher is not actually to be trusted, will be strongly tempted just to sit and say nothing, avoiding the issue and trying to change the subject as quickly as possible. There is a great emotional pressure to look for any little sign of encouragement and to say things which we think are faith-building to help the person to fight the sickness. For this reason above all we would caution friends to hold back on all prophecy in such circumstances.

A prophetic word from someone totally unaware of the sickness might have more significance, however. One who has great experience in this has written: 'Probably 99 per cent of all healing and miracles . . . happened through personal prophecy . . . when the one prophesying had no prior knowledge of the existing condition.'[3]

The same high risk of wishful thinking or best intentions pertains in the case of a prophetic 'word' given in the congregation where it is taken home to a particular dying person with insistence that this word must be for him/her. Nor should such a 'word' be pressed on to a sick or dying person even when the person has been present. We must allow the sick person in such cases to let the Holy Spirit witness secretly to his/her own heart without the slightest manipulative gesture on our part.

30 Never add to the prophetic word. There are subtle temptations here to exaggerate or flatter those who accept your word. On the other hand there is a temptation to give negative words to those who challenge you.

31 Never prophesy concerning a romance or marriage where you are emotionally involved in any way with either party.

32 Never prophesy over any other situation where you have natural knowledge, are emotionally involved or have strong opinions.

33 Never pretend to be prophesying when you are speaking simply from the conviction of Scripture rather than the quickening of the Spirit.

Receiving a prophetic word from a prophetic person

In the Old Testament guidance came through the prophet, as did healing and the gift of miracles. Under the New Covenant (Jer. 31:31–4, Heb. 8:8–13) things were radically changed. After the death and resurrection of Christ the believer had direct access to God the Father through the Holy Spirit. Jesus gave considerable time to teaching the disciples about this (cf. John 13–16).

George Canty is a wise and experienced teacher, and a one-time worldwide president of the Elim Pentecostal

Church. He warns us to beware of those who are using their gift to control others:

> We should submit to nobody who professes by the word of the Spirit to know better than we ourselves what God's will is about our personal affairs and business. It is in fact out of accord with, even a contradiction of, the glorious promises of God and the provisions of covenanted and blood bought freedom . . .
>
> To bring people into the bondage of hardly moving foot or finger without permission from some person claiming Divine command from prophetic powers is totally outside the whole concept of prophecy both in the New and the Old dispensation.[4]

Although directional prophecy is capable of being greatly abused there are occasional examples of it in the New Testament (e.g. Acts 27:10). It needs treating with great care and should certainly be tested with the leadership present.

The word to the prophets in Acts 13:2 seemed to come as a confirmation rather more than a direction. The church was to let Paul and Barnabas go to the work to which God had called them. It would appear that both Paul and Barnabas already knew what the Lord had called them to do next.

The word Agabus brought to Paul in Acts 21:11–14 did not cause Paul to stop or change direction but simply confirmed to him that he was on course, and the warnings of what were to come were simply confirmation (Acts 20:22–4) that all was going according to God's plan. Because of that they were, in fact, words of comfort (1 Cor. 14:3).

We should never act on any prophecy until the Lord has clearly confirmed it from a completely different source. Obviously there are times when the prophecy itself is a clear confirmation of what the Lord has been saying in other ways and will need no further reinforcement. There are other times where something in the future is predicted and nothing can be done; the prophecy needs to be put 'on hold' (Luke 2:19).

'*Beware* of any words, dreams, visions about oneself where it involves something like *finding a treasure, marrying "a film star", taking a leadership role in the church, giving up a job which has become frustrating.*'[5]

Revelations are not usually plain, but when they are or become plain, and have been suitably tested, they should, if possible, be received with faith (Heb. 4:2) and acted upon in the appropriate way (Acts 26:19).

9

HOW IS PROPHECY EVALUATED?

Introduction
Following a spiritual outpouring in North America during
the late 1940s and early 1950s, a surge of prophecies
accompanied a new 'Latter Rain Movement'. Without
endorsing all the teaching of that movement it has to be
said that many were astonished by the depth of revelation
given about people, situations and churches. Thousands
were blessed by the prophetic words to themselves and
their families.

Serious problems arose, however, when prophecy became
the 'in' thing and people began to manufacture prophetic
words out of their own conjecturings (Ezek. 13:2). It was
a repeat of the old story: 'I did not send these prophets,
yet they have run with their message; I did not speak to
them, yet they have prophesied' (Jer. 23:21). Little was
apparently done to correct all this and the 'Latter Rain
Movement', whatever its merits, was greatly undermined
by such unbridled 'prophetic utterances'. Men and women
were prophesying all kinds of words over people but were
not operating under authority. Their prophecies went
untested.

God is not the author of such confusion, which could
not but end in despair and delusion. There is a divine
order for such things (1 Cor. 14:31 and 40). We all need
to learn how to behave ourselves in the household of God
(1 Tim. 3:15). Because these principles were overlooked,
the whole movement was eventually banned from the

Assemblies of God. Onlookers were left reflecting ruefully that if the AOG who promote the gifts of the Spirit can't handle this, who can?

Once again God's true gift of prophecy, which could have been restored for the great blessing of the Church, was rejected.

With the so-called 'Charismatic Movement' beginning in the early 1960s there was a rediscovery in Britain of the gifts of the Spirit (1 Cor. 12) – and once again there have been some serious mistakes over prophecy.

Professor Verna Wright reports the tragic case of a couple from a Sheffield church who had had a severely disabled child with cystic fibrosis. Their specialist medical advice strongly discouraged them from having any more children. It was explained that in their case there was a 'one in four' chance that any future offspring would be affected.[1] The parents were almost reconciled to this situation when a member of their church gave them a 'prophecy' saying, 'You will have a normal child!' The wife soon conceived again and their next baby was more severely affected than their first.

There are of course bound to be mistakes but it would be irresponsible indeed if we did not try to learn some of the lessons of the past.

Paul enjoins his readers to treat prophetic utterances with respect and not with contempt (1 Thess 5:20). John Stott writes that we are neither to accept them outright nor to reject them outright. We are to listen to them and test everything (1 Thess. 5:21a) – to sift them and to weigh carefully what is said (1 Cor. 14:29).[2]

Varying mix of the human and divine

It may be appropriate to repeat a purely human and subjective conjecture at this point. God has chosen to use humans as his spokespeople so it is reasonable to assume that some of the humanity comes with the prophecy, and this seems to match with our experience of it! This is also why we are told to sift and weigh prophecy. The most pure prophecy given publicly is probably only 80 per cent God and 20 per cent human. In some cases it may be 80 per cent human and only 20 per cent God.[3]

While there is no specific gift of discernment, but rather distinguishing of spirits, there is nevertheless the gift of wisdom which God gives generously to those who ask for it (Jas 1:5). Some tend to be very fearful about the whole area of discernment lest we should be easily deceived. We should be encouraged by John's words when he said: 'the one who is in you is greater than the one who is in the world' (1 John 4:4). We have a greater discerner than the greatest deceiver!

How should we filter prophecy?

There are at least eight possible tests. Individually applied they may not prove conclusive, but several taken together act as a good guide.

1 *Scripture*. Like the Bereans (Acts 17:11) we are to examine the Scriptures to see if what is said is true (Deut. 13:1ff). 'All Scripture is God-breathed and is useful for teaching, rebuking, correcting and training in righteousness' (2 Tim. 3:16). 'For the word of God is living and active. Sharper than any double-edged sword, it penetrates even to dividing soul and spirit, joints and marrow; it judges the thoughts and attitudes of the heart' (Heb. 4:12). This two-edged sword applies both to the truth of the prophecy itself and also the effectiveness of the prophecy.

Prophecy may reveal something through Scripture or apart from Scripture but never in contradiction to Scripture. 'My sheep,' said Jesus, 'do not recognise a stranger's voice' (John 10:5).

Problem: It is possible to find places where the prophetic gift is exercised among Christians who have such a limited knowledge of the Bible – even the leadership – that they cannot use this test adequately. This was especially the case in Third World countries but could well be true in the UK today.

It is salutary also to note that there are genuine cases of revelation where the prophet is sometimes told to do things quite contrary to the accepted wisdom and tradition, e.g. Ezekiel in Ezek. 4:12–13 and Peter in Acts 10:4.

2 *Jesus* – the divine-human person. We are *not to believe every spirit*, but test the spirits to see whether they are from God. 'This is how you can recognise the Spirit of God: every spirit [prophet claiming inspiration] that acknowledges that Jesus Christ has come in the flesh is from God, but every spirit that does not acknowledge Jesus is not from God. This is the spirit of the antichrist' (1 John 4:3). 'The testimony of Jesus is the spirit of prophecy' (Rev. 19:10). Are the words and the 'feel' of the prophecy honouring to Christ?

Problem: Demons can be so deceiving that *sometimes they even speak the truth* (Mark 1:24). 'Whenever the evil spirits saw him, they fell down before [Jesus] and cried out, "You are the Son of God." But [Jesus] gave them strict orders not to tell who he was' (Mark 3:11, cf. Acts 16:17).

3 *The gospel*. This is God's free and saving grace through Christ. Anybody who perverts this gospel (whether preacher, prophet, apostle or even angel) deserves to be 'eternally condemned' (Gal. 1:6–9).

Problem: This is pretty clear, but *some deceivers carefully avoid any reference to the gospel but cover this up by couching their words in pious jargon*.

4 *The character of the prophet*. Jesus warned his disciples to watch out for false prophets, saying that they are wolves disguised as sheep. He said they would be known by their fruits (Matt. 7:15–20).

Just as a tree is known by its fruit (the taste of the fruit etc.) so the testing of a prophet is his/her character or conduct and the fruit of his/her ministry. One example might be that the prophet's followers were opposed to authority. That would leave a bad taste among healthy church members. If a prophet were to be doing or saying something for personal gratification rather than the glory of God, that, too, would leave a bad taste.

Problem: God pronounced *Abraham* a prophet even though he had just blatantly deceived Abimelech by telling a lie about his wife (Gen. 20:7).

Balaam had a beautiful prophecy regarding Christ and it is recorded in Scripture (Num. 24) that though he resorted to sorcery (Num. 24:1), the Lord used Balaam to deliver Israel out of Balak's hand (Josh. 24:10) and he fell from grace (Jude 11).

David committed adultery and murder, but we are still edified by his Psalms and his prophetic ministry is owned by the New Testament Church (Acts 2:29–30).

The old prophet lied to the man of God from Judah, but gave a prophecy to him, which was almost immediately and literally fulfilled (1 Kgs 13:14–26).

5 *Fulfilment of the prophecy.* 'Will this come to pass?' (Deut. 18:22). If the thing prophesied comes to pass, it would seem to be self-authenticating.

Problem:

a) The devil baits his hooks with truth (Deut. 13:1–3) – New Agers will sometimes be right!

b) Had the Ninevites waited for Jonah's prophecy to be fulfilled, they would all have been dead. As it was, they repented (Jonah 3:4–5).

c) Hezekiah received a word from Isaiah that he was about to die, but he repented and lived another fifteen years (Isa. 38:8).

d) Jeremiah points out that so much will depend upon our attitude to the prophecy for its effect (Jer. 18:7–8).

6 *Edification.* Paul insisted that prophecy was for the edification of the Church – to strengthen, encourage and comfort (1 Cor. 14:3), to bring conviction of sin and an awareness of God (1 Cor. 14:25), to be exercised in a fitting and orderly way (i.e. under authority) (1

Cor. 14:40) and in love (1 Cor. 13). 'Prophecy which is frightening, harsh, condemning or critical seldom comes from the Holy Spirit.'[4]

7 *Resonance test*. This is the inner witness that also seems to confirm the prophecy.[5] Bruce Yocum explains how 'objects have certain characteristic frequencies at which they vibrate near another object with the same characteristic frequency [my example – two wineglasses of the same size and shape]; the second object will begin to vibrate by itself'. That is something similar to what happens when we truly discern the voice of the Lord. There is a vibration of resonance; a sense of moving in the flow of what God is already doing; a witness among the faithful (*sensus fidelium*) that the prophecy will lead into freedom from bondage (rather than the reverse) and there is a delightful anticipation that this is for the glory of Jesus.

8 *The love test*. This test could be placed first as the chief foundation or last as the crowning conclusion to all the tests. Paul puts his famous chapter on love right in the middle of his treatise on the gifts, and all who believe they have prophetic gifting, and those who want to discern, should not only soak themselves in 1 Corinthians 13 but seek wholeheartedly to live it. 'If we love one another, God lives in us and his love is made complete in us' (1 John 4:12). A simple way of testing this if one is giving a prophecy is to put oneself in the other person's shoes. How would you react if someone said the same thing to you – even if it were true?

Confirmation

Prophecy may pass all the tests or at least not run counter to any of them, but it would still be unwise to act in more than a tentative way in response to any prophecy *without confirmation* from some completely independent source. This is especially true if the prophecy speaks of a *radical* or *irrevocable change of direction in the life of an individual or the church.* It may be, of course, that the prophecy comes as the *culmination* of things revealed by God in other ways and at different times and is itself, therefore, a clear confirmation. In all prophecy concerning direction or a moral problem in another person, the leadership should be consulted first.

10

HOW IS PROPHECY MANAGED IN THE LOCAL CHURCH?

Introduction

Hermas, a former slave turned farmer, was known as a sub-apostolic Christian Father who wrote 'The Shepherd' (between AD 90 and 150). In that work there are five visions, twelve mandates and ten similitudes. Hermas reveals himself as a prophet of mediocre intellect and narrow interests, who receives revelations from the 'angel of repentance' in shepherd's guise.

His particular concern was the impact so-called prophets were having on newly committed Christians, the young and the spiritually immature. He notably singled out those who prophesied on the fringe of the congregation, unnoticed or disregarded by the larger body. He argued against the usefulness of privately given 'personal' prophecies. Typically they were nothing more than 'empty words' that often left the immature at the mercy of the false prophet.[1]

Clearly there was a problem there which needed to be addressed. Where order is required it must be the responsibility of the leadership to sort things out constructively. We are meeting the same problems over prophecy today and too many leaders have no idea of how to handle them. A clumsy approach can easily snuff out prophecy altogether and often has. In this chapter and the next we try to encourage leaders who are unsure about their authority where prophecy is concerned.

Authority and potentiality of leaders

1 Leaders may need to follow the example of Paul on occasions when he said, 'I magnify mine office' (Rom. 11:13 KJV), without disregarding Peter's admonition against 'lording it over those entrusted to you' (1 Pet. 5:3). The one who speaks *'ex officio'* (out of his office) has *higher authority* than the one who speaks *'ex dono'* (out of his gifting). A prophetic anointing which conveys a kind of authority is not the same as *governmental authority* over the church, which the leader/elder/minister/rector/vicar has.

The *leader* must remember that he/she has the *proper responsibility* and *full authority* to deal with any matters concerning prophecy. (1 Cor. 14:40: Everything should be done in a fitting and *orderly* way.) *Order* must be maintained by the *governmental authority* of the Church.

2 Leaders who are properly appointed may not have the anointing of the prophet, but they do have the experience of leadership, an overview of the whole local church and a relationship with the wider church, which enables them to handle prophecy sensibly and sensitively. Leaders are usually more aware of the *pack mentality* and the dangers of the *cult personality*. The God-given cognitive process is of no less value, and the intuitive gut feelings should never be despised, where the leaders know they are being truly open to God. They may have a lesser sense of unction but they should have a greater sense of obligation.

3 Prophecies for particular individuals (especially when they concern correction or direction) should be given preferably with the church leaders present, or after counsel with them, having other witnesses present in the giving of them.

Obviously there needs to be a little flexibility here. Since spontaneity and surprise are sometimes part of God's sovereign purpose, there must be some leeway on this point. Provided there is a wholesome recognition in the church that all prophecy needs testing and there is a genuine submission by both the one prophesying and the one receiving the prophecy, it should be possible to avoid potential dangers. A wise leadership will ensure that intermediaries – such as home group leaders – are available, with whom such prophecies can be readily discussed. These intermediaries must themselves have easy access to the leadership.

4 Once the person who has the prophecy has given it to the leaders, then *s/he has discharged* his/her responsibility. Leaders will not necessarily act on it immediately. They may simply ponder it, as Mary did (Luke 2:19) or not act at all!

A significant factor often will be the prophet's track record. Has s/he established any real credibility as a prophet? Some people want a *prophet's visibility* (recognition and authority) without having established a *prophet's credibility*. In Acts 27, the centurion on board ship did not take Paul's prophecy in v. 10 seriously, but once the first prophecy was clearly fulfilled (vv. 21–6), then he did.

5 Leaders may be confident. They may safely trust God to give the wisdom (Jas 1:5) as to when to stop something gently but firmly, or better to guide things positively in a new direction if unease is felt *at any time* about the way things are going. If there is any uncertainty about the propriety of something it may quite simply be explained that time and counsel needs to be taken with others before making any definite or final decision about what has been 'prophesied'. Always seek to keep things low key. Usually just quietly stopping something tactfully and firmly, without making heavy weather of it, will be all that is needed.

6 Leaders must not allow themselves to be spiritually manipulated against their better judgment, nor should they retreat into a false humility which may lead them to *abdicate from their responsibilities* – seemingly the error of Edward Irving[2] treated in fuller detail in chapter 20.

7 Churches are *not normally* led by prophets. Peter tells the churches to be subject to their elders, not their prophets (1 Pet. 5:5). Paul and Barnabas did not appoint prophets to govern the churches, but elders (Acts 14:23). Paul refers to elders who rule well (1 Tim. 5:17).

8 However, an elder who has the authority to govern *may also have an anointing to prophesy*. Moses was both a leader and a prophet (Deut. 18:18), as was King David (Acts 4:25). Both Ezekiel and Jeremiah were priests as well as prophets (Ezek. 1:3, Jer. 1:1). See also Isaiah 28:7. James Ryle, the author of a book on prophecy called *The Hippo in the Garden*,[3] is both a pastor and a prophet. His double role enhances the value of his teaching on the whole subject of prophecy. Where a prophet exercises sole rule over a church, there is a much greater danger, in certain circumstances, for that church to become a cult. It does not have to be, and it would be quite wrong to suggest that it was necessarily so, but it could easily happen, unless the prophet is very wise and walks humbly before the Lord.

9 Leaders must remind themselves that all prophets or persons who minister in the gift of prophecy are fallible. Some people are waiting to meet the infallible prophet before they can believe that prophecy is for today. Some prophecies are purer than others and this means all prophecy needs sifting.

To help with this process, there are good biblical guidelines available (and already demonstrated in this book), but it must be said that most leaders and laity are doing their own sifting almost automatically without any prompting from others. 'The ear tests words as the tongue tastes food' (Job 34:3).

10 From time to time leaders will receive prophecies concerning themselves given to them directly or in writing. They should deal with these in the same way they do the others, but being always aware that some people are greatly tempted to use 'prophecy' to manipulate their leaders with

their chips on the shoulder and wishful thinking, as in (3) above.

11 It may be deemed right sometimes for the leader to invite a visitor with a proven track record in prophetic gifting to come to the front to offer some words of encouragement publicly to individual members of the congregation. This is not a good model for normal prophetic ministry but it does help (especially after church members have had time to check things over with the people concerned) to show the reality and the relevance of some prophecies.

I remember once in California how helpful it was simply to hear Paul Cain naming a couple unknown to him and asking them to stand up. He then addressed the wife and said, 'It's all over – it's all over! . . . The Lord has shown me that your son is safe with Christ.' It was not until we had time to hear their side of the story that we understood and indeed rejoiced that the Lord could minister such words of comfort in this way.

Apparently they were missionaries on furlough. They had come home early because of a tragedy. The husband worked very hard 'on the field' and one day when he was planning to take a day off to go hunting, his wife insisted that he take their two boys with him as they had been seeing so little of him recently.

The husband felt very uneasy about it but gave in because he knew he should be spending more time with them. Out in the forest with their father the older boy accidentally shot the younger one dead. They carried him home, weeping. The father blamed himself for taking them hunting in the forest; the son for killing his younger brother. And this was horribly compounded on arriving home when the wife blamed herself for insisting the boys should go with their father.

On leave back in the USA the wife was still finding no comfort in her mourning and the husband felt it important for her to attend this conference in the hope she would receive there the help she badly needed. He had taken her there by car, but outside she resisted coming in, saying she could not face it. The husband begged her saying, 'Darling, it's all over – it's all over!' The latter were the very words Paul Cain had given out, but he, knowing only what he sensed the Lord was telling him, had been able to assure her that her boy was safe with Jesus. We were just amazed that out of thousands of people present Paul was led to pick out that couple who so needed the comfort of those words.

This kind of ministry to individuals should be very limited because in a public meeting few are able to verify the accuracy or the effectiveness of such prophecies to others. It is likely too that there will be many others present with their own pressing problems who may tend to think that God is not concerned with their difficulties.

Alternatively it may seem right to allow a visiting prophet who is well tried and trusted to prophesy after the service to individuals. Those who want this ministry simply form a queue in front of the prophet.

These kinds of ministry do have their place occasionally for catalystic purposes.

Lessons from church life

Beware of shaming
If we shame those who aspire to prophesy we can be sure that both they and those who witnessed such shaming will be very reticent about ever prophesying again. Just to know, however, that a leader will tackle something if it becomes a real problem creates the kind of relaxed atmosphere for the use of the gifts which can be such a blessing to the church.

The leader's love for his people means that great care must be taken to avoid any hint of shaming. Most people who make mistakes in public already know where things went wrong and it is counterproductive to drive the point home too heavily afterwards, though if it ever has to be done that is usually the best time to tackle it.

Beware of Theopaths

In almost every church there will be some who see significance in everything that happens – they are searching for the will-o'-the-wisp.

In her 'Fanaticism Papers', the commonsensical Quaker lady Hannah Whitall Smith describes the case of a woman who claimed that each morning, having consecrated her day to the Lord as soon as she awoke, 'would then ask him whether she was to get up or not', and would not stir till the 'voice' told her to get dressed.

'As she put on each article she asked the Lord whether she was to put it on and very often the Lord would tell her to put on the right shoe and leave off the other; sometimes she was to put on both stockings and no shoes; and sometimes both shoes and no stockings. It was the same with all the articles of dress . . .'[4]

Such people are almost impossible to convince. They are 'theopaths'. This is a word used by Dean Inge to describe a confusing condition most of us have met from time to time in certain good Christian people who seem to have abandoned their God-given common sense.

Real prophetic gifting sometimes comes to strange people in strange ways, but there are others who are so strange about the whole area of hearing the Lord that we are unable to discern any real gifting. Indeed we sense it is unsafe to heed their messages at all. This painful perplexity we may experience with some brothers and sisters in Christ is part of the price we have to pay for encouraging prophecy.

We must be patient and kind. Theopaths are often very good spiritual people who are constructive members of the local church. Listen to them, thank them, and simply keep their words by you for later review if you feel in your spirit that they are not relevant or significant or safe to follow through just then.

It is good to ask such people to keep copies of the prophecies they give to you and to check them through as time goes by. Maybe after a while it will be possible to evaluate them together. Let them draw their own conclusions realistically and responsibly!

Lessons from Church history

It is important to keep in mind that history often repeats itself. A quick perusal of Ronald Knox's slightly cynical but well documented book *Enthusiasm*[5] reveals a number of directions God's people have been falsely led to take down the ages, following supposed divine revelations or their inner light, where the normal double checks to counter possible delusions have been neglected.

Somewhat randomly we select the following pitfalls from Knox's book, although there are others not included in this list: licence for immorality and claims to sinless perfection; both legalism and rigorism; revolt against either ecclesiastical or civil authorities; disregard for the Bible; anti-intellectualism and neglect of Christian theology; date-fixing for the Second Coming or the end of the world leading to cynicism, pessimism and despair among God's people when such prophecies are clearly not fulfilled. Two final pitfalls are sectarianism and prophetic despotism, such as was recently illustrated in the 1970s at the People's Temple in Guyana under Jim Jones where the cult annihilated itself, and the Branch Davidian cult in Waco, Texas under David Koresh which ended in 1993 after a clash with the civil authorities with many including children being killed. Who knows what tragedies still lie in store as I write?

It would, however, be a mistake to imagine the worst and to condemn any prophecy too readily. Let no one attempt to cut the tree down before it can be seen clearly what the fruit is going to be. John Wesley, who certainly had to cope with plenty of off-beat prophets in his day, cautioned his readers with Paul's words when dealing with such situations: 'Judge nothing before its time' (1 Cor. 4:5, KJV).

11

PRACTICALITIES FOR PUBLIC WORSHIP

Practicalities for leaders

Once a leader thinks of introducing prophecy into any of the main services of the local church a number of practical issues immediately come to mind:

Space for prophecy

There is no doubt that prophecy was expected to take place when the Church of God was gathered for worship – even at the Lord's Supper. The idea of the Body of Christ being assembled (1 Cor. 12:27), coming together as a church (1 Cor. 11:18, 20, 33, 34; 1 Cor. 14:23, 26), suggests that space was allowed for the exercise of the gifts of the Spirit which would have included prophecy (1 Cor. 12:10 and 14:5).

Using any liturgical structure in such a way that it inhibits the exercise of the spiritual gifts would seem to be contrary to the plainest practical spelling-out in the New Testament (1 Cor. chs 11–14) of what actually might take place in worship.

Order for prophecy

'The order of Christ's church must . . . be an *order of freedom*.'[1] The freedom for the exercise of the gifts of the Spirit is in no way incompatible with orderliness and that which is fitting. Paul is expecting both the use of the gifts in worship and the exercise of order (cf. 1 Cor. 14:39, 40) implies the need for authority. The leader is responsible

for restoring order if things become disorderly which they
sometimes may. But a leader can soon learn to cope with
that. A young parent soon learns to do it.

No doubt this is why Paul insists that leaders should
know how to manage their own families and have children
who obey with proper respect (1 Tim. 3:4). Such leaders
would have discovered the value of the nursery where
there is room for spontaneous response, allowance for
mistakes and acceptance of untidiness at times, while
at the same time so many lasting lessons are learned
there. Parents welcome this and do not really resent the
problems involved. They are the normal problems of life.
The rewards for learning through the freedom to make
mistakes are so worthwhile.

A new order

However, every now and again things have to be tidied up
and brought back into order, though not necessarily the
same order as before; often a new order fitting to the new
situation is necessary.

Order is not really a matter of strict rules so much as a
sound relationship. I remember talking to an archdeacon
from overseas who told me that when he was asked by
his bishop to consider the job he felt he must decline
because there were some matters of churchmanship where
he disagreed with his bishop on principle. The bishop
listened and then sent him away to make a list of things on
which, in all good conscience, he felt they would disagree.
When he returned with his list the bishop looked at it and
said, 'Good, I can understand this. I still want you to be
my archdeacon. Do not feel that you have to do any of
these things. Good order does not come out of rules but
out of a relationship.' That bishop knew something! A
good relationship creates the basic elements for freedom,
spontaneity and creativity. A leader, like a parent, may
not know exactly how he is going to handle a certain
situation before he comes to it, but he can be relaxed

because everybody knows he has the authority to deal with any disorder in the best way he is able, where and whenever it becomes necessary.

Announcements in church concerning the prophetic

Since we usually have a number of visitors at St Andrew's we have found it best in public worship to make an announcement during the service about the use of the gifts for those who are not used to them. At this time we usually say that there may be tongues and if that is the case we shall pray and wait for the interpretation which could either be a prayer to God or a word from God. If there is no interpretation we do not allow more tongues as that contravenes the principle of edification (1 Cor. 14:5). Or there might be some prophecy. We make it clear that we reserve the right for ministry in this way to those who are regular worshippers in the church *for the sake of decency and order*.

This should forestall any 'weirdo' charismatic who, being forbidden to hold the floor in his own church, decides to take a liberty in another. So far it has worked! When one knows the people it is much easier to discern which words are likely to be chips on the shoulder, wishful thinking or vested interests. Again, in over seventeen years in St Andrew's, we have rarely sensed any such abuse, neither have we ever discerned a lying spirit manifesting in this way (Ezek. chs 13–14). This may encourage any worried leader!

Other churches we know of have a prophetic team who are called upon to prophesy on occasions when it is felt to be appropriate.

Number of prophecies permissible at one time

So as not to overbalance the worship and following good Pauline precedent, we should limit the number of prophecies to two or three (1 Cor. 14:29). There may be one or two extra 'words' thrown in which the leader discerns simply as good blessed thoughts but not 'anointed'. The leader makes a note of the main burden of each prophecy and then reflects them back through the microphone to the congregation.

One can usually pick something positive or fairly bland out of any message so if one of them is ever a little dubious it is allowed to fall to the ground, but the speaker is not publicly put down. This seems a simple and merciful way of dealing with the problem and saves embarrassing the rest of the congregation. It also seems to work well.

The use of the microphone
We do not normally give the microphone to those who want to prophesy, though in some churches this is done. This could be counterproductive and serve as an inhibiting factor for some who would find it difficult to hear their own voice ringing out too loudly round the church. Also it's very hard to take a microphone away from someone once s/he has it and so many possible problems can be avoided by a little careful forethought here.

Of course, it may be that someone clearly has a 'word' from the Lord which s/he has spoken to the leader about beforehand, and it may be thought desirable that the person who has been given the 'word' should deliver it over the microphone. In that case plans can be made before the service of worship for the person to come forward at an appropriate time. A few churches have microphone points available around the building or microphones on long cords so that it is not even necessary to move from one's place to prophesy. A church officer simply moves with the microphone, as the leader directs, to the persons indicating they wish to prophesy.

Testing: where and when
There is an immediate testing by the majority of the congregation. The Holy Spirit bears witness with our spirit (Rom. 8:16). Someone once asked my colleague

Barry Kissell how he weighed a prophecy when he was out at the front of the church and he half-jokingly said that he measured how far people's heads were sinking between their knees! The 'cringe factor' can often be a spontaneous indicator! If a prophecy is clearly misguided and the church's response has to be clarified, then the leader can simply say something like 'I think we shall need to pray about that one and deal with it later,' or 'We, on the leadership, will need to pray over that one, and if we feel it needs to be taken further we will bring it back to the church.'

Some prophecies may call for immediate positive action, whether it be for individuals or the whole congregation. Maybe the Lord is challenging the whole church about loving neighbours; maybe he is chiding the church over coldness towards himself. The leader can call for a time of reflection or perhaps invite the Spirit of God to come and warm our cold hearts. In the case of warnings or blessings the church can be encouraged to respond appropriately. This prophetic ministry opens a whole new dimension to worship and prompts both visitors to reflect on the fact that our God really is a living God and regular worshippers to search their hearts before him.

Other prophecies cannot be tested there and then and can simply be left. There may be nothing more to be done about them for the time being. No one could possibly say whether they were right or wrong – either time will show, or there needs to be more clarification. If there is still real concern then they can be discussed by the leader with other responsible people in the church at the time, applying the tests we have already suggested in chapter 9. Further weighing may take place later among the staff or at the next Parish Church Council meeting.

Some prophecies will be consciously picked up and definite action will be taken in the life of the church. Others have unconsciously motivated developments in the church's programme, but their impact has been observable only in review.

Anyone who has had experience of gold-washing will have discovered that a lot of common dirt and rubble has to be washed away for every tiny nugget of gold! Within my limited and luckless experience at that pastime in South America, I never heard any serious complaints on that score, it being accepted quite simply as the way these things worked. So it may be with prophecy.

What if there are no prophecies?
Even if on some occasions opportunity is given for prophecy and this is not taken up, the time of silence is profitable and the very fact that space is deliberately allowed for this speaks its own message – that we serve a living God who speaks today and we are trying to listen to him! Allowing for this dimension in worship is a powerful statement in itself.

Application in the church
Sometimes the message may seem commonplace and one thinks that anybody could have got it from Scripture. I was once greatly humbled because I was inwardly dismissive of a 'word', but later I found that it had gone right home to the heart of a visitor who was seeking the Lord and it revolutionised her life. (It seemed to be a case of 1 Cor. 14:24.) She was converted through it and has since been playing a leading role in this church.

Four different kinds of response
1 *Individual response*: Some words are for individuals who receive them secretly and inwardly, immediately or later (perhaps after some spiritual struggle).

2 *General response*: Other prophecies are plainly for the whole congregation and it may seem appropriate to say so from the front and suggest a short time of silence

to allow the Holy Spirit opportunity to apply the 'word' to our hearts.

3 *Delayed response*: Sometimes there is a word given and the leader does not immediately sense what he should do about it and lets it pass. This happened once in our case. It was a word about youth work. It was picked up later by a member of the PCC who asked what we were doing about it. We put it on the agenda for the next meeting and this led to a new development in our youth work and also a new development for the PCC. From that time we have always had one item each month on the agenda of the PCC under the heading of 'What is the Spirit saying to the Church', in case there is something we have not picked up. We do not often sense that we have missed things, nor do we feel obliged to deal with them all immediately. If it was a big thing, we would put it high on the agenda for the next meeting. If it seemed an urgent matter we would try to deal with it then and there.

4 *The trickle-down factor*: It has been possible to discern that new programmes launched in the church have been almost unconsciously derived from a particular trend in the prophecies delivered to the church over a period of time. It is not necessarily easy to identify the particular prophecies (unless one has kept a special record which we do not officially do, though some keep these records privately) but there is a consensus that these have been things that God has been speaking to us about through prophecy in the church over a period of time.

Because of possible hardness of heart or difficulty in discerning what is of God and what is just human, the Lord often seems to repeat what he wants to say until the message has got home to us.

12

WHAT ABOUT
CHURCH ORDER?

One of the first apparent obstacles to a prophetic ministry
in the life of the church is the possible conflict with order.
I have already touched on this to some extent in a previous
book called *Come, Holy Spirit*, with a special chapter
headed 'Operating within a liturgical structure' to help
those who wanted to establish a regular healing ministry
in the local church. Liturgy happens to be something many
church people value highly for very wholesome reasons,
and the intention there was to show how a healing ministry
could be developed within such a structured environment.
The same principles apply in the case of prophecy. Here
we suggest reasons why there should be sensitivity towards
change, so that we understand as well as we are able what
we are up against.

Traditional reasons for order

Even before the conversion of the Emperor Constantine,
the Christian churches had procedures and customs to
regulate individual behaviour and community life. This
was something which had developed out of the New
Testament writings (cf. Acts 15), particularly the letters
of Paul (1 Cor. 5 and 1 Tim. 3:1–13). By the second and
third centuries churches had developed rules for admitting members, for expelling sinners, for choosing clergy,
for performing liturgical services and for administering
property.

There was considerable diversity from one end of the

Mediterranean to the other, but the leading bishops and the decisions of councils gradually introduced some similarity of practice at the regional level. This was all revised, refined and developed over the years and became known as 'canon law'.

Canon law

One of the prime movers for bringing order to the Church's own internally created canon law was the learned monk Dionysius the Short, who was active at Rome from AD 497 to 540. Dionysius was the man who calculated, apparently with an error of between four and seven years, the date of Christ's birth, which is used in the modern dating system using AD for 'anno domini' – 'in the year of our Lord'. As the Christian movement grew it encountered new problems, new situations and new cultures. They in turn called for new decisions, some of which were eventually incorporated into canon law.

There were changes and additions to this over the years and probably the influence of the pious King Charles the Great ('Charlemagne', 768–814), crowned emperor by the pope in 800, was most significant. He gave canon law such precedence that certain bishops were not past forging canon laws to their own advantage. These became incorporated in a grand accumulation of canon law known as the Pseudo-Isidorean Decretals (850).

The monk Gratian at Bologna in the 1140s, Pope Gregory IX in 1234, Pope Boniface VIII in 1298 and Pope Clement VI in 1317 were some of the greatest contributors to canon law during the Middle Ages. Doctors of canon law were soon being authorised to sort out the complexities and counterfeits.

Anyone reading these laws soon becomes aware of how stern the punishments were. In fact they were often so harsh as to be mostly symbolic – an expression of indignation towards the offence. In practice they were rarely exacted in their full force, particularly if the offender was penitent. For centuries the Eastern and Western Church had acted on the principle that if the strict application of the law would do more harm than good, it could be relaxed or dispensed with.

A simple example

Canon law said that mass was to be celebrated in a church by a priest who was fasting. But if, in an emergency, a priest had to say mass in the open air (for instance, with soldiers on the battlefield) or if he had already eaten, not expecting to be called upon to say mass, then common sense demanded that he could be dispensed from the law.

In the same way, in their effort to enhance the dignity of the clergy, the eleventh-century reformers had forbidden the ordination of illegitimate children. However, if the young man (possibly himself an orphan reared in a monastery) was otherwise suitable for the clergy and if there was no danger of seeming to approve of the fornication or adultery of his parents, then canon law was commonly dispensed with unless the Church needed reasons for wanting to block an otherwise suitable candidate's promotion.

It was quite clear that, so long as man-made laws were helpful, they were good, but once they could be seen to hinder the life of the Church they could be dispensed with. It was recognised that the letter kills but the Spirit gives life.

When the English Church broke away from Rome, during the time of Henry VIII, a new situation was created and eventually in 1603 a new Code of the Canons was produced. In 1904 the Catholic Church began to overhaul and codify its canon law once more and this resulted in a new code being published in 1917.

As far as the Church of England was concerned there was ongoing frustration over canon laws which could so quickly become outdated. In his introduction to *The Canon Law of the Church of England*, Dr Garbett, then Archbishop of York, wrote:

At the present time the Church of England, alone among the Churches of the Anglican Communion, lacks a body of Canons which has been revised and supplemented in the light of modern conditions, and which is regarded as authoritative by its members . . .

This state of confusion and uncertainty is profoundly humiliating and unsatisfactory, and until it is remedied it will be difficult to secure order and cohesion in our Church . . . Through the very nature of the case there can be no final body of canons. For a living Church will frequently desire, both to amend existing canons and to add to their number as new needs arise.

The most recent revision, with simplification and clarification, was brought out in 1969 under the title *The Canons of the Church of England*[1] as a response to that challenge.

British particularly sensitive

The British churches are particularly sensitive about order. One glance at an old book of *Homilies and Canons* first published in 1562 conveys the idea forcefully. Following the Reformation certain exhortations were supplied to be read in the place of a sermon where the parish priest was too ignorant of the Scripture, or perhaps too busy, to prepare a suitably edifying address. One of the exhortations concerns good order and obedience to rulers and magistrates.

It begins with an extravagant appeal to the example of order in creation – the position of angels and archangels, the sun, moon and stars, the seasons (which keep their comely course and order). Then it refers to the order within man himself, 'with all and singular corporal members of his body in a profitable, necessary and pleasant order'.

Finally it addresses order in society: 'Every degree of people, in their vocation, calling and office hath appointed to them their entry and order. Some are on high degree and some on low.' There are echoes here of 'the rich man in his castle and the poor man at his gate'; people had to learn to know their station in life! 'So that in all things is to be lauded and praised the goodly order of God: without which no house, no city, no commonwealth can continue and endure [or last]; for, where there is no right order, there reigneth all abuse, carnal liberty, enormity, sin and Babylonian confusion.'[2]

Good order in our society has come to be exemplified by military precision, pomp and ceremony at the national celebrations and good order has become the traditional ethos as far as church worship is concerned. Although liturgy has in fact been evolving considerably over the years, the general impression that nothing must be changed is positively cultivated. The familiar words 'As it was in the beginning, is now and ever shall be, world without end. Amen' might almost be part of the creed! Of course, order in itself is deadly: 'The letter kills, but the Spirit gives life' (2 Cor. 3:6).

Psychological reasons for order

There are psychological reasons to explain why some people are so insistent about order. Order ensures predictability. Change exposes vulnerability. Many in our churches may be hiding behind carefully cultivated masks, the protective creations of a lifetime.

C.S. Lewis illustrates something of what we mean here when he reflects upon his loathing for *interference*. No word in his vocabulary expressed deeper hatred than that word.

> Christianity placed at the centre what then seemed to me a transcendental Interferer . . . There was no region even in the innermost depth of one's soul (nay least of all) which one could surround with a barbed wire fence and guard with a notice 'No Admittance'. And that was what I wanted; some area, however small, of which I

could say to all other beings, 'This is my business and mine only.'[3]

From a lifetime of practice, masked people appear well-defended. They are fearful lest something should catch them unawares: all would then be revealed, they believe, if the mask was shattered! Their shame and guilt (real or imagined) and the scars of emotional hurt might be laid bare for all to see. The only defence would seem to be the guarantee of order.

The mask is something we make ourselves, partly out of our own creative cunning and partly through copying others. It provides a kind of security behind which a person can adjust to some of the painful realities from which there is apparently no relief. It enables those who have found the business of life hard, to cope with its realities and with other people.

The mask wearers form a substantial portion of our congregations and they, above all, can be guaranteed to insist rightly on decency and order in worship – that which is traditionally accepted and rubrically directed. (The minister may easily count himself among them.) Liturgy can become part of the mask. Like good manners in a social context, it can be regarded as the accepted form of address and communication. It is edifying for a large number of people and acts as an insurance against doctrinal error and spiritual malapropisms. Anything outside the liturgy could be dangerous.

Through openness to the Holy Spirit, loving care, gentle coaxing, patient teaching and firm leadership, people will gain the confidence to remove their masks. Sooner or later some will begin to discover that emotional hurts openly exposed heal more readily than hidden ones. Some of the newly healed will begin to minister effectively with those still hurting.

In a church where the order has been a thing 'received' rather than 'evolved' there has often been no real model of leadership in the minister officiating. When selecting their ordinands, traditional churches are more often looking for spiritual and cultured people who are pastorally gifted and will not rock the boat – they are not really looking for leaders.

Many of our traditional clergy do not lead. They are often godly and hard-working, but they follow the leadership of others in the church – the choir master or the organist, a warden or some socially prestigious lady. Such men shudder at the very idea of taking a real lead. They have never witnessed the exercise of the gifts in church and their minds recoil at the parodies of charismatic worship they have heard about from others who are hostile to such openness. They have almost certainly never seen such things handled easily and maturely by the church leadership.

The biblical mandate for order

There is, of course, a proper biblical mandate for order (1 Cor. 14:40), but we must distinguish between the unpredictable and sometimes embarrassing order of the nursery and the neatly whitewashed order of the cemetery. A cemetery is so much more peaceful and tidy – there can be no doubt about the order there. But the choice is between an order for life and an order for death.

The great preacher Martin Lloyd Jones once feigned shock at the very idea of good order being disturbed even by God himself: 'Fancy upsetting the clock-like mechanical perfection of a great service with an outpouring of the Holy Spirit. The thing is unthinkable!'[4]

Understanding biblical order

We all have our preconceived ideas of what order is all about. Many see it as something 'given' – a traditional order of worship, a noun. Others see it as a verb – a process of bringing things into order. The latter would seem to be the biblical meaning. St Paul is first of all urging that 'all things be done'; that is, that the gifts of the Spirit are given proper space in worship.

This, as anyone knows (and as has already been spelt out in chapters 10 and 11), will require some ordering. The opportunity must be made, the explanation of what it is all about must be given and any limitation felt necessary must be imposed. (In St Andrew's we allow only the regular members, those known to the church leadership, to exercise the gifts and even some of these might be privately requested not to do so for one good reason or another.)

Once there has been any manifestation of the gifts the leadership will need to help filter out what was of God; how the Lord might want to minister further in any area highlighted; whether it is too much of the flesh and to be ignored; whether the word was for some individuals in the church or for the whole church; whether it requires immediate attention or if the matter would be better handled at a later time. This will require wise leadership.

A constructive policy for the Church

The traditional Church has yet to frame a constructive policy for developing and regulating prophetic activity within its ranks. This need was first frankly recognised in the *Didache* (written some time between the first and the third century AD, probably in Syria), but which, it must be said, dealt with the phenomenon too crudely to be helpful.

This is perhaps not surprising because so often in the past priest and prophet have been in opposition, instead of in submission to each other for the edifying of the Church and the glory of God. Our main sources for information on the prophets in Church history come from the establishment itself and not surprisingly have tended to be critical, hostile and negative. As Dean Inge has aptly commented: 'A priest was never so happy as when he had a prophet to stone.'

It took the Church five hundred years to change its stance on the fifteenth-century prophetess Joan of Arc – from condemnation in 1431 when she was burned to death for heresy to canonisation in 1920! Incidentally, in the introduction to his play *Saint Joan*,[5] George Bernard Shaw provides a most readable discussion on the Church's dilemma over prophecy.

What attitude should we adopt today?

There are a number of basic attitudes the Church needs to adopt:

1 To accept positively the place of the prophet and prophecy today in speaking to individuals; to the Church; to the community and to the nation (this latter would be limited to those few who had means of personal access to the media and/or the nation's leadership).

2 To define clearly the essential place of leadership in the Church with regard to prophecy. The prophet ranks second to the apostles in the various ministries (Eph. 2:20, 1 Cor. 12:28). 'They are equal to the apostles because both are agents of revelation, but subordinate to the apostles because they cannot go behind them to an independent interpretation of Jesus. The apostles' witness defines the faith.'[6] Because the apostles rank first they must therefore have the final responsibility for order as we have already seen in chapters 10 and 11.

3 To pray both publicly and privately, corporately and individually for the gift (Jas 1:17). It may seem right to lay hands on some in prayer (Acts 19:6). But the warning principle of laying hands suddenly on no man would seem to apply to gifting as much as to ordaining. If the Holy Spirit anoints a person sovereignly without the laying on of hands, that is one thing; rushing to lay on our own hands independently is another.

4 To teach the Church about the role of prophecy today. It should be stressed that gifts are not rewards; they are tools to do the job, not trophies for having done some

other job well. All the gifts, except for tongues (unless interpreted), are for the benefit of others. It should also be made clear that gifting is not a sign of spiritual maturity.

5 To provide the environment to encourage those with potential gifting to start by sharing their revelations in their home groups or by bringing their prophecies (reduced to one side of a sheet of paper!) to the leadership.

6 To teach the Church the reasons why and how good order can be maintained while at the same time allowing the freedom of the Spirit. 'Everything should be done in a fitting and orderly way' is an injunction where the context clearly shows it has a particular application to the gifts of the Spirit' (1 Cor. 14:39). Teach also the fundamental causes for disorder: 'Where you have envy and selfish ambition, there you find disorder and every evil practice' (Jas 3:16).

The order Paul urged was never to rule out prophecy. He intended that all the gifts of the Spirit should be exercised and tested under authority. Those who rightly insist upon decency and order should be equally pressing about the place prophecy should have in the coming together of God's people for worship (1 Cor. 14:40).

13

TOWARDS A BETTER
THEOLOGY

Over the last three centuries theologians have shown an
increasing degree of scepticism towards the idea that
God reveals himself directly to our senses. Where has
this scepticism come from? What are the implications for
prophecy? In this chapter we must trace the history of
scepticism from its roots in classical Greece to its expression in twentieth-century existentialism. The difficulty for
a number of readers here will be their unfamiliarity with
some of the theological and philosophical jargon. For
others it will be the degree of superficiality required for
the condensing of so much into one chapter.

It is not often realised outside academic circles how
widely our Western culture has been influenced by Greek
thought. We can see hints of it in our form of government
(democracy), our architecture ('Corinthian' porticos and
pillars), our medicine (the Hippocratic oath) and our ath-
letics (The Olympic Games), to give a few examples. We
have tended to adopt without question the Greek division
of sacred and secular, eternal and temporal, spiritual and
physical.

The Greeks considered flesh and spirit to be incompatible – almost synonymous with evil and good. Hebrew
thought, by contrast, began with the understanding that
God created the physical world and declared it to be
'good'. When he made human bodies he made them male
and female and pronounced them 'very good'. In Hebrew
understanding the physical and the spiritual are intercon-

nected. God made the human body and breathed life into it so that it became a 'living soul' or an 'animated body'.

Three of the major Greek thinkers, Socrates, Plato and Aristotle, lived at least three centuries before Christ and their philosophies were already well circulated among the Gentile cultures surrounding Palestine long before the earliest churches were planted there.

Socrates

Socrates (469–399 BC), the well-known Athenian philosopher, advocated a method for reaching the truth through repeated questioning. A few of the disciples who flocked to his side used his method on public dignitaries, making them contradict themselves. Socrates was eventually sentenced to death for corrupting youth – teaching the younger generation to humiliate their elders by such questionings. Refusing all opportunity for compromise, Socrates drank the statutory cup of hemlock, believing with Plato, his disciple, that death brought total and final release to the soul. Justin Martyr (c. 100–c. 160) believed that Socrates, like Abraham, was a Christian before Christ, and his death was an example for Christian martyrs.

Plato

Plato (427–347 BC), a wealthy Athenian aristocrat, was Socrates' best known student. After years of travelling abroad he returned home to set up an academy in a garden outside Athens. His method followed that of Socrates; he encouraged people to cross-examine him to elicit the truth on any subject. His favourite interrogator had been his former teacher Socrates himself. Plato had propounded many radical ideas, such as the abolition of private property and the family – even eugenic mating. Some of these ideas were obviously contrary to Christian teaching but others were to be deemed compatible with the New Testament, such as the Christian hope of immortality.

Plato believed that the human soul was immortal but a prisoner of the mortal body. He taught that the world we see with our eyes and perceive with our senses is in fact a world of shadows, a copy of the eternal world of spiritual Forms which the pure soul can attain only by philosophical contemplation. He believed in two realities, the spiritual and the material, each interacting upon the other, and at the head of these two realities was the Form of the Good. Subsequent thinkers have criticised or modified Plato's teaching but his influence has continued unabated down the centuries.[1] Some of the Church Fathers claimed that he was a secular John the Baptist, sent to prepare the way for Christ.

Aristotle

Besides the various forms of Platonism (which have been developed as Neoplatonism – 'rehashed' Platonic thought), medieval philosophy was also to be deeply influenced by Plato's pupil Aristotle (384–322 BC). This 'Father of Logic' became tutor to the future Alexander the Great. After travels abroad Aristotle opened a new school in Athens called the Lyceum.

In the early period of his life he had taught Plato's view of the soul's immortality and his doctrine of the Form of the Good. Later he became critical of Plato, especially his idea of the Forms. Finally he became an exponent of empirical science by which knowledge is acquired through the senses and reason. By the end of his life he had dispensed with all the essential features of Platonic other-worldly metaphysics.[2]

Aristotle represented a complete explanation of reality without any reference to the Christian God; his 'first cause' was a principle of existence, not a personal being. The Arians in the fourth century and many Muslims in the seventh had already adopted Aristotle's world view once his works became available in Arabic. It was not until the twelfth century that they were translated from Greek into Latin.

It has been said that Christianity is a religion in search of a philosophy. Theology speaks of mysteries and must communicate these through the most culturally relevant framework and language. The prevailing philosophy of the day has frequently appeared to be the most appropriate means for communicating the truth of theology, especially when that philosophy talks of ways of knowing what we think it is necessary to know. The risk is always that the false assumptions of the 'flavour-of-the-month' philosopher will be absorbed into the bloodstream of the theology of the Church.

Aristotle in vogue for theology

Thomas Aquinas (1225–74) was a French aristocrat and member of the newly founded Dominican Order. He soon acquired the nickname of the 'Dumb Ox' because of his bulk, his seriousness and his slowness. Aquinas was a formal thinker. He developed his theology (later called 'Thomism') out of Aristotle's teaching. Basic to this was the theory that we can know reality only through our reason and our sense experiences. Aquinas' works were very orderly. He tidied his theology into manageable units which made his thinking easily digestible. Accepting Aristotle as a guide in reason, and Scripture as a rule in faith, he harmonised faith and reason – at least to his own satisfaction. He was a prolific writer. His *Summa contra Gentiles* was designed for the conversion of Muslim Arabs. His *Summa Theologica* was the highest achievement in medieval theological systematisation. In this latter work and also his *De Veritate* he addressed himself to the nature and workings of the gift of prophecy at some length. He believed that the prophetic revelation came principally through the rational mind and revelation supplemented, but never contradicted, reason.

Aquinas differentiated between sense experience and heavenly knowledge. The apostles and prophets could receive revelation in a mystic fashion now, but for the rest of us this was something reserved until after death. Aquinas was making a clear distinction between science and the Christian hope.[3]

Throughout the Middle Ages (AD 500–1400) thinking had been characterised by an interest in metaphysics (supernatural or abstract) rather than physics. By and large, the great minds of the Middle Ages were not interested in the physical universe for its own sake: they were interested in the reality of the Absolute which they believed lay behind it. They were not so much concerned with scientific questions about natural phenomena. What interested them was the relationship between the supernatural and the natural, beginning with God. Theirs was a theocentric rather than a cosmocentric world view. All this was gradually being reversed. This was the period when the idea of the university materialised. Many infant sciences of the future were spawned. The extensive task of working out the relationship between religion and human knowledge was being developed.

The Renaissance

The crowning effect of Aristotle's rationalistic influence (mediated by Aquinas) in Western Europe was the Renaissance which marked the end of the Middle Ages. This switched the focus on to the individual instead of the Absolute, thus setting the stage for Renaissance humanism with the ensuing problems of its tolerance for a pagan world view. It sought to reproduce the life of antiquity with its vices as well as its virtues.

When society started with the Absolute it could then relate this to mankind. Starting now with the individual, humanism had no way of reaching that Absolute which alone gives meaning to existence and morals. The climate was becoming increasingly hostile to the supernatural in religion.

The gradual projection of the Aristotelian approach

into the critical studies of the Old Testament compelled students to doubt the miraculous and the possibility of long-range predictive prophecies. The same arguments were applied to the supernatural elements in the New Testament.

The over-riding influence of philosophy was not only evident in the University theological faculties but in the local church services. Erasmus (*c* 1466–1536) complained that 'Aristotle is so in vogue that there is scarcely time in the churches to interpret the gospel'.[4]

The Renaissance movement fostered the desire to master the treasures of the East by bringing Greek and Latin scholars together. Greek was taught in Florence by Manuel Chrysoloras (?1355–1415) who had also translated Homer and Plato into Latin. The study of Plato was ardently pursued by the Italian philosopher Marsilio Ficino (between the years 1463 and 1477). A resurgence of Neoplatonism created a reaction to this humanism.

The Reformers

The Reformers rejected the place of God's revelation in any current prophetic ministry because this would seem to violate man's reason and God's natural law. Luther (as we shall see in chapter 17), was particularly disturbed by the excessive abuses of the Zwichau prophets. He urged his readers to stand guard against them in his tract *Against Heavenly Prophets*. In a letter to Melanchthon, Luther wrote: 'No! The Divine Majesty (as they call it) does not speak directly to man, so that man may look upon his presence.'[5] Again he said, 'The Scripture is so full, that as for visions and revelations, "Nec curo, nec desidero"' (I neither regard nor desire them). And when he himself had a vision of Christ, after a day of fasting and prayer, he cried out, 'Avoid Satan, I know no image of Christ but the Scriptures'.[6] According to Luther's preface to his book *On Zechariah*, prophecy was to be understood as the gift of all those who expound the Scriptures and ably interpret and teach difficult books.

Calvin expressed a similar view in his *Commentary* on Romans (12:5), that 'Prophecy . . . is simply the right understanding of Scripture and the particular gift for expounding it.' The prophetic, in the view of the Reformers, was rather akin to the illumination of Scripture: it consisted in the correct interpretation and application of existing revelation.

The Enlightenment

It would be wrong to suggest that there had ever been a sudden cut-off point to mark the out-moding of the belief in the supernatural and the supra-rational dimension in Christianity. But it would be true to say that from the time of the so-called 'Aufklärung' (the eighteenth-century 'Enlightenment') a marked hardening along such lines became noticeable amongst leading theological thinkers.

Liberals had served a useful purpose in freeing minds from the dominance of authority – an authority which had silenced Copernicus (1473–1543) and Galileo (1564–1642). This eventually led Giordano Bruno to the stake in Rome in 1600 for maintaining that there must be a place in society for a spirit of free enquiry against the deadening authority of the establishment.

The desire to find the Platonic heart beneath its Aristotelian head was carried through into the seventeenth century as an attempt to recreate philosophical space for the supernatural and the mystical. We are thinking here of the Cambridge Platonists (1633–1688) with their mystical view of reason. The Aristotelian head, however, was still strong and kept the door open for rational Enlightenment. This was to combine opposition to all supernatural religion and the belief in the all-sufficiency of human reason with an ardent desire to promote the happiness of mankind in this life.

The Enlightenment was soon under way in Europe

with its watchword 'courage to make use of one's own understanding'. Again it was philosophy which had set the scene for this. John Locke's *Reasonableness of Christianity* (1695) was the pacemaker for the rationalisation of the Christian faith. Matthew Tindal then produced his most competent exposition of natural religion in his *Christianity as Old as the Creation* (1730). Immanuel Kant, a monumental thinker, followed with a book whose title spoke for itself: *Religion Within the Bounds of Reason Only* (1793). Kant argued forcibly for the priority of reason and conscience over the authority of Jesus Christ. Where Jesus endorsed what reason had to say he was to be respected; where he went against or beyond reason he was to be rejected. Kant published his own programme for bringing the Christian faith into line with 'Christian' thought, although in all his writings he was apparently unable to bring himself to pronounce the name of Jesus. Kant's aim was to strip Christianity of such extras as faith and belief in a supernatural God who personally intervened in human affairs.

The Enlightenment gave the freedom for the emerging scientists to build on the hypothesis that all 'matters physical' operated in an orderly manner. In the process faith was destroyed and man's rationality viewed with a false optimism.

The current new theology was Deism, which treated God as a kind of absent landlord. God made the world in the beginning and set it in motion, but then left it to run on its own accord like a clockwork toy. A fixed critical and negative tradition was developing among the new Christian thinkers. Part of a recent critique of Anglican Evangelicalism by Richard Holloway would have been equally applicable to the Enlightenment theologians: 'Social, as well as intellectual history is bedevilled by the craving for a single explanation of complex realities. There is a strong urge towards a theory of everything, an explanation into which we fit all facts. The opposite of this monistic craving is what John Keats called "negative capability", and that is when man is capable of being in uncertainties, mysteries, doubts, without any irritable reaching after fact and reason.'[7] Enlightenment theologians, like their scientist contemporaries, were becoming trapped into the theory that all 'matters physical and spiritual' operated in an orderly and recognisable manner.

Could be then – can't be now

The Reformers had also adopted the rational world view of Aquinas. In fact, Aquinas himself had experienced something, whilst saying mass in the morning of December 6th, 1273, which caused him to leave his monumental *Summa Theologica* where it stood, unfinished. 'I can write no more,' he told his friends. 'All I have written seems like so much straw compared with what I have seen, and what has been revealed to me.' Clearly Aquinas had received some kind of revelation which he believed to be from the Holy Spirit that was beyond his intellect or field of sense perception. Where would he put this experience in his neatly defined system? He had met that of which he could not speak. He determined to consult the Pope.

On his way to Rome he fell ill and died with his questions still unanswered. The *Summa Theologica* was never finished and its Aristotelian view of man was rounded out by others.[8]

The Reformers may have experienced a supernatural encounter with God in their new birth experience through faith in Jesus Christ, but they did not develop a system of thought to integrate that experience. They did not anticipate further divine encounters in their time, but their belief in the authority of the Bible placed them in a dilemma. They resolved it by the theory of dispensationalism. It was undeniable that God had broken through in the past and would do so again at the end of time. But it was not to be expected today. This was essentially the view of Calvin and Luther, both of whom simply maintained the Thomistic distinction between the natural and the supernatural. It was also the general view of the Puritans. Richard Sibbes wrote, 'There is a particular revelation of God's Spirit. This the Apostles and the Prophets had but now we have no such rule'.[9]

Commenting on this form of thinking, Morton Kelsey observes that there is 'a direct kinship between the theology of Karl Barth and that of the dispensationalists. Barth, whose emphasis on the transcendence and "otherness" of God has been of tremendous theological value, expresses it, however, with infinitely greater dialectical subtlety.'[10]

After 1945 the influence of Karl Barth began to give way to the theology of Rudolf Bultmann. The latter, following tradition, believed that theology needed a philosophical base, and he found this in the Existentialism of the Danish writer Søren Kierkegaard (1813–55), and the atheistic German philosophers Friedrich Nietzsche (1844–1900) and Martin Heidegger (1889–1976).

Revolt against current world view

As Colin Brown explains,[11] 'Existentialism' is a 'characteristically continental movement' which sprang up in Germany after the First World War and has flourished in France since the Second. It is 'not so much a movement as a tendency or attitude'. The word itself is a translation from the German *Existenz-philosophie*. We talk about things and people 'existing' but in the context of Existentialism the word 'existence' has a more specialised meaning. It is not as much concerned with the fact that this or that person or thing is there, as with the fact that as human beings we have lives to be lived.

The term has been described as an attempt to philosophise from the standpoint of the actor, rather than, as in classical philosophy, from that of the detached spectator. It is best regarded as an approach rather than a fixed body of philosophical doctrines. In Kierkegaard's

philosophy Existentialism is an attack on absolute ideal-
ism and individual existence. 'Existentialism represents a
revolt against external authority, ready-made world views,
authoritarianism, conventional moral values and codes of
conduct.'[12] Man has to make his own way in the world,
creating his own values and determining his own existence
as he goes along. It is this which distinguishes man from
things and animals. Existence is a big responsibility. Each
person exists and chooses in time. There can be no putting
off making choices because that in itself is a choice. We
have only a limited amount of time in which to make the
right decisions that are so vital to us. The thought of just
how much depends upon our decision makes our freedom
a source of anguish.

This philosophy dominates the lugubrious writing skills
of the Russian F.M. Dostoevsky and the stark despair
reflected in the works of the French communist Jean-Paul
Sartre. Existentialists may have grappled honestly with
their own problems and difficulties, in a way with which
many people could gratefully identify, but in the end
they drive us to despair and have brought disaster to
the Western world in which we live today. They brought
us seemingly into a dead-end street with no way out.

Myth-eaten theology
Rudolf Bultmann (1884) was one of the pioneers of form
criticism (from the German *Formgeschichte*). The form
critics endorsed the documentary criticism of the Bible
of the nineteenth century but believed that this was not
enough. They believed that further analysis was needed
of the various oral forms, such as the controversy story,
the miracle story and the pronouncement story, etc.,
which constituted the biblical literature possessed prior
to its being written down. In the case of the Gospels,
these forms tell us not so much what Jesus actually said
and did but what the early Church believed about him.
Bultmann taught that much of what was believed (forms)

was consciously or unconsciously invented by Christians of differing outlooks to suit their own views or needs. From Bultmann's analysis we know next to nothing about the historical Jesus but a great deal about the beliefs of the Christian Church. There is no such thing as an objective word of God, in Bultmann's view. He believed that it is our decision about Jesus which enables us 'to interpret our own existence'. Truth is supposed to emerge in this subjective response.

In 1941 Bultmann circulated an essay among his friends entitled *The New Testament and Mythology*. In this he propounds the theory that every description of a non-physical reality in the New Testament is mythical. He reflects his Existentialism when he defines myth in the Bible: 'The real purpose of myth is not to present an objective picture of the World as it is but to express man's understanding of himself in the world in which he lives.'[13] No objective word of God, no objective truth and now no objective picture of the world! What had theology come to?

Obviously we must have theologians but the tragedy is that during the twentieth century thousands of promising students have actually lost their faith through the study of theology. Hundreds have gone out into the ordained ministry uncertain of what to believe. If the leaders cannot lead, where will the rank and file be found? 'If the trumpet does not sound a clear call who will get ready for the battle?' (1 Cor. 14:8).

The significance of Bultmann (in relationship to prophecy) is that he led a whole generation of scholars into a hermeneutic of scepticism with regard to the supernatural. There was no real openness to the transcendent in Bultmann. Hence prophecies on the lips of Jesus himself were never regarded as *ipsissima verba* (his actual words) but as *vaticiniae ex eventu* (prophecies read back into the teaching of Jesus by the early Church). It is no surprise that Bultmann once remarked that in his whole life he had never begun to understand the Holy Spirit.

Revival movements

Down the centuries of Church history there have been many movements of God's Spirit in revival power since the first Pentecost in Jerusalem. To quote John Zizioulos' famous dictum: 'The Church is instituted by Christ but is constituted (and needs to be) by the Spirit'. There have been many more and varied revivals than most of us appreciate.[14] We are talking also of revivals long before the sixteenth-century Reformation, which has always appeared as the watershed for revival as far as many Protestants are concerned. These revivals have frequently occurred during times of socio-political upheaval and their occurrence has, not surprisingly, always provoked reaction. This has not been restricted to physical persecutions but has extended to theological and ecclesiastical objections and open rejection.

Outstanding examples of this may be seen in the revivals under George Fox or John Wesley in the seventeenth and eighteenth centuries respectively. Fox was imprisoned many times and Wesley was forbidden to preach in more than one diocese in England. When revival occurs there are often unusual manifestations of God's power. Some surprising public people demonstrate a change of heart. Whole communities turn to the Lord. There may be 'new' teachings, moral reformation, speaking in tongues, healings, prophecies, expressions of emotion and other phenomena. Questions concerning authority, orthodoxy and morality are raised. Although not every revival creates a challenge in all these areas, there is always a reaction, some of it very sincere and well-meaning, coming from people whose genuine concern is the glory of God. Others react out of fear, and whether or not they realise it, they are resisting the Holy Spirit. Often their appeal is solely to a traditional view of good order and reason.

An 'alternative' Christianity begins to flourish but is unable to generate new life. History has never been quite as simplistic as this, of course, for God can never be boxed into any one of our theories, but it would seem that the 'alternative' Christianity in fact becomes a parasite which survives by living off the 'revived' church for which it professes dislike.

This 'alternative' Christianity eventually destroys the regenerating element by its overwhelming systems and criticisms; the revival life is being snuffed out and the fire of the Spirit quenched. The rational, anti-supernatural 'alternative' is by then well in control. The Church motors along for a while with the respectable 'parasitic' element somehow surviving on the spiritual reserves of the past.

Then, once again, people begin to realise that there is no new life in the Church. Although the rituals, the programmes, the order and the authority structures with all their committees and councils are there, the gospel is rarely preached with conviction and commitment, and there are few conversions. Church-going declines; family life disintegrates. Meanwhile the world is sinking in chaos. Violence, terror and disaster begin to stalk the land. Finally, driven to their knees in desperation, a godly remnant begin praying for revival once more until in God's own good time it comes, as it always has in the past.

Then the backlash follows and the cycle begins once again. From the establishment there come cries of 'Order! Order!'; from the intellectuals, with their Aristotelian mindset, cries of scorn and contempt for the supra-rational and the supernatural.

Towards the year 2000
No theologian in the twentieth century has written as much theology as Karl Barth. Writing of the Holy Spirit, Barth highlights the problem in essence: 'As a foolish church presupposes His presence and action in its own existence, in its officers and sacraments, ordinations and absolutions,

so a foolish theology presupposes the Holy Spirit . . . [but] only where the Spirit is sighed, cried and prayed for does He become present and newly active.'[15] In one of Barth's last words, he said he dreamed of a new theology which would begin with the third article of the Creed – the Holy Spirit.[16]

Thirty years ago, the late Karl Rahner wrote that 'orthodox theology has never paid any serious attention to the question whether there are prophets even in post-apostolic times, how their spirit can be recognised and discerned, what their role is in the church, what their relationship is to the hierarchy, or what is the import of their mission for the exterior and interior life of the Church'.[17] Rahner also wrote of the gulf fixed between mystical and orthodox theology, taking note, by inference, that mystical theology does have a place for prophecy (as we shall see in chapter 21) and for the direct encounter of God with men.

The world view of Aristotle is becoming gradually deconstructed today, but being rational and humanistic, it is the natural line of approach for those theologians who acknowledge no experience of the supernatural and whose appeal is to the natural man and his latest philosophy. It would seem that this is what Paul was referring to when he wrote to the Christians at Colosse: 'See to it that no one takes you captive through hollow and deceptive philosophy, which depends upon human tradition and the basic principles of this world rather than on Christ' (Col. 2:8).

This is always a dangerous path to follow, but never more so than with the influential German philosopher Friedrich Nietzsche (1844–1900), 'whose starting point was the non-existence of God'.[18] Not surprisingly those who came under his influence would soon reduce their theology to the theory that God was dead! A small step for some theologians but a disastrous step for theology, the Church and society. We are now discovering first hand what it is like to live in a culture where there is no longer any fear of God. Devilish manifestations of this have been seen in Nazism, Marxism and today's widespread lawlessness and terrorism.

Whilst theology had reached its nadir in the 1960s, science had already recognised the fallacy of a philosophy which dictated that 'matters physical' operated in an orderly manner and that knowledge was purely rational and objective. Einstein gave the game away when he revealed that he discovered his theory of relativity through intuition – a kind of leap of faith – which brought him to the conclusion that space might not be what it seemed to be in ordinary sense experience. Michael Polanyi has clearly demonstrated the fallacy of traditional Enlightenment thinking in his book *Personal Knowledge* published in 1958.

Rise of Pentecostalism

The only large group of Christians today who take the idea of direct divine encounters seriously, along with visions, healings, prophecies, tongues, and dealings with the demonic, are the Pentecostals. These Christians, though often bound into their own culture, are freed from the restrictions of rationalism and ritualism, and therefore liberated to engage these God-given gifts for the enrichment of minds and hearts where and whenever this may seem appropriate.

Because of their supra-rationality, the Pentecostals have come in for derision from every side since they first emerged as a movement at the turn of the twentieth century.

If we include Charismatics of all denominations within the label 'Pentecostal' then, according to the *World Christian Encyclopedia*, the Pentecostal element was a total of 352 million souls in 1982. They are currently the fastest growing group of Christians in the world. It is estimated that there were 372 million in 1990 which is 21.4 per cent of the total number of Christians in the world.[19] 'The

Pentecostal Movement . . . is the most important source of world-wide renewal of Christianity,' says David Ford, the current Regius professor of theology at Cambridge University.[20]

Pentecostal leaders in the early decades of the twentieth century believed that they could not withstand (they certainly could not understand) the powerful rationalistic and naturalistic thinking of modern society and so they withdrew into their own structural sub-culture, discouraging contact with the secular world and non-Pentecostal denominations.

They even developed their own forms of religious language. John Sherrill, a popular writer who worked with David Wilkerson on *The Cross and the Switchblade*,[21] has admitted that one of his major problems was translating the language of the original manuscript into words that would have meaning for the general public.[22]

Since the rise of the Charismatic movement in the 1960s there has been very significant theological output from those within the movement or those who have had close contact with the movement who have been used to communicate to non-Charismatics. The contributors who come most readily to mind would be Gervaise Angel, Richard Bauckham, Roger Cowley, Frederick Dale Bruner, James Dunn, Herbert Carson, Michael Green, John Gunstone, Michael Harper, Peter Hocken, Walter Jacob Hollenweger, Morton Kelsey, Lesslie Newbigin, Karl Rahner, John Rea, Vinson Synon, Thomas Smail, Robert Warren, David Watson, Rodman Williams down to the 1990s with Cyril Ashton, Ken Bleu, Mike Butterworth, Christopher Cocksworth, Charles Kraft, Graham Cray, Graham Dow, David Gillett, John Goldingay, Douglas McBain, Graham McFarlane, George Malone, Jürgen Moltmann, Leanne Payne, Martyn Percy, Rich Nathan, Nigel Scotland, Mark Stibbe, Don Williams, Andrew Walker, John Wimber, Peter Wagner and Nigel Wright.

A few Pentecostal theologians have obtained positions

on the faculties of main-line study centres and universities. Academics with Pentecostal experiences are rubbing shoulders with traditionalists and writing papers which can be understood in main-line churches.

Writing the preface to the English translation from the German of Arnold Bittlinger's *Gifts and Graces* in 1967, Michael Harper comments:

> One of the chief handicaps, which has confronted commentators who have sought to deal adequately with these chapters [1 Cor. 12–14] in the past, is the lack of practical experience of these phenomena. In some sections they have been writing about purely hypothetical matters. However the significance of this book lies in the fact that it is one of the first to be written, outside Pentecostal literature, by someone who has fairly wide experience of these manifestations in West Germany. Even if scholarship is dedicated and inspired, it will obviously lack some quality if it is denied the experience of the very matters being dealt with.[23]

Significance of the New Age movement

A major feature which demonstrates how the scene has changed today has been the New Age movement. 'The rise of the New Age movement,' writes Mark Stibbe 'shows that people are looking for a theological philosophy which is furthest removed from Enlightenment rationalism.'[24] Though today's New Age thinkers have embraced a 'gnostic' mindset (which New Testament Christianity rejects – see chapter 14), 'their presence highlights the enormous paradigm shift in late twentieth century thinking which has allowed Charismatic and Pentecostal scholars far more freedom to do their theology from a perspective open to the supernatural'.[25]

Though our world seems more full of tragedy than ever before it is also a challenging age in which to be living. We are rediscovering the role of revelation and faith; we can refocus on 'that realm of the numinous where the divine and the human intersect and relate'.[26] No longer does it seem imperative to fit the Christian faith and divine revelation into the rationalistic strait-jacket of that secular world view emanating from Aristotle.

It was the prophet Isaiah who warned us centuries before that God's thoughts were not our thoughts (cf. Isa. 55:8, 9). Paul underlined this when he wrote that no one knows the thoughts of God except the Spirit of God. The natural man cannot understand the things that come from the Spirit of God (cf. 1 Cor. 2:11–14).

A Pentecostal hermeneutic

While highlighting the limitations of a traditional Western world view in evaluating the work of the Spirit, we would never discourage critical thinking and truly biblical theology. The Pentecostal/Charismatic spirituality has its own particular limitations. Religion can so quickly degenerate into superstition, unbiblical assumptions and ungodly practices. There is the need for a biblical theology which can embrace the tensions of both revelation and reason, healing and suffering, faith and doubt, conviction and compromise, victory and failure, power and weakness, the love of God and the judgment of God – a theology which is faithful to both the Word and the Spirit in exalting Christ and building up the Church.

'Today we are seeing the rise of a new generation of biblical scholars whose Pentecostal/Charismatic spirituality is informing critical research in all the theological disciplines.'[27] A new Pentecostal hermeneutic is at last on course to make its proper contribution to Christian theology. In Britain (the North American field is more advanced) there are hopeful signs that the current spiritual renewal movements will be well undergirded with robust theology. Scholars at Mattersey Hall (Doncaster, S.Yorks), the Assemblies of God Bible College, have their own studies. At the beginning of this decade the London Bible College at Northwood, which is interdenominational, opened a new post-graduate course on 'Spirit and Spiritual Gifts' taught by the Rev. Drs Max Turner and Graham McFarlane.

Pentecostals and Roman Catholics have been having theological discussions together for the last twenty years or more. Reports of these have appeared in various numbers of the journal *One In Christ* since 1974. Charismatic and Pentecostal scholars are meeting together in study groups in various parts of the country. Brighton saw a major conference in 1992 for scholars interested in the Person and Work of the Holy Spirit.

The first *Journal of Pentecostal Theology* (*JPT*) was started in October 1992, published by the Sheffield Academic Press, and it offers an intellectually rigorous explanation of the issues faced by Spirit-filled believers today. This is being supplemented by a number of new theological volumes from Pentecostal scholars. There are official plans by the Sheffield Academic Press to produce a new series of Pentecostal commentaries on the Bible which will be both scholarly and practical. As Mark Stibbe writes, 'Here at last is an opportunity to give scholarly foundations to the most powerful movement of God in the 20th century.'[28]

Of course, prophecy is among the gifts of the Spirit coming under theological review and a number of serious scholars such as David Aune, M.J. Cartledge, D.A. Carson, Y.J.M. Congar, Wayne Grudem, David Hill, Clifford Hill, Michael Green, Graham Houston, C.M. Robeck Jr and Max Turner have, among others, all produced valuable studies, covering this specific area over the last few years. These are currently circulating in Britain, Europe and beyond.

PART TWO

PROPHECY YESTERDAY

14

PROPHECY IN THE EARLY CHURCH

Those eager to develop a prophetic ministry, and those church leaders concerned about handling prophecy constructively, would do well to take to heart the history of prophecy (both the way it was exercised and the way it came to be marginalised) in the early Church.

Early prophetic movements

Breakaways, for whatever excuse, were occurring quite early on in the history of the Church (2 Tim. 1:15). Prophetic movements have prevailed far more than many popular Church histories would seem to indicate. Many of those early prophets founded movements which were short-lived, it is true, and in themselves they were hardly significant for the main-line historian.

The major motivation for most of the early Christian prophets was to prepare the world for the Second Coming of Christ and to challenge the current spiritual apathy and worldliness of the Church. Some breakaway groups were led by men with the spirit of Diotrephes 'who loves to be first' (3 John v.9), a simple egotistical motive, but others were more highly motivated.

In most cases these founding prophets were converts from surrounding cultures where there was already a prophetic tradition (even the Apostle Paul on one occasion quotes a pagan prophet with approval – Titus 1:12). Understanding of the faith could be easily distorted by alien philosophies and deceptive spirits (1 Tim. 4:1).

The Greeks had their oracles, where their deities were consulted. Homer mentions the existence of prophetic activity at Dodona and Delphi (otherwise known as Pythea). It is significant that the slave girl at Philippi who harassed Paul with her prophecies (Acts 16: 16–18) had what the Greek text describes as a 'pythian' spirit, which Paul cast out in the name of Jesus. Prophetic activity in the Greek world was generally associated with Zeus (at Dodona) and Apollo (at Delphi, where young virgins prophesied in metered verse). The Greeks also hosted the shrine of Asclepius which promoted the pagan practice of seeking foreknowledge by ritual incubation.

The gospel spread fast into those pagan cultures where prophecy (albeit non-Christian) played a prominent role. Robert Brow writes: 'It is not often realized by Christians in the West that, during the first three hundred years after Christ, the Christian Church expanded very rapidly across Persia to India and even into China. One reason for this was that since Rome was persecuting Christians the Persians felt the Christians must be their allies. As Christian churches multiplied a second Persian Empire arose and in reaction to Christian teaching Zoroastrianism (hitherto prophet-led) was made a state religion. The old Magi priesthood incorporated Zoroastrianism into its system.'[1]

When Constantine turned Christian in AD 312 the Persians naturally decided to persecute the religion adopted by their enemy, the Roman emperor, and the Persian Christians now had to endure two centuries of brutal oppression.[2]

Familiar pagan practices

Early Christian prophets trained themselves (1 Tim. 4:7) to 'see' and 'hear' what they thought God was communicating and quite properly to value that highly. Just as so many Christian teachers have appealed to the pagan philosophies of Plato or Aristotle, so it must have been a great temptation for some of the prophets to fall back on familiar pagan practices (like Balaam in Num. 22:7), hoping in this way to improve their prophetic gifting.

In the process some were attracted to 'gnostic' teaching (from the Greek *gnosis*, to know) – a mistaken belief that in the possession of secret knowledge there was a form of life. This led to the heresy that knowledge was the door to eternal life. In some respects 'gnosticism' can seem to be very near the gospel but it is certainly not the gospel and therefore most misleading. It is the Spirit who gives life and it is only by grace that we are saved through faith in Jesus Christ (cf. Eph. 2:8). Knowledge may be obtained through 'cheating' (see chapter 25 on the occult) and the claim that the possession of knowledge gives life is not valid.

It needs to be said that the Fathers of the Church were unanimous in their condemnation of prophetic activity in the Greek and Roman religions. Justyn Martyr saw their source as demonic, as did also Origen and Tertullian.

Not much theology about

Like gnosticism, another attractive path for the prophet was the local mystic cult. The prevailing mystic cults proclaimed that the object of the soul's striving was an immediate vision of God. The early Christian prophets spawned out of the local church could so easily be side-tracked from the truth, as it is in Jesus, if they were not well grounded in the faith. Something as high and holy as the vision of God would certainly seem right to prioritise and strive for. Often, outside the experience of Christ through lay evangelism, the early Christian converts would have had very little follow-up teaching to help them, though in some of the larger central churches there were instruction courses for the candidates for baptism who were known as catechumens.

Theological vacuum

It is important to bear in mind that in those early stages many Christian theologies had yet to be clearly thrashed out. The creeds which served such a useful purpose in crystallising the essence of Christian doctrine had yet to be formulated and agreed by the general Councils of the Church. There was a lack of clear and satisfactory definitions over good and evil, the God-head, and the Person of Christ.

It was not until Origen came on the scene (born c. AD 185) that we meet one of our first notable Christian theologians. He was a profound thinker and biblical scholar who drew thousands of disciples to his school in Alexandria where he exemplified an ascetic and extremely pious lifestyle – even to the extent of having himself castrated. With his philosophical background he attempted a systematic presentation of Christian doctrine called *De Principiis*, though some of his teaching, especially the concept of human pre-existence, was later to be rejected by the Church.

If *he*, of such massive intellect, had problems, is it any wonder that some of the local Christian prophets sometimes floundered and brought the Christian ministry into disrepute?

Half-enlightened prophet

Zoroastrian prophets had been popular in Mesopotamia and Egypt since the sixth century BC. Zoroaster was a Mede whose Persian name was Zarathustra. He lived more than a century after Isaiah and Ezekiel and was a contemporary of Daniel. He seems both to have been influenced by Israel's belief in one true God, and in turn, directly or indirectly, to have influenced Cyrus (cf. Isa. 45:1) who overthrew the Babylonian Empire in 539 BC. It was Cyrus who sent the first group of Jews back to Palestine to rebuild their temple (cf. Ezra 1).

Zoroaster had a life-changing experience at the age

of about thirty in which he met the 'Wise Lord'. This experience, besides other revelations, led him to become the prophet of a new and purified religion. He taught that the world was made by the same 'Wise Lord' with the help of his holy Spirit and six other divine spirits, or attributes of God. These spirits work against the Evil Spirit who is also helped by six other spirits, and tempts man to do wrong. He also taught that after life on earth a virgin-born Saviour God will finally triumph over Evil and all souls eventually pass over the 'bridge of decision' (from which some must first fall into purifying flames) and enjoy eternal bliss. He stressed the importance of truth and the value of mercy.[3]

This was the dominant religion of Persia for more than a millennium preceding the Muslim invasion of AD 636. Zoroastrianism (a layman's religion) became the spawning ground for Mithraism (a mystery religion opposed to Christianity) and Manichaeism. It created the spiritual environment for the primitive Christian Churches being planted in Mesopotamia and Babylonia.

Grappling with light and dark

A classic example of a prophet heading off into heresy is the case of Mani (AD 216–76), the founder of Manichaeism. He was a Persian, born in Mesopotamia, who began preaching in Babylon in 242 and was crucified or decapitated in 276 or 277. Mani had been brought up in a Jewish-Christian sect but left it when he received 'revelations'.

Calling himself an apostle of Jesus Christ, he converted members of his own family and commenced his far-flung ministry which lasted over thirty years. He delivered people from demons and diseases. His teaching had elements of Zoroastrianism mixed in with his version of Christianity.

Mani was also grappling with the problem of good and evil; something very much on the agenda of the Christian Church (cf. Origen above) and debated in the surrounding

cultures. His bottom line was that light and darkness, good
and evil are eternally at war – very like the 'dualism'
of Zoroastrianism, that both God and the devil endure
for ever.

Another element in Mani's teaching was similar to the
'gnostic' belief that the material part of man was evil
and represented a kind of dark prison-house in which
some of the realm of light was confined. Salvation was
in knowing the nature of this bondage and desiring to
return to the light. In the process man needed to adopt an
ascetic lifestyle to deaden physical appetites and desires.
Manichaean worship was simple and its asceticism was
strict. Its membership was of two classes, the perfect who
were relatively few, and the hearers who accepted the
teachings but practised them with much less strictness.

Manichaean organisation was centralised and rigid.
It spread rapidly, absorbing remnants of the Christian-
gnostic sects and other early heresies. Manichaeans carried
their 'gospel' to Africa, to Europe and even to China
(Mani himself reaching India). The sect numbered among
its adherents Augustine before his conversion, and experienced its greatest growth in the fourth and fifth centuries.
Its influence continued to be felt late into the Middle
Ages through Christian sects such as the Paulicians and
the Cathars (mentioned later).

Getting back on course

Through a link with Tertullian, the historian Eusebius has
provided a significant reference point for a classic type of
prophetic movement by highlighting Montanus (c. 170),
a Christian in Phrygia, Asia Minor. There are no records
available of direct contributions from Montanus himself
to help the modern day researcher. We do not even know
if Montanus ever committed his own prophecies or views
to paper, though we know of some sixteen prophecies
attributed to individuals among the Montanists.

The movement included two notable prophetesses,

Prisca and Maximilia, and extended to North Africa. In its ascetic strictness, its apocalyptic fervour and insistence on the infallibility of its own prophetic utterances (making prophecy an end in itself rather than a help for the church to function properly), the movement clearly made serious mistakes.

It was not until the latter half of the fourth century that it was formally rejected by the Council of Laodicea. But for all its faults Montanism won the allegiance of Tertullian (c. 160/70 – c. 215/20), the African moralist and theologian who blamed Praxeus (c. 200) for turning the Pope against the Montanists.

All this is by way of saying that, though the mainline Church had some responsibility for the decline of prophecy, the prophetic movements themselves must take some blame for their own rejection because they had too often been carried off into extremist positions leading into heresy.

Some find it hard to understand how this could be if the prophet was truly receiving revelation from God. It needs to be said that prophets do not know everything. Revelations which come from God do not give the whole picture by any means, but are simply glimpses 'behind the scenes' of matters relevant for the moment in the purposes of God.

It is a natural assumption but a mistaken one, to believe that because the Lord has revealed something he must have revealed everything.

Sound doctrine
The Church was having to clarify its position on doctrine, as seen by Tertullian's tract against Praxeus whom he charged with 'serving the devil by driving away prophecy and bringing in heresy; he put to flight the Paraclete and crucified the Father'. In the same cause Novatian produced a treatise on the Trinity.

During the first two hundred years of the life of the

Church there was a flood of written works, including gospels, letters, apocalypses, sermons and treatises. Almost all were written under the name of a prestigious apostle or apostles and claimed to carry the authentic teaching of Jesus.

Internal divisions in the Church were reflected in written works which presented diametrically opposite views of who Jesus was and what he had said. The Church was having to define a canon for the Bible by determining which of these writings should be included and which excluded so that yet another door to heresy could hopefully be closed. In the process the door was almost closed on prophecy also.

Limiting revelation to the Bible

'The chief effect of Montanism on the Catholic church', according to Henry Chadwick, 'was greatly *to reinforce the conviction that revelation came to an end with the apostolic age* [my italics], and so to foster the creation of a closed canon of the New Testament'.[4] Thereafter believers came to assume that the Bible (and tradition) was the limit of God's revelation in all things. To all practical purposes it became accepted wisdom that God spoke only through the pages of the Bible (with tradition to interpret it) or possibly later, if one was a Catholic, through the Pope (when speaking ex cathedra).

Tertullian had once remarked that there were two ways of nullifying Scriptures. 'One is Marcion's way; he used the knife to excise from the Scriptures whatever did not conform with his own opinion.' Marcion was a wealthy shipowner and a prominent lay heretic of the second century who differentiated radically between the God of the Old Testament and the Father of Jesus. He was in Rome shortly before AD 140 and was excommunicated four years later.

'The other way', said Tertullian, 'was that of Valentinus who seems to use the entire *instrumentum*' (which here means the New Testament), 'but he perverts its meaning by misinterpreting it.'[5] Valentinus was a contemporary of Marcion who came from Alexandria in Egypt and lived in Rome from about AD 135 to 160 (expecting to become the bishop there). Valentinus accepted not only the four versions of the gospel, but many additional documents professing to contain traditions of the secret sayings of Jesus, like the *Gospel of Thomas* recently recovered from the sands of Egypt.

Irenaeus (Bishop of Lyons AD 177) is credited with being the first to articulate the felt need of the Church to have a canon or a fixed list of authoritative writings of the New Testament. Hitherto the dividing line between books accorded the status of being read in the Church lectionary and books that were of approved orthodoxy had not been decisively drawn. Irenaeus drew his own line, and is the first writer whose New Testament virtually corresponds to the canon that became accepted as traditional.[6]

A process was commenced by which the Church could establish a canon of Scripture – 'something accepted, always, by all' (although in fact the Church has yet to agree over the full limits of the canon). It is ironical that in the process towards solving this problem another problem emerged. Once the canon was closed a view was quickly assumed that God's voice was clearly limited to Scripture (interpreted by tradition). From henceforth God could write but he could not speak! The canon could de facto be regarded as a system to silence God from speaking at all apart from the Scripture!

Irenaeus is 'the last writer who can still think of himself as belonging to the eschatological age of miracle and revelation'. In his work *Against Heresies* he wrote:

For which cause also His true disciples, having received grace from Him, use it in His name for the benefit of the rest of mankind, even as each has received the gifts from Him. For some certainly do drive out demons so that those who have been cleansed from evil spirits frequently both believe and join themselves to the church.[7]

Others have foreknowledge of things to be, and visions and *prophetic speech*, and others cure the sick by the laying on of hands and make them whole. Yea, moreover, as I have said, the dead even have been raised up and remained among us for many years. And what shall I say more? It is not possible to name the number of gifts which the church throughout the world has received from God in the name of Jesus Christ.[8]

The New Testament canon was not finally fixed until AD 367 by the Eastern Church (see Athanasius' thirty-ninth paschal letter) and in AD 397 by the Western Church at the council of Carthage. Both churches were now in agreement that the twenty-seven books which today we call the New Testament should be accepted as inspired by God.

Limiting God to speaking only through Scripture was the last thing Irenaeus would have intended for the canon. While it was needed for exposing the heretic, it was all too soon to become a means for excluding the prophetic.

Limiting the anointing for ministry in the gifts of the Spirit to the sacrament of baptism

A second means for silencing prophecy was the gradual equating of the anointing of the Holy Spirit and the gifts (charisms) of the Spirit with the Christian initiatory sacrament of baptism. Admittedly it was believed that those baptised in infancy might actualise the full richness of baptismal grace only years later either as a separate experience or through the laying on of hands in confirmations. (This latter seemed integral to the baptism rite in many places during the sub-Apostolic age but was beginning to appear as a separate rite by the time of Tertullian (c. 160–c. 220), Pope Cornelius (d. 253) and St Cyprian (c. 300) and came to be understood as the grace of God being conveyed in a new and fuller way to those already baptised.)

This was a theological position which seemed best to square with Scripture even if it could never be made to square with the sovereign work of God's Spirit. It was adhered to by an impressive array of early Church fathers – to wit: Hilary in Gaul at Poitiers (c. 350), Cyril in Palestine at Jerusalem (c. 364), Basil in Cappadocia at Caesarea (366 and 374–75) and Gregory Nazianzus at Constantinople (380); in Syria there was Philoxenus at Mabbug (end of the fifth and beginning of the sixth centuries), John the Solitary at Apamea (430–50), Theodoret at Cyrrhus (c. 444) and Joseph Hazzaza (eighth century) at Qardu (in present-day Iraq) who all placed the charisms (gifts of the Spirit) within or in reference to initiation. John Chrysostom (c. 392–3) and Severus of Antioch (end of the fifth and beginning of the sixth centuries) 'also recall the apostolic paradigm, that is that the prophetic charisms are implanted during initiation'. Almost the whole seaboard bears witness, representing Latin, Greek and Syriac cultures. The witnesses were not minor personalities.[9]

The gifts of the Spirit were being fused into one formal sacrament (even if divided into baptism and confirmation). The problem was not solved, however. The sovereign Lord can do whatever he wills and we can never force God into a formula. This, of course, is well understood by our theologians but the body of believers is left with the impression (usually for the sake of convenience) that their God has been brought into order by such teaching from the Church. For God to appear to move in other than familiar ways is immediately suspect and certainly threatening. And so another door to prophecy appeared to be gradually closing.

Limiting prophecy to Church authority

As if this was not sufficient to silence lay folk from
exercising spiritual gifts in the congregation, the theory
was developed that these charisms were now limited to
the Church authorities. By the last stages of the Didache
(compiled somewhere between the first and the third
centuries) there appeared a new morphology: 'Appoint
for yourselves, then, bishops and deacons . . . for they
also are performing for you the task of the *prophets* and
the teachers.'[10] Bishops and deacons were taking over the
charism of prophecy!

The priest and the prophet were being merged into one
office. The anointing for the gifts was being channelled
into a formal sacrament. From now on the voice of God
could only be heard through Scripture when interpreted
by the Church's ordained authorities. As Yves Congar
has written, 'prophecy declined to some extent in the
early church . . . because of an increasing emphasis on
the authority of the bishops.'[11] The established Church
seemed at last to have God and prophecy nicely ordered.
But the problem still existed; the wind will always blow
wherever it pleases.

After reading an old book called *The General Delusion
of Christians with Regard to Prophecy*, John Wesley
ruefully reflected in his journal:

I was fully convinced of what I had once suspected:
(1) That the Montanists, in the second and third
centuries, were real, scriptural Christians; and (2)
That the grand reason why the miraculous gifts were
so soon withdrawn, was not only that faith and holiness
were well nigh lost, but that dry, formal, orthodox men
began even then to ridicule whatever gifts they had not
themselves, and to decry them all as either madness or
imposture.[12]

Conclusion

While we have traced some of the adverse effects of prophecy upon the traditional Church in its early days and equally the adverse effects of the traditional Church upon prophecy, it would not be correct to assume that the gifts of the Spirit had been completely withdrawn. Many independent sects thrived on the exercise of these gifts. Though some of their leadership were immature, often unlearned and even tending to heresy, their followers, usually uncomprehending or even unaware of the finer points of doctrine, would be faithful to the Lord they knew and fervent in their faith – even unto death.

15

PROPHECY DURING THE DARK AGES

Centralisation of authority

A process towards the centralisation of authority followed the conversion of the Roman Emperor Constantine. Before attacking his rival Maxentius at the Milvian Bridge (AD 312) he had invoked the aid of the Christian God already worshipped by his half-sister Anastasia. Victory gave Constantine sole political power in the West. It also changed his attitude towards the Christian Church which would eventually become entrusted with the role of public state religion.

During the sixty or more years prior to Constantine's conversion, the Church, by then widely scattered round the Mediterranean basin, had been suffering considerably. These Christians were unauthorised groups and technically illegal but the Roman central government had shown relatively little interest in them for the first two hundred years of their existence.

The change of attitude was brought about by several developments. The Christians had grown more numerous and prominent. The empire had suffered military defeat and economic problems: a scapegoat was required. But the most important issue was the clash of kingdoms highlighted in the Christians' refusal to worship the emperor, who was regarded as a god by his pagan subjects. The Christians proclaimed: 'Jesus is Lord.' The state declared: 'Caesar is Lord – Jesus is cursed.'

Emperor worship was a form of patriotism. Refusal to

participate seemed to threaten the well-being of society from within. This was seen as particularly reprehensible when the empire was being severely threatened from without. Three Roman emperors made systematic attempts at forcing the Christians to conform through persecution. They were Decius (249–51), Valerian (253–60) and Diocletian (284–312).

The last named ordered every citizen of the empire to offer the traditional sacrifice to the emperor and to obtain a certificate from witnesses. Many Christians who still refused were executed. Others were cruelly mutilated and sent off to work in the imperial mines till they died. But the Church, as it always will, survived all these sufferings.

Now, within one lifetime under Constantine the Christian Church had moved from a position of illegality and ferocious persecution to one of favour. 'The church was no longer organized in independent and voluntary fellowships; it was ordered according to regions and territories, sees and parishes for the care and welfare of the people.'[1]

In search of spirituality

But there was a legacy which caused considerable unrest. Just before the persecution ended, and peace for the Church should have ensued, the Christians had become seriously divided over those among their leadership who had compromised with the State. Matters had come to a head in 311 when Caecilian, a new bishop for Carthage (the old one had been a doughty defender of compromise), was consecrated by three bishops, one of whom had apparently compromised his faith by co-operation with the persecuting Roman authorities.

The question was raised: 'Could one who had lost the Spirit confer the Spirit's gifts?' Divisions over this continued for almost two hundred years. The main opposition came from Bishop Donatus, a rival of Bishop Caecilian.

Emerging options

Persecution can be made to serve a good purpose. Without it the Church found itself sinking to a low ebb. There were *three possible options* emerging for those who wished to express any residual religious fervour. All were radical.

The cloisters

One option was the cloisters or the isolated seclusion of the desert hermit. Antony (c. 251–356) was a pioneer example of this latter course. Born in Coma in middle Egypt, his well-to-do Christian parents were not long dead when Antony, aged about twenty, heard the reading from the Gospel 'If you want to be perfect, go, sell . . .' (Matt. 19:21) followed by 'Do not worry about tomorrow' (Matt. 6:34). Seeking isolation, Antony took to the bush – *anachorein* in the Greek, from which we have 'anchorites'. One of our best-known English equivalents was Julian(a) of Norwich, an 'anchoress', living alone in her 'anchorage' cell of timber or stone, at Conisford near Norwich, in the fourteenth century.

Antony eventually crossed the Nile eastwards to a disused fort at Pispir which he occupied alone for twenty years. Then in AD 312 he retreated still further to the remote Mt Colzeim, near the Red Sea. There he was still sought after by visitors, some of whom he settled into a colony of hermit cells back at Pispir. Antony was the first person known to withdraw to the depths of the desert for Christian reasons. His model of the anchorite life was one of severe austerity, incessant prayer, supernatural healings and prophetic 'perceptions', and above all perpetual warfare with the demons of the desert. Thousands of men and women followed Antony's example, seeking God in the desert, either alone or in communities.

Pilgrimages

A second option was to go on a pilgrimage or later one of the Crusades. Constantine's mother started a trend, being one of the first to make a pilgrimage to the Holy Land (in AD 326–7). But these pilgrimages removed good people from the local congregation and the local community.

Sects

A third option was to join one of the sects. *There were many of these* which may generally be classified as 'reforming sects' and 'prophetic sects'. The 'reforming sects' glorified the golden age of the primitive Church and protested against its take-over by the state. The 'prophetic sects' did not go back from the decadent forms of Christianity to its supposedly pristine beginnings, but claimed, rather, to anticipate Christianity's consummation, beyond its beginnings and its history.

New prophetic movements sprang up continually as the bearers of the Spirit promised by Christ. 'Because Christianity, by virtue of its messianic hope points beyond itself and the church, prophetic and messianic sects always come to the fore whenever the church surrenders its hope for the coming kingdom.'[2]

To gain a more truly holistic perspective of the early Church it is useful to read main-line Church history and that of the sects at the same time; to see both forms of Christianity together. It is then easier to understand the godly motivation for some of the sects. 'A Christianity that departs from its beginnings in order to adapt itself to the present day state is bound to evoke the Christianity of reform. A Christianity that surrenders its messianic hope is bound to evoke the Christianity of prophecy.'[3]

In the schism between the mainstream churches and the sects, the 'mainstream churches' themselves became sectarian, because they repressed fundamental elements of the Christian truth. On the other hand, both the reforming and the prophetic sects, with their criticism of the Church's worldliness, tended to repress certain elements of Christian mission and love expressed in the mainstream churches by their openness to the world.

Some pedigrees

There are a number of reforming and prophetic groups that could be considered with interest.

The Novatianists (after the martyr Novatian (210–58?) who was a rival bishop in Rome) were a small puritanical group which eventually split from Rome over its supposedly lax attitude towards those who had 'reneged' on Christ during the persecutions. Bishop Novatian has given the West its first full treatment of the Trinity (completely orthodox) in which he writes of the Spirit:[4]

> This is He who places *prophets* in the Church, instructs teachers, directs tongues, gives powers and healings, does wonderful works, offers discrimination of spirits, affords powers of government, suggests councils, and orders and arranges whatever other gifts there are of *charismata*; thus makes the Lord's Church everywhere, and in all, perfected and completed.[5]

Support groups known as Cathari (pure ones) were known to exist in places like Carthage. It is possible that these in turn influenced the Paulicians who can be traced back to the mid seventh century (possibly earlier) in the eastern part of the Byzantine Empire, and still survived in Armenia in the early nineteenth century. They helped to spawn the Bogomiles in Bulgaria, and the Cathari (or Cathars), a larger heretical movement which may have been a revival of the old group in Carthage (but this is unlikely) or a new puritan group politically active in Italy and Western Europe in the twelfth century. There are also links between the Paulicians and the Albigenses of Southern France, the Beguines and the

Beghards of the Netherlands, the Apostolici in Brittany, the Petrobrusians of Toulouse, the Henricians of Lausanne and the Familists of Munster who developed an unusual prophetic ministry.

Equally there were prophetic trends within the more mystical wing of the Western Church from St Francis (Italian), Meister Eckhart, Johannes Tauler and Henry Suso (Germans), and the Jansenists, named after Cornelius Otto Jansen (French). The same was true of the Eastern Church, whose Russian hermits, the staretz, were clearly given to prophecy.

In Benedicta Ward's *The Lives of the Desert Fathers*[6] there is a typical story of seven religious brothers who went to visit the hermit John Thycopolis. The old man asked if anyone in the party was a cleric. They all replied that none of them was. But one in fact was a deacon, though he felt unworthy even to be called a Christian and had only revealed his office confidentially to one other member of the party, asking him to keep it a secret. But nevertheless the old man pointed to him and said, 'This one is a deacon,' and then kindly but sternly admonished him for his deception.

Russia's most beloved 'staretz' and saint was born in 1759 with the name Prokhor Moshnin and canonised St Serafim of Sarov in 1903, seventy years after his death. After thirteen years of silence followed by a powerful healing he began his prophetic ministry to those who visited him in his cell. He read people's thoughts, predicted their future, and healed their spiritual as well as physical ailments. In his old age he had a revelation of the approaching tragedy coming upon his beloved country – the terrible loss of life through the Revolution, the religious persecutions, the participation in the world wars. 'Life will be short,' he prophesied tearfully, 'the angels will hardly have time to gather up the souls.'[7]

All this goes to show that the prophetic ministry,

though often misled and just as often misunderstood, has remained a recurring feature in many ways and in various traditions throughout the ages of the Christian Church.

16

THE FRENCH PROPHETS

There are a number of movements it would be fascinating to trace, but there are three which have particular interest for us because they make plain that manifestations of the gifts of the Spirit are not limited to the early Church or to our twentieth century.

They make plain too the mistakes which were made by those who had the gifts, those who led them and those who opposed them. They concern us also because remnants of the first and second groups certainly drifted over to England as 'Ranters' and 'Seekers'. The latter two groups are also of interest because of their association with some famous Christian personalities whose thinking has influenced theology. The first group were Calvinist, the second group Arminian and the third group Catholic.

The Huguenots

The Huguenots (supposedly a nickname from the German word for 'confederates') sprang from remnants of the Vaudois, a branch of an earlier revival movement known as the Albigenses, who have otherwise been known as Camisards, Prophets of Dauphiny, prophets of Cevennes, French or Inspired Prophets, 'Church in the Desert' and 'Children of God'.

Two million membership

In spite of a turbulent sequence of outlawry, persecution, defeat in war, and massacre (St Bartholomew's day 1572 being the most terrible), the Huguenots numbered about two million of the population of France by 1706. Those in the south (from the counties of Albi, Quercy, Raverque and Costres) were involved in continuous civil wars in which religious differences between Catholics and Protestants were entangled with political ambition.

John Calvin (1509–64) escaped from that region to Basle during the first persecution. Those he left behind later out-calvined Calvin with their extreme views on election, which made them fatalists and led to their fearlessness and marked ferocity in battle. Their leaders believed that the Spirit informed them when traitors were present. At least two, discovered in this way, are reported as confessing to such treachery.

Prophets as chaplains

Their military forces had prophets attached to serve as chaplains. The latter were regarded as supreme commanders when under the power of the Spirit.[1] It was also reported of them that 'an infectious ecstasy seized people of all ages and of both sexes. They claimed to hear supernatural voices. They spoke with tongues . . . Quite uneducated persons gave utterance when "seized by the Spirit" to prophecies in the purest French.'[2] This was significant since most were unable to speak anything but the Romance patois of the Cevennes. It was also claimed that between 5,000 and 6,000 children prophesied at one time (1689).

Extreme manifestations

They had extreme manifestations. Some were said to be able to fall from places as high as twelve feet without injury; drove sharp knives into themselves without any trace; were able to pass through fire without burning; could quote long passages of Scripture correctly and prophesied events which were to occur some distance away – predictions which were afterwards confirmed by fulfilment. One man by the name of du Serre even recruited students for a school of prophecy where they were taught how to exercise the gift.

Holy kiss baptism

A unique feature of the Huguenots was the manner by which some were known to receive the 'baptism' of the Holy Spirit. This took place after the candidate had first fasted for several days and was then greeted with a holy kiss. This was followed by physical agitations and tongues lasting for up to two hours. Candidates were taught to expect such a result.[3]

Serious mistakes

They made some serious mistakes: 'what contributed most to their publicity was the announcement made by several prophets that a certain Dr Eames, then on his death bed, would be raised from the tomb five months after his burial. The French prophets never did things by halves,' wrote Ronald Knox with his wry cynicism.[4]

According to contemporary sources these were sincere and godly people. Though some were poor many were educated and better off. All their leaders were prophets and it was believed that it was prophecy which held them together for the two hundred years of their political power, which terminated with their military defeat in 1704. As a religious entity, however, they continued on, though some became widely dispersed. It was not until the French Revolution that they finally achieved full toleration and civil rights.

'The last prophet of Doopsgezinden'

Galenus Abrahamsz de Hann, usually called Galenus Abrahaams, was known as 'the last prophet of Doopsgezinden'. He was a Mennonite pastor and belonged to a group called the Rhynsburger Collegiants of Holland. This group contained some of the most intellectual minds of Europe. Jacobus Arminius (1560–1609), professor of theology at Leyden, was delegated by the Reformed Church to refute their free-will tendencies, but having studied some of their writings, Arminius was persuaded by their doctrine. He soon became their leader and gave his name to the theory that man served God by his own free choice – Arminianism. Arminius insisted that biblically it was possible to believe in God's sovereignty while allowing for real free will in man.

'Prophetic openings'

The group formulated doctrines which showed traits of 'enthusiasm' and they encouraged a ministry of 'prophetic openings' based on 1 Corinthians 14. They believed that free prophecy was the highest form of ministry and held that God, by his grace, could pour out his Spirit upon men in the seventeenth century as he did in the days of the apostles. But they also valued dignity and propriety of behaviour.[5] Abrahaams and David Spruyt drew up their 'Nineteen Articles' in 1658. 'These documents present the apostolic pattern or model as the ideal of the visible church for all ages . . .'

Hastings claims that the Seekers (see chapter 18) were an English version of these Collegiants and that they were waiting for a further revelation and a new demonstration of the Spirit. These Collegiants also had a clear connection with the continental Anabaptists, some of whom had crossed over to England.

The Jansenists

Cornelius Jansen gives his name to a spiritual movement of the seventeenth and eighteenth centuries which has been termed Jansenism and has kept within the Catholic Church. Jansen was born in Accoy in the province of Utrecht on October 28th, 1585 and became the Bishop of Ypres.

Another leader of the Jansenists was Jean du Vergier de

Hauranne, a fellow student at the University of Louvain who became the Abbot of Saint Cyran.

Augustinus

In his desire to promote spiritual renewal in the Church, Bishop Jansen, with the help of Saint Cyran, wrote a book called *Augustinus* highlighting some of the teachings of St Augustine of Hippo.

The book, which was not published until after Jansen's death, advanced the call to evangelism, explained that faith was not subject to the limitation of reason, encouraged Catholics to seek an experience of God and proclaimed clearly (following Augustine's 'City of God' theory) that maintaining incorporation in the visible Church was essential to salvation.

The book also found a ready response from those who were disillusioned with the current life of the Church. The Jesuits were incensed and Saint Cyran was imprisoned (1638), not to be released for five years.

Angélique Arnauld

A third who had a significant role in this movement for renewal was the beautiful and godly Angélique Arnauld, Abbess of the Cistercian Abbey of Port Royal des Champs, who instituted a reform movement in Port Royal which was to have an impact upon the whole continent. Saint Cyran had been appointed supervisor over this Cistercian Abbey.

Provincial letters

Antoine Arnauld, Angélique's brother, assumed active leadership of the movement at this stage. Trained as a lawyer he turned to writing a defence of the Jansenist position. His 'Provincial Letters' were the first of forty-two volumes. He was eventually driven into seclusion in both Holland and Belgium and died in 1694.

Another spiritual leader who was never actually a

member was the brilliant Blaise Pascal. 'It is true that as a mathematical genius, inventor and father of the modern computer he is one of the greatest human thinkers of all time – a Renaissance thinker, well versed in mathematics, physics, philosophy and theology – he wrote what . . . Voltaire . . . hailed as the greatest masterpiece in French prose.'[6] One of his choice sayings, frequently quoted, was 'The heart has its reasons that reason knows not of.'

Pascal and Port Royal

Pascal was introduced to the convent of Port Royal des Champs, south of Paris, by his sister Jacqueline. After her father's death, she entered the convent as a nun. Pascal found there a community which sought spiritual renewal by striving to live a self-abandoned life of devotion to God in response to God's irresistible grace.

In *The Memorial* Pascal tells of the 'night of fire' beginning on the evening of November 23rd 1654, when he was thirty-one years old and had just experienced a close brush with death in a driving accident. This encounter with God changed the whole course of his life. Lasting from 10.30 to 12.30 that night the experience strained and exhausted language; he could only describe it in one word – 'Fire'.

The experience was so precious and pivotal to him that he sewed the parchment record of it into the lining of his doublet and for the remaining eight years of his life took the trouble to sew it into every new doublet he bought.

That experience is sometimes referred to as Pascal's 'second conversion', following the first in Rouen in 1646 in his twenty-fourth year, the year when Pascal first became sickly. This infirmity stayed with him for the rest of his life, the last six months of which were intensely painful.

Jesuits attacked

Pascal attacked the Jesuits whom he, with the Port Royal party, blamed for the decadence of the Church. He disputed the whole basis of the Jesuit religious casuistry, with its moral laxity and mental reservations known as 'probabilism'. He believed the Jesuit position was realistic about human nature but in error about God's grace.

He defended the Jansenists who believed in the radical nature of conversion, the need for repentance for sin, and the irresistible grace of Jesus Christ – an emphasis which rang true to Pascal's own experience.

The Church's response

The Catholic Church's concern about the Port Royal community is best expressed through a chance word of St Francis de Sales to Mother Angélique. Her nuns maintained a standard of sanctification which appealed to a few choice souls but left so many others, full of good dispositions, out of the running – 'Could she not be less exacting and cast her nets a little wider?'

Jansenism had a reputation generally for harsh moral rigorism. It was condemned by the Pope first in 1653 and later in 1713. Many French Jansenists found refuge from the ensuing persecution in Holland. In one form or another (e.g. the Old Catholic Church in the USA) they still exist today. They continued for many years in Paris as a strict group. Their headquarters are maintained in Utrecht.

It is a fact that the tendency to elitism and even rigorism is a temptation to the prophetic groups, just as there is the temptation to take to extremes other good things in the Christian Church, such as fasting or the possession of a fine church choir. But as with all temptation it must be recognised, resisted and, whenever it has been given in to, repented of.

17

THE GERMAN PROPHETS

In 1521 a radical party arose in the small town of Zwichau on the borders of Saxony and Bohemia. The town had already accepted the Reformation, but this group wanted to move much faster and further than the Reformation leaders themselves. Though not necessarily directly or organisationally linked, this radicalism was part of a much wider Anabaptist tradition.

Social oppression

There was a history of appalling oppression in the whole region of Saxony and Bohemia. This had produced such abortive movements as the 'Bundshuh' (from 1493) on the Upper Rhine and the 'Armer Konrad' in Wurtemberg. The peasants still awaited a 'messiah' to take up their just cause.

Claus Storch, who was the foremost among the prophets in Zwichau, is described as a local weaver. This may refer either to his actual occupation or to his membership of one of the Christian guilds. These were interconnected across Europe from Portugal to Bohemia, from England to Sicily. One did not need to practise the craft to belong to the guild but it gave protection for public reading of the Bible and open prayer.[1]

Storch claimed to be led directly by God and gathered together followers to help him extend Luther's Reformation into the area of social reform. There was no question about the rightness of their cause; it sorely needed urgent attention.

Leadership problem

There was one immediate problem, however, and this concerned the suitability of the local leaders, who showed so much courage but seemingly little wisdom.

When they were challenged on the authority of the Bible for what they claimed, Storch is reported to have replied:

> For what good purpose is it to attach oneself so exclusively to the Bible? The Bible! Always the Bible! Can the Bible speak to us? Is it not insufficient for our instruction? If God had wished to instruct us by means of a book, would he not have sent us a Bible from Heaven? It is by the Spirit alone that we can be enlightened. God himself speaks to us. God himself reveals to us what we ought to do and what we ought to say.[2]

Undermining the Reformation

This was seen as undermining the very foundations of the Reformation and its appeal to *sola scriptura* – the unique authority of Scripture.

It was claimed that Storch believed the Angel Gabriel had appeared to him one night communicating things which he had no permission to reveal, but one thing he could tell was that the angel had said, 'Thou thyself shalt sit upon my throne'! These may simply be allegations from enemies of the Anabaptists, but it is important to note here that prophets before and since have so easily deluded themselves.

Enter Thomas Munzer

Storch was joined by a former student called Mark Stubner of Wittemberg and later by Thomas Munzer (1490–1525) who completed his leadership party. Munzer had a gift for organising and was the most educated of the three.

He had studied latterly at Frankfurt but previously at Leipzig where he first came under the personal influence of Martin Luther. Munzer was also greatly influenced by the 400-year-old writings of Joachim de Fiori (1130–1202), a Cistercian abbot whom Dante described as *di spiritu profetico dotado* (gifted with a spirit of prophecy).

Influence of Joachim de Fiori

Joachim de Fiori had taught that there were to be three ages in the world's history: that of God the Father (the Old Testament Church), of the Son (the New Testament Church) and the Holy Spirit. This last was still in the future for Joachim de Fiori and was not expected to begin until the year 1260 when the Spirit would come in full power. This was to be an age when men would truly understand 'the eternal gospel': not a new gospel but the old gospel spiritually interpreted. This was the age Munzer believed had now been entered.

Joachim's millennial vision of this third age became the rallying point for many of the disaffected elements that existed in and around the Church of the day. His optimistic expectations for new religious orders destined to convert the whole world and to usher in the 'Ecclesia Spiritualis' had a far-reaching influence in the following centuries among groups who often carried his ideas to revolutionary conclusions.[3]

Influence of Jan Hus

In fourteenth-century Prague a reform movement[4] was begun through the magnetic preaching of an Augustinian canon from Vienna, Conrad of Waldhausen (d. 1369). The movement continued through to the Bohemian reformist Jan Hus (1374–1415), who had been influenced by John Wycliffe (1329–84), a Catholic priest and a doctor of theology from Oxford whose writings had been circulated in Bohemia. Munzer had imbibed much from Jan Hus through his life, teachings and finally martyrdom. Munzer became a Lutheran preacher in Zwichau in 1520, and believed himself, like Storch and many of the charismatic communities already mentioned, to be directly inspired by the Holy Spirit.

He also demanded radical religious and social reform like Storch. It was in Zwichau that Storch, with good precedent, had chosen twelve apostles and seventy-two disciples.

Apostles and prophets restored

The cry went up that apostles and prophets were at last being restored to the Church of God. The Zwichau prophets declared that a Catholic Church governed by men so corrupted as their bishops could not be the Church of Jesus Christ. They prophesied a universal judgment within the space of five or so years. No impious person would be left alive.

After the earth had been purified by blood God would establish a new kingdom with Storch in supreme authority! (Did Storch actually claim that or was it a detractor's embellishment?) He would at last bestow upon the saints the government of the people.

Storch preached repentance and, in the tradition of a growing movement of Anabaptists, taught that infant baptism was invalid. He invited all men to come and receive from his apostles and prophets 'believer's' baptism as a witness to their initiation into the new Church of God.

Not surprisingly this style of preaching made considerable impact. Rightly or wrongly the prophets were accused of 'Montanism'[5] and they soon found themselves strongly opposed in Zwichau. After a near riot many of their followers were imprisoned.

Expelled from Zwichau

The leaders were expelled from Zwichau and, believing that prophets had no honour in their own country, Storch, Munzer and Stubner moved hastily on to Wittemberg, arriving there on December 27th, 1521. Hoping for support, they called upon the university professors Philip Melanchthon and Andreas Carlstadt, introducing themselves as men ordained directly by God.

Melanchthon, who with Carlstadt was the main leader of the Reformation in Luther's absence, was at a loss to know how to react to them.

Extraordinary spirits

'There are,' said Melanchthon, 'extraordinary spirits in these men, but what sort of spirits? . . . Only Luther can decide this question . . . on the one hand let us beware of extinguishing the Spirit of God, and on the other of being seduced by the spirit of the devil.'

The two academics were not really prepared to grasp the nettle. Melanchthon was godly but weak. Carlstadt was enthusiastic but agreed with Melanchthon to leave it for Luther to sort out on his return.

Incidentally Carlstadt, regarded as the most extreme of the Reformers, himself joined another group of Anabaptists later (March 1522) and went to Zurich. Unfortunately we have a very limited knowledge of the Anabaptists of the sixteenth century as they have left little account of themselves.[6] They may have been misjudged on some matters.

The delay over Luther's return brought its own solution. Running out of patience, the restless Storch soon moved off with Munzer, leaving only Stubner behind to be roundly denounced by Luther when they met soon after.

Luther's scorn

'Those who are expert in spiritual things have gone through the Valley of the Shadow,' he said. 'When these men talk of sweetness and of being transported to the third heaven, do not believe them. Divine Majesty does not speak directly to men. God is a consuming fire, and the dreams and visions of the saints are terrible . . . Prove

the spirits and if you are not able to do so then take the
advice of Gamaliel and wait.'[7]

Peasants' revolt

Storch now disappears from view but Munzer went on
to preach to the peasants in Thuringia and Saxony.
There his eloquence stirred them to demonstrations which
eventually led to armed revolt, the burning down of castles
and monasteries, and a proposal to destroy all authority.

By 1524 Munzer was in Zurich, a thorn in the flesh
to the Reformers there also. Once more he soon gained
disciples with his radical doctrines, claiming that through
the priesthood of all believers each disciple was specially
taught of God, and that all rules of life outside heart and
conscience were quite unnecessary. What a mish-mash of
truth and falsehood! This confusion was compounded by
reports that Munzer's followers were even publicly burning
their Bibles.

Among many other new opinions held was the strange
belief that since Christ had said his followers should
become like little children they must behave like little
children. This accounts for the reports that they were
playing with dolls on the streets of Zurich! The embarrassment caused by this kind of teaching and concern over
their role in the threatened peasants' revolt caused the city
council finally to expel them.

Everything Luther had worked and prayed for seemed
threatened by this political crisis. The Reformation was
in danger of a speedy dissolution. Intolerable conditions
for the peasants prevailed and nothing was being done to
help them. A large-scale revolt was in process.

Appeal to Luther

An appeal was made to Luther, himself a peasant's son,
to use his influence. Luther was already disturbed by
the peasant leaders' claims to direct revelations from
God and now he was further embarrassed by requests

to identify with their just cause in the name of the gospel.

Nevertheless, he did take up their case with the authorities, at the same time begging the peasants to submit to the powers-that-be and in so doing avoid further bloodshed. Luther believed that both were in the wrong. But when all the peasants' reasonable requests had been totally ignored for so long nothing but a decisive victory could stop the revolt.

Luther eventually sided with officialdom to save what was left of the Reformation. He penned a hasty tract, 'Against the Murderous and Thieving Hordes of Peasants', in which he wrote: 'Let everyone who can, smite, slay and stab, remembering that nothing can be more devilish than a rebel.'

Some 5,000 peasants were cruelly massacred in their tragic struggle against their oppressive landowning princes. Munzer escaped but was eventually caught, tortured and beheaded in May 1525.

Rejection of hotlines from God

It is no surprise, then, that those who have a feel for history are inclined to reject out of hand all 'hotline' messengers from God. For them it seems mostly déjà vu; history quite simply repeating itself. There are too many instances from the past where it has all turned terribly sour. Some questions remain. How far did the prophetic become discredited by the sheer folly of the leadership? And how far did the prophetic become discredited because of its over-identification with political revolt and anarchy?

It has to be readily admitted that the leadership, while having the cause of justice on their side which they defended bravely with their lives, certainly appear to have acted very foolishly (adults playing with dolls in the streets one minute and burning their Bibles the next!). The brave prophets of Zwichau seem to have thrown wisdom to the wind in their practice of prophecy.

18

THE RANTERS

Ranter pedigree

It is not easy to make out a proper pedigree for the origin
of the Ranters, who appeared as a 'plague' of prophets
to invade our mid seventeenth-century English towns and
villages. Some of them may have been known originally as
'Friends of the Free Spirit'. Questions have been raised by
serious historians as to whether Ranters ever existed[1] but
George Fox, the founder of the Quakers, describes many
disagreeable encounters with them in his journal.

The following are typical extracts:

> A great company of Ranters came in . . . and they
> began to call for drink and tobacco; and I desired them
> to forbear it in my room . . . and one of them said 'All
> is ours', and another said 'All is well' but I replied how
> is all well when thou art so peevish and envious and
> crabbed? for I saw that he was of a peevish nature and
> I spake to their condition, and they knew it and looked
> at one another wondering.

> On another occasion, when Fox had a meeting appointed
> at a great man's house, 'An abundance of Ranters and
> professors [i.e. professing Christians] there were that had
> been so loose in their lives that they began to be weary
> of it and . . . the Lord's Truth catched them all and their
> power and understanding were opened by his light, spirit
> and power, through which they came to be settled upon
> the Lord.'

He mentions a visit to Weymouth in 1655, saying that 'some that had been Ranters came to own the truth and came to be very sober'; the following year he referred to a meeting at Edge Hill that 'was very rude, for there came Ranters, Baptists and several sorts of rude people, for I had sent word to have a meeting there a matter of three weeks before . . . and many that day were turned to the Lord Jesus Christ by his power and spirit, and came to sit under his everlasting, free teaching and feeding with his eternal and heavenly food'.

He had similar problems in New England: 'Then I had great travail concerning the Ranters for they had been rude at a meeting where I was not at. I appointed a meeting among them and I knew that the Lord would give me power over them and he did to his praise and glory.'

Another extract tells of a visit back in Dorset: 'And this Rose was like to have cut a child's throat (as we were informed), and he that went for her husband did stab the gaoler, but not mortal, and after they were out of prison he hanged himself. Now these people had prophesied in London when the city was fired, that the rest of London should be burned within fourteen days. And they much disturbed our meetings.'[2]

Bunyan versus Ranters

John Bunyan is another reliable witness who refers to 'some Ranter books that were put forth by some of our countrymen, which books were highly esteemed by several old professors'. Ranters were certainly very much alive and active as far as Bunyan was concerned. He first mentions them by name in the third edition of his *Grace Abounding* (1672–4),[3] though he clearly refers to their doctrines earlier.

Without always naming them, Bunyan was still attacking them to the very end of his life, which shows that Ranterism was neither a figment of the imagination nor a feature of the past. In the areas which he knew best –

Bedford, the surrounding countryside and London – the Ranters were a thorn in the flesh to him. Bunyan also tended to confuse Ranters with Quakers because in fact there seems to have been no Ranter organisation at all; just a 'Ranter milieu'.

There seemed to be several streams flowing into the Ranter river. Besides these streams there were a growing number of independent self-styled prophets and lunatic fringe associations of radicals, libertines and others who formed drinking groups that dissolved and re-formed. Though seemingly a contradiction in terms, these constituted a kind of radical wing of English Puritanism. Doubtless it is the fact that Ranters were never an organised entity which has led to the view held by some historians that they never existed. That view is incorrect. Ranters were reported in more than twenty counties.[4]

A third reliable witness to the existence of Ranters is the early Quaker theologian Robert Barclay whose book *The Anarchy of the Ranters* traces the roots of Ranterism back to the prophets of Zwichau.[5]

Family of love

Mixed up with the Ranters was a Familist stream. The Familists or Family of Love (nothing to do with the recent Children of God sect which went by this name also) was founded by Henry Nicholas (Hendrik Niclaes, ?1501–?1580), a native of Munster and devout Roman Catholic, a child visionary who grew up to grieve because the redeeming death of Christ had yet to conquer the world's sin.

The movement he began in 1541 had an exaggerated form of 'Inner-Light' teaching which caused members to regard themselves as God incarnate. They were accused of pantheism, but this may have been simply a common assumption because they had mystic tendencies. They had no faith in outward ordinances and were reviled for being antinomian. There were many rumours about them – they were accused of 'sexual communism' – but the evidence is hopelessly contradictory.

Some of them may have claimed perfection or infallibility, partly because they were selective in their choice of Scripture and partly because some were cranks. They renounced war and violence. In 1552 Cranmer examined the tenets of the English branch known as the 'David George' sect. David George was said to have made himself out to be sometimes the Christ and sometimes the Holy Ghost. His followers were spreading their doctrines in Cambridgeshire in 1574, paying their way as travelling basket-makers and musicians. The next year, in response to the unfriendly reports circulating about them, they published an 'apology'.

They were reported as active in Norfolk and Suffolk in 1579,[6] and as being strangely orthodox. Little reference is made to them again until 1647 when a certain Randall was preaching 'Familist' doctrines publicly in Bishopsgate and 'many people were flocking after him.'[7] Cromwell allowed them liberty of publication. Generally they appeared to be an inchoate grassroots movement of humble folk, though at least one Anglican clergyman, John Everard, turned Familist. He was also associated with alchemy, using chemicals (today's drugs) for spiritual revelation. The Familists have been linked to a mystical occult sect, the Cabalists.[8] They were also accused of practising astrology: 'The Familists are very confident,' wrote their contemporary Mr B. Bourne, 'that by knowledge of astrology and the strength of reason they shall be able to conquer the world.'[9] They were not of the stuff of martyrs and tended to recant easily under questioning without changing their beliefs. It is possible that they degenerated into the seemingly godless libertines who were associated with the Ranters in Bunyan's dialogues. Those who were still serious seekers after the truth probably ended up with the Quakers.

A Lollard link

There is another stream which apparently flowed down from the Lollards (literally 'mutterers' or 'mumblers' – did they pray in tongues, we may ask?). These were the pre-Reformation disciples of John Wycliffe (1329–84). Wycliffe had preached widely across England. By 1395 his disciples were formed into an organised group with their own ministers and received much popular support. They believed in prophets, as we see from the response of Henry VIII. He had 'taken firm measures against all kinds of political prophecies and action had been taken against Welsh bards and the prophetic utterances of the Lollards'.[10]

'Sacred' literature in English produces side-effects

Wycliffe is regarded as a forerunner of the Protestant Reformation and was the first to attempt a translation of the Scriptures from Latin into English. He was followed by William Tyndale who translated from both the Hebrew and the Greek. Parts of the Bible in the English language were soon beginning to circulate more widely. Literate individuals were beginning to put their own interpretations on biblical texts. These were often quite independent of the accepted understandings of the traditional Church.

Added to this was the appearance of the first English translation of the Koran (1649) which caused some who were uncomfortable about the plain teaching of the Bible to question why the Bible should be considered more worthy of respect than the Koran if the wide acceptance of the Bible was a main argument for its authenticity and authority. This (along with the current religious pluralism) created the climate for latent religious liberalism to vocalise itself.

Seekers

Some of those known as Seekers constituted a small sect of Puritan Independents who appeared in England in the seventeenth century. They were otherwise known as the 'Scattered Flock' or 'Legatines' after one of three brothers, Bartholomew Legate (c. 1575–1612). Legate was a cloth merchant trading with Holland who became a preacher and was burnt at the stake at Smithfield for Arian heresy. It may have been the same group, or another branded with the same name, also from Holland, who were linked with the movement led by Arminius (cf. chapter 16).

Godly men

Unlike some other streams identified with the Ranters, the Seekers were seen to be more spiritual and less anti-state. Some of their members exercised considerable influence during the Commonwealth period. They were godly quietists who were dissatisfied with both the Established Church and the various religious sects and movements of their day. They were waiting upon God for fresh light and guidance.

In some respects they shared the same idea as some of the Ranters. The visible Church with its 'notions' (i.e. doctrines), organisation and ceremonies was repudiated, while the true believer waited, 'seeking' the Church of apostolic power, which God was yet to establish. Some Seekers had already formed themselves into organised groups, meeting together for silent worship. They appear to have had large meetings in Bristol and New England.

Oliver Cromwell had once written, 'And thus to be a Seeker is to be the next best thing to a Finder, and such shall every faithful, humble Seeker be at the end.' With the arrival of George Fox some of these Seekers soon merged into Quakerism. One group in Westmorland were 'converted' in the 1650s and formed the power base for aggressive evangelism led by Fox preaching his gospel of the New Age of the Spirit. Other Seekers simply lost their identity among the rag-tag Ranters.

The Camisard element

There was almost certainly some influence from another quarter across the Channel. The early 1700s saw the first Camisard prophets (as already mentioned in chapter 16) coming over to Britain as refugees or missionaries or both, following their persecution in France. The origin of 'camisard' is uncertain – possibly it is derived from *camise*, a French word, describing the kind of shirts they wore. The Camisards, also known as Huguenots or the Protestants of Cevennes, were militarily defeated in France in 1704.

The French Colonel John Cavalier and two of his colleagues had arrived in England as refugees in 1706 and published their prophecies which included a number by children.[11] Cavalier described their former life in France: 'All our possessions were in common; we were of one heart and one soul. Swearing, cursing, filthy conversation were wholly eschewed; and the overseers whom we had appointed to preserve order had the poor and the sick especially under their care.'[12]

Although of separate origin, the Camisards showed similarities to the Ranters which led inevitably to their being casually lumbered with the same identity. These French Protestants were from the Cevennes district and had risen in revolt after the rigorous steps taken by Louis XIV to suppress them in 1702. The Camisards would fall down under the power of their anointings and were pilloried in London for announcing that the Last Days had begun. By 1707 it was said that there were over four hundred of them prophesying in different parts of the country.[13]

The Ranter phenomenon surely owes much to the particular circumstances of the times, the main one being the emerging religious pluralism in England. A number of streams were seen to be merging into Ranterism, a 'garbage dump' name into which were tipped all those troublesome groups that were difficult to classify.

Extraordinary tolerance

'The Protector' Oliver Cromwell (1599–1658) had extended extraordinary tolerance to all Christian denominations, except the Church of England, the Church of Rome and the Quakers. (The Quakers refused to take up arms in the Civil War and were therefore persecuted.) Three times Fox had occasion personally to address the issue of Quaker persecution face to face with Cromwell.

Apart from the exceptions already mentioned the door was now opened to religious pluralism in England, a door which would never again be quite closed. For a brief period also there was room for some of the radical Christians to take a more centre-stage role on the religious scene.

Cromwell appointed 'prophets' to chaplaincies in his army and invited others to minister to his Council. On at least a half dozen occasions between 1647 and 1654 the council meetings of Oliver Cromwell and his colleagues were interrupted by one obscure prophet after another – often women. Was not this the age of the Holy Spirit? Could not any believer receive a word from the Lord and declare it?

All sorts of weird accusations have been laid to the charge of these prophets, some cynically invented and others fantastically exaggerated. Having said that, however, there were undoubtedly yet other charges which, it has sadly to be admitted, were only too true. England had had her fill of these strange free-lance prophets.

Two weavers

Two weavers, Richard Farnham and John Bull, attracted a good deal of public attention in 1636. They claimed to be divinely inspired prophets with the knowledge of all things to come and armed with powers to inflict plagues upon mankind. 'I am one of the two witnesses spoken of in the

11th chapter of Revelation,' declared Farnham. 'The Lord has given me the power for the opening and the shutting of the heavens.' Notwithstanding, both men were locked up in very earthly prisons and died there in 1642. This was not before they had issued promises to their followers that they would rise again and reign for ever.

The claim to be the Two Witnesses of Revelation (ch. 11) was revived later by the tailors John Reeves and Lodwick Muggleton who established a small sect during Cromwell's time, announcing themselves to be the forerunners of Christ endowed with the keys of heaven and hell.

A prophetess

The best known of the prophetesses before the Civil War was Lady Eleanor Davis, the daughter of the Earl of Castledown, who was married first to Sir John Davis and then to Sir Archibald Douglas. In 1625 she claimed to hear a word, a 'Voice from Heaven' early in the morning, speaking, 'as through a trumpet': 'There is nineteen years and a half to the Judgement Day.' From then on until her death in 1652 she was continuously given to such prophetic utterances and spent many spells in prison for her pains.

She was believed to have accurately predicted the deaths of several leading public figures as well as that of her first husband. Her ecstatic and utterly enigmatic pronouncements were frequently printed, and as frequently suppressed. In a commentary she wrote on Daniel in 1633, she made dark predictions about the fate of Archbishop Laud and King Charles I. Her commentary was published illegally in Amsterdam, and for this she was fined and imprisoned by the High Commission.

Some years later she went berserk in Lichfield Cathedral, defiling the altar hangings and proclaiming from the bishop's throne that she was the Primate of All England! No one could be deceived, of course, but she had to be restrained. However, she was not without serious supporters, including the politician Edward Dering who fully accepted that she had genuine foreknowledge. The refugee Queen of Bohemia and the Anglican divine Peter de Moulin were also her champions.

Short cut to free speech

Prophetesses were becoming quite the thing. This might have been partly because within the culture of the times women had no other accepted medium for public expression. The same was true for the ordinary working-class man and probably explains why so many of them also adopted the convenient but counterfeit guise of the prophet. A readily available 'word from the Lord' gave the message immediate authentication and was assumed to be the best guarantee that one's voice would be heard whenever and wherever one wanted.[14]

Theology of the Holy Spirit

The Church was unprepared for the novelty of free-lance prophets. Some were for believing them; others for banning them. Something had to be done. John Owen, a moderate and scholarly Puritan and vice-chancellor of Christ Church, Oxford by Cromwell's appointment, was the first to produce a thorough doctrinal treatise on the person and work of the Holy Spirit which he entitled *Pneumatologia*.

For those who did not have access to university libraries there were the more accessible and digestible works of John Bunyan, who found both the Ranters and the Quakers difficult to handle, partly because he himself shared their disillusionment with the Church of England and the Church of Rome, and because he believed, like some of them, in the millennium. Bunyan could also testify to supernatural dreams, revelations and experiences, such as 'a great wind' at the time of his conversion, but of course he disagreed with the Ranters on many counts.

He found that most of those he met were 'mortalists'

who taught that the soul dies with the body, and does not revive until the final resurrection – if then. They regarded the resurrection as a symbolic rather than a historical event: 'nothing but the resurrection from a sinful to a holy state in this life'.

Many of the Ranters whom Bunyan met denied the Scriptures to be the Word of God, believing the Bible to be simply a historical document which could be criticised just like any other. Many of them denied the historical existence of Jesus Christ, or at least held that 'the mystery' was more important than 'the history'; the Christ within was more important than the Christ who died at Jerusalem.

Ranters were also sceptical about Christ's Second Coming, regarding that, too, as a metaphor for the transformation within believers. Bunyan attributed 'mocking at the Second Coming of the man Christ' to Ranters, who also rejected, like the Quakers, both Baptism and the Holy Communion.

Two Ranters, Lawrence Clarkson and Abiezer Coppe, extended their brand of antinomianism to cover sexual licence and promiscuity, and taught that sin existed only in the imagination.[15] Clarkson eventually came to believe there was no God but nature.[16] This is not to say that all Ranters went as far as that.

Variety of doctrines

It is difficult to know what the Ranters really believed. Sympathetic sources are unavailable and critical sources may easily have distorted any good they did. In Bunyan's pamphlet *The Holy City* (1665), he attacks 'Ranting opinions', and in *The Resurrection from the Dead* (written probably the same year), his concern throughout is with 'mortalism', which for Bunyan is the chief doctrine of the Ranters.

Clearly there was considerable variation in their teaching, with the stress on individual thought and action, though they all made common cause against the Church of England and the Church of Rome. In doing so many of them professed to share with the Puritans (sadly without their measured scholarship) an expressed desire for a restoration of primitive apostolic Christianity.

Fifth Monarchy Men

There was yet another major element among the Ranters. In January 1661 there was an uprising of the 'Fifth Monarchy Men'. These were a handful of fanatics who had supported Cromwell during the time of the Commonwealth. After the beheading of King Charles I it was believed that the time had come for the fulfilment of Daniel's prophecy concerning a fifth and messianic kingdom to follow those of Babylon, Persia, Greece and Rome.

The execution of King Charles opened the way for King Jesus! Their hopes of such a thing ever happening under Cromwell, however, seemed to be slipping away so they rose suddenly and terrorised London with strange cries of 'King Jesus and their heads upon the gates'! The leaders were arrested and it was soon their own heads upon the gates. Unfortunately for the Quakers they tended to be lumped together with these fanatics, perhaps not entirely without justification as even George Fox, their founder, could be rather a fearsome public speaker – a ranter by nature if not by name. Many innocent people suffered from the public reaction which followed the 1661 uprising of the Fifth Monarchy Men.

Restrictive legislation

From all this, a generally unfavourable impression has remained. Prophecy was obviously seen as a dangerous practice which could lead even to revolution if directed against the powers of state. The long spate of prophecy was sharply checked at the Restoration of the Monarchy and the return of power to the Church of England. The governing classes were determined to prevent the possibility of any reversion to the social anarchy of the interregnum years. They felt their security lay much more with a king than with Cromwell.

Prophets were associated with the Protectorate and the Royalists had had their fill of all that. The remainder of the Fifth Monarchy Men melted away. Some of the Ranters (a number of the Seeker stream) were absorbed into the early Quakers, while others carried on independently for a few more years.

The prophetic element among the Ranters had become almost exclusively focused on eschatology, but with no discipline and no clearly defined doctrine this semblance of a movement could not survive much longer. It may be that both Bunyan and Fox had wounded the Ranters, but it was the state which finished them off. A spate of political prophecies provoked the hierarchy to react strongly and swiftly. In 1662 a wave of restrictive legislation issued from Parliament as a result: the Corporation Act, the Quaker Act, the Act of Uniformity and the Five Mile Act. These acts struck at the very roots of the religious freedom which English people were learning to prize.

A question remains: how should this kind of prophetic folly be avoided in the future? Great wisdom would be needed, should the Lord reveal some significant future event of a political nature; wisdom concerning just how such a revelation should be interpreted, publicised and applied. Even Jesus speaking of the abomination of desolation standing in the holy place, spoken of by Daniel the prophet, would not be more explicit than to say simply, 'Let the reader understand' (Matt. 24:15).

There is much wisdom in that for our prophets today. To proclaim from the rooftops the downfall of the highest powers in the land led inevitably to the charge of sedition. The heretical teachings and corrupt lives of some of the so-called prophets increased prejudice against the Ranters, not to mention the anarchical character of uncontrolled prophecy. All this meant that a supernatural gift of God was widely discredited.

These are the lessons today's would-be prophets need to learn. It could be argued that a worse example of a so-called prophetic movement could not be found in history. This is true. Ranterism was the prophetic movement run rampant. But if we are to learn and if we are to understand the genuine concern of good Christians who fear the revival of the gifts of the Spirit, we shall help neither them nor ourselves by hiding our heads in the sand.

There are many reasons why prophets need to walk humbly before the Lord. Their reputation historically is a major reason. The Ranters were a clear example of arrogant anarchy: there was no real respect for the authority of the Bible, the Church or the State.

19

THE QUAKERS

The search

George Fox (1624–91) was the founder of the Society
of Friends, soon nicknamed Quakers. 'Justice Bennet
of Derby first called us Quakers,' wrote Fox, 'because
we bid them tremble at the word of God.' His journal,[1]
first edited by Thomas Ellwood, is one of the most
remarkable documents of the seventeenth century. Fox
was 'an original, being no man's copy'. Born at Fenny
Drayton, Leicestershire, not far from Lutterworth, famed
for its one-time reformist rector John Wycliffe, Fox came
of a good Christian family belonging to the Church of
England. His father Christopher, nick-named 'Righteous
Christer', was a weaver – a trade that always gave a
certain independence. His mother, a woman of higher
than average accomplishments, was descended from a
family which had suffered martyrdom for the faith.

The shepherd boy

Caring for his father's sheep, the boy grew up with
little formal education though he read widely, studying
the various Protestant sects (over a hundred of them
apparently). The apathy of the established Church and
the extreme Calvinism prevalent in the sects was causing
people to leave the churches in droves. From the age of
nineteen Fox spent four frustrating years as a 'seeker',
visiting one minister after another in his search for inner
peace. One counselled smoking tobacco, another singing
psalms and getting married, while yet another suggested

blood-letting. Finally, after this time of 'sorrows and troubles', while out 'walking solitary abroad' in prayer, he heard the Lord speaking to him: 'There is one, even Jesus Christ, who can speak to thy condition.'

The living Christ was revealed to him 'in light, spirit and power':

> Now was I come up in spirit through the flaming sword into the paradise of God. All things were new, and all creation gave another smell unto me than before, beyond what words can utter. I knew nothing but pureness, and innocency, and righteousness, being renewed up into the image of God by Jesus Christ, so that I was come up into the state of Adam which he was before he fell . . . even into the state of Christ Jesus, that should never fall.

Sacred self-confidence

Fox now began preaching in power to any group who would listen. Often he found his audience in the churches, where he would stand up after the sermon and attack the church leaders for their worldliness. Thomas Carlyle wrote of Fox that he had an 'enormous sacred self-confidence'. His mission took fire in 1652 in the North West of England. He was incredibly bold. When he learned of a community that threatened some action against him if ever he should dare to return, he would return immediately if possible and denounce their wicked rebellion against the message of the Gospel.

From 1652 Judge Fell allowed his home in Westmorland to be used as a regular meeting place for the Quakers. The movement grew and so did the persecution. They were frequently confused with Ranters – possibly a deliberate ploy of their enemies.

But though they had contradictory teachings, they shared with the Ranters a common dislike of both the state Church and the Catholics. They rejected the ordained ministry (theirs being essentially a lay ministry) and traditional forms of worship. Disliking the fuss between Anglicans and Baptists over infant or believer's baptism, they rejected baptism altogether. Reacting to the fierce quarrels between Anglicans and Catholics over the sacrament of the Lord's Supper, they rejected that means of grace as well. It was no wonder if there was confusion, since many of the Ranters rejected the sacraments as well.

Power in prayer

Both Fox's personal courage and his prayer life inspired his followers. 'Above all he excelled in prayer,' wrote the aristocratic William Penn:

> the inwardness and weight of his spirit, the reverence and solemnity of his address and behaviour, and the fewness and the fullness of his words, have often struck even strangers with admiration, as they used to reach others with consolation. The most awful, living, reverent frame I ever felt or beheld, I must say was in his prayer. And truly it was a testimony that he knew and lived nearer to the Lord than other men, for they that knew him most will see most reason to approach him with reverence and fear.

Fox had a vision of a people being gathered into victory over Satan. 'Christ has been too long locked up in the Mass or in the Book,' he said. 'Let him be your prophet, your priest and king. Obey him.'

The yeomen of the North West

Fox held, with Oliver Cromwell, that 'God speaks without a written word sometimes, yet according to it.' He urged men to attend to the words of the Spirit of Christ still speaking to their hearts. His message appealed to the yeomen of the North West of England, though not many mighty nor many noble folk were called through Fox. He was an incessant labourer completely undaunted in his services for God and his people:

> And a report went abroad of me that I was a young man that had a discerning spirit; whereupon many came to me from far and near, professors, priests, and people.
>
> And the Lord's power brake forth [a frequent expression in the journal] and I had great openings, and prophecies, and spake unto them of the things of God, and they heard with attention and silence, and went away and spread the fame thereof.
>
> Then came the tempter, and set upon me again, charging me that I had sinned against the Holy Ghost, but I could not tell in what. And then Paul's condition came before me, how after he had been taken up into the third heaven and seen things not lawful to be uttered, a messenger of Satan was sent to buffet him again. Thus I got over this temptation also.[2]

Frequent raptures

Fox frequently had raptures: 'I was come up in the Spirit through the flaming sword into the paradise of God.'[3] In a further revelation, Fox claimed:

> Now the Lord God hath opened to me by his invisible power how that everyman was enlightened by the divine light of Christ; I saw it shine through all, and that they that believed in it came out of condemnation and came into the light of life and became the children of it, but they that hated it, and did not believe in it, were condemned by it, though they made a profession of Christ.
>
> This I saw in the pure openings of the Light without the help of any man, neither did I then know where to

find it in the Scriptures; though afterward, searching the Scriptures I found it.[4]

Again he writes in the same vein and it is included here because it illustrates the kind of prophecy he is talking about:

These things I did not see by the help of man, nor by the letter but I saw them in the light of the Lord Jesus Christ, and by his immediate Spirit and power, as did the holy men of God, by whom the Holy Scriptures were written. Yet I had no slight esteem of the Holy Scriptures, but they were very precious to me, for I was in that spirit by which they were given forth, and what the Lord opened in me I afterward found was agreeable to them. I could speak much of these things and many volumes might be written, but all would prove too short to set forth the infinite love, wisdom, and power of God, in preparing, fitting, and furnishing me for the service he had appointed me to; letting me see the depths of Satan on the one hand, and opening to me, on the other hand, the divine mysteries of his own everlasting kingdom.[5]

The Valiant Sixty

Within six years Fox had gathered an enthusiastic group known as the Valiant Sixty (some of them originally Seekers from Westmorland and others formerly Franciscan Friars) and within eight years his membership was 50,000 strong. Quaker missionaries were soon reaching the continent, while two of their women had gone to Barbados and from there to the mainland of North America.

The early Quaker preachers were likened to the Old Testament prophet Amos. They proclaimed Christ as truth and challenged that the truth be allowed to stand over current evils. They wanted people to live by Christ's righteousness (in today's jargon 'realised eschatology') rather than to speculate about his imminent Second Coming – this latter was a prevalent preoccupation among the prophetic people of Fox's day, such as the Fifth Monarchy Men in chapter 18.

Mystic influence

Fox had been greatly influenced by the teaching of the Waldenses, St Francis, the Beguines and the Beghards, Meister Eckhart, Rulman Merswin of Strassburg, John Tauler, Thomas à Kempis and the Philadelphians – a strongly mystic intake. Fox proved a powerful preacher with the eyes of a seer. Men commented with fear, 'Look at his eyes!' and 'Don't pierce me so with thy eyes! Keep thy eyes off me!' He looked at men and knew what was in them. Sometimes he saw people, not only as they were, but as they would be. He was minding 'the light within'. He was also 'a discerner of other's spirits,' said William Penn.

Given to visions

Fox was given to visions. On various occasions he would see scenes like 'a bear and two great mastiff dogs, that I should pass by them and they should do me no hurt'; of 'a desperate creature like a wild horse or colt that was coming to destroy me; but I got the victory over it'; of 'a black coffin, but I passed over it'; of 'an ugly slubbering hound'. All of these apparent presentiments of danger came to him often, and the warnings were seldom without good cause.

One vision, which was omitted from the first *Journal* published twenty years after his death, runs as follows:

And I had a vision . . . that I was walking in the fields, and many Friends were with me, and I bid them dig in the earth, and they did and I went down. And there was a mighty vault top-full of people kept under the earth, rocks and stones. So I bid them break open the earth and let all the people out, and they did, and all the people came forth to liberty; and it was a mighty place.

And when they had done I went on and bid them dig again. They did, and there was a mighty vault full of people, and I bid them throw it down and let all the people out, and so they did.

And I went on again, and bid them dig again, and Friends said unto me, 'George, thou finds out all things', and so there they digged, and I went down, and went along the vault; and there sat a woman in white looking at time how it passed away. And there followed me a woman down in the vault, in which vault there was treasure; and so she laid her hand on the treasure on my left hand, and then time whisked on apace; but I clapped my hand upon her, and said, 'Touch not the treasure.' And then time passed not so swift.[6]

Philadelphian influence

A distinctly middle-class Society of Philadelphians was emerging in Britain around the 1650s. Their teachings were derived originally from Jakob Boehme (1575–1624), sometimes referred to as the 'Father of Protestant Mysticism'. He was a German Lutheran (a one-time shoemaker and glover, with no formal education) who claimed mystical experiences which he described in his writings *The Beginning of Dawn* and *The Way to Christ* (1623) as coming directly from God. Boehme was difficult to understand and so shifted his doctrinal position that no single theory fitted all his works. In places he was surely heretical, but Cromwell's chaplain, Peter Sterry, a Cambridge Platonist and Puritan divine, took his mystical experiences seriously, as did John Smith, Simon Patrick, Bishop Jeremy Taylor (most famous for the two books *Holy Living* and *Holy Dying* but also *The Liberty of Prophesying*, 1647), William

Law, John Wesley, Isaac Newton and Samuel Coleridge among others, who all respected him for pointing the way towards the rediscovery of spirituality in their formal Christian religion.

Boehme's influence is seen in his followers' tolerance and their belief that reason could judge the data of revelation by virtue of the indwelling of God in the mind (their inner light – John 1:9) since the spirit in man is the candle of the Lord (Prov. 20:27). The Cambridge Platonists, however, made a clear distinction between 'the spirit in man' and 'the inner light' as Fox proclaimed it. They saw the spirit in man as reason while the inner light was revelation.

John Pordage (1607–81), a Berkshire rector (ejected from his living by the 'Triers' – Cromwell's commissioners – in 1655), was the main propagator of Boehme's mysticism in England. His disciples became known as 'Behemists' while simultaneously retaining their respective ecclesiastical allegiances. In an age of sectarian strife, Boehme advocated mutual tolerance based on the love of the Christian brotherhood – hence 'philadelphia'.

The other main promoter of the movement in England (formerly known as the Philadelphian Society for the Advancement of Piety and Divine Philosophy) was the author of *A Fountain of Gardens*, Mrs Jane Leade (1623–1704), who recorded in the book the visions experienced in her childhood. After her death the society in England began to decline rapidly. Most of the remaining members amalgamated with the Quakers, because of their similar views regarding the direct illumination of the soul by the Holy Spirit.

Confused doctrines among Fox's followers

John Bunyan found the variations in teaching among some of the Quakers, Seekers and Ranters confusing. He had frequent brushes with them all. Ranters and Quakers 'knowingly, wilfully and despitefully rejected the atonement of Christ, the Resurrection and the Second Coming', he wrote. 'Their errors', declared Bunyan in *The Strait Gate* (1676), 'meant that they will seek to enter in [to heaven], and shall not be able.'

Bunyan regarded the Quaker 'inner light' as simply that law of nature which is universal in every individual man in the world. He was even more indignant over supposed Quaker disparagement of those ministers 'who preach up sin'. Edward Burrough sought to correct Bunyan's confusion of the Quakers with the Ranters.

Bunyan may have misjudged the Quakers at times but some of them certainly left themselves open to serious misunderstanding. As with all Christian traditions there appeared inherent weaknesses in their attempts to correct the imbalance they saw in the prevailing theologies of their day.

Doctrinal clarification

Actually, from 1660 (the restoration of the monarchy under Charles II) we find Quakers clarifying a number of issues and working out their theology more thoroughly. They also proclaimed pacifism and abstained from politics. They withdrew from making the kind of antisocial gestures they had previously indulged in, such as going naked for a sign (except for a loin cloth – Isa. 20:2) and upsetting religious services. 'They reinstated sin and the Bible. They came nearer to the Bible as Bunyan came nearer to them.'[7]

They became pioneers in the movement for the abolition of slavery in North America and prison reform in Britain. Though pacifist, they have a notable record of valiant service on and off the battlefield. Quakers have been found at the forefront of many good social causes. They have been respected for their consistent moral stance. Along with the Ranters they were regarded as the radical wing of English Puritanism.

Quakers may have been seen by some as antinomian

but they themselves would have stoutly refuted it. At times they have boldly defied the law when it was clearly prejudicial to human rights and in violation of the plain teachings and example of Jesus. Their commitment to the cause of social justice has been an example and challenge to the wider Church.

They have survived because they allowed, not without difficulty, a healthy discipline to develop. The Quakers began to stress the importance not only of the indwelling Spirit but also of the fruits of the Spirit (whereby that Spirit could be recognised). Moreover, they imposed the wholesome check of a strong sense of community upon individual guidance.

An able theologian

The British Quakers were to be fortunate in having an able theologian and apologist come to their aid in the person of a Scot, Robert Barclay (1648–90). Barclay had followed his father in becoming a Quaker in 1667. After years of persecution he eventually became a favourite of the Duke of York (later James II).

Among his many works, the better known are *A Catechism and Confession of Faith* (1673), *The Anarchy of the Ranters* (1676) and *An Apology for the True Christian Divinity, Being an Explanation and Vindication of the People called Quakers* (1678). Always insisting upon inward revelation from God as necessary for true faith, Barclay also spelt out the humanitarian and pacifist ideals still followed by the Society of Friends.

Naylor's London leadership

Another of the Seekers who became a Quaker was James Naylor, a yeoman farmer who had served with distinction in the Parliamentary Army. We tell the sad story here because of the salutary warning it could give to any misguided prophets. He was already a noted preacher and after hearing Fox's teaching on the 'inner light' he left his home to wander the world, 'not knowing today what I was doing tomorrow', but always preaching. Judge Fell (whose widow later married Fox) found Naylor a most reasonable man and was greatly impressed in spite of himself.

By 1656 James Naylor was taking responsibility for the work in the London area having recently returned from Yorkshire, but it soon became a heavy burden. His very popularity made things difficult for him. He was in great demand everywhere, both among the aristocracy and with humbler folk.

He was the sort of man who found it extremely hard to say 'no'. His charm of manner, ready sympathy and reckless generosity in self-giving attracted many to him, whereas George Fox, with his brisk, common-sense approach and his impatience with many people's 'notions', seemed much less sympathetic.

By March Naylor realised he could not continue without assistance. Overtired and overwrought, he was living on his nerves. Edward Burrough and Francis Howgill arrived to help in the London area.

'Ranting' women

Among Naylor's admirers were a number of women who resembled Ranters rather than Quakers in their religious beliefs. 'Ranting' women began to exercise an undue influence on him. He had always shown a deep understanding of the opposite sex. This was appreciated by all the women Friends, to such an extent that many of the wisest and most sensitive would continue to support him with their friendship through all his trials and difficulties. These troubles grew swiftly enough. Hysterical Ranter women began disturbing public meetings whenever they were addressed by Friends other than James Naylor. They would interrupt the speakers, chanting or calling out incessantly, sometimes for hours on end.

Naylor clearly had sex appeal and the adulation of sycophantic women and their dissensions caused a constant strain. His very tenderness of spirit and reverence for the inner light, which he believed to be in others, disarmed him before their flattery and warped his better judgment.

One of his most ardent admirers, Martha Simmonds, was an impulsive married woman who felt herself slighted by the London Friends. They strongly discouraged her from travelling with Naylor in the service of truth. She began to oppose the local authority of Edward Burrough and Francis Howgill and the Friends' patience was severely tried. Eventually they reproved her (publicly at a meeting) and Edward Burrough followed this up with a letter containing some plain speaking. All who truly cared for Naylor's welfare were becoming alarmed for him because of her.

Martha Simmonds next visited George Fox in prison at Launceston, Cornwall, during one of his frequent confinements (he had spent three and a half of the first four years of his married life in prison). She began taunting him that he must yield the leadership of the Quakers to James Naylor, for Fox's heart was rotten, she said.

Dorcas, arise!
Meanwhile frenzied scenes were taking place elsewhere. A girl called Dorcas Erbury had fainted or died (reports are not clear) and it was afterwards claimed that Naylor had raised her from the dead with the words, 'Dorcas, arise!'

Women now began to kneel before Naylor singing 'Holy, Holy, Holy!' and his admirers wrote him letters full of adulation, one even calling him 'The Everlasting Son of Righteousness'. Fox arranged a meeting with Naylor at Exeter to warn him of his danger but something went sadly wrong and the latter walked out.

One letter from a supporter described Naylor as 'the only begotten Son of God' and ended with a postscript, 'Thy name shall be no more James Naylor but Jesus'. An awful fear struck Naylor when he read these words, though he did not destroy the letter. (Before we become too judgmental at this excess, let us take note that there is a fine point here for those Christians who truly believe they are sons of God (Gal. 4:7 among other texts). It could be difficult 'on the hoof', as it were, to know how to address this obvious blasphemy without denying a fundamental truth of the Bible.)

Naylor headed for Bristol on horseback. A party accompanied him, some on foot chanting their trisagions, 'Holy, Holy, Holy!' and throwing down their garments in the muddy way. Though there were over a thousand Quakers in Bristol not one would now come near him. Naylor was seeking to teach the inward coming of Christ into the heart and he had staged this 'Triumphant Entry' into Bristol, complete with donkey and hosannas, hoping to illustrate the point. This had scandalised the Friends, who feared for him. But a large crowd followed him through the streets of the city, where Naylor was eventually arrested and committed to prison.

Terrible punishment

He was sent to London to be tried by Parliament and was convicted of 'horrid blasphemy'. He escaped the death penalty only by a narrow majority. But the savage punishment which was actually inflicted upon him fell little short of death.

On December 18th, 1653 James Naylor was made to stand and for two full hours with his head in the pillory, was stripped and whipped at a cart's tail, from Palace yard to the Old Exchange and received three hundred ten stripes . . . then on December 27th, he having stood 'till two, the executioner took him out, and having bound his arms with cords to the pillory, and he having put forth his tongue, which he freely did, the executioner, with red hot iron, about the bigness of a quill, bored the same, and by the order of the Sheriff, held it a small space . . . then having taken it

out, and pulled the cap off that covered his face, he put
a handkerchief over his eyes and putting his left hand
to the back part of his head, and taking the red hot
iron letter 'B' [for blasphemy] in his hand, put it to his
forehead 'till it smoked: all of which time James Naylor
never so much as winced.[8]

Naylor was finally released from prison and after some
frustrations a longed-for reconciliation with Fox took
place. He then made public confession in Bristol which
drew Friends to him. Finally he set off north to his
faithful wife and his children, but died of exhaustion
before reaching home.

A new denomination

Fox had never envisaged a new denomination and certainly not one by the name of 'Quaker', but it became
obvious that some kind of a framework was necessary.
Based on principles already worked out by the Friends
in Westmorland, Fox – who, besides being a visionary,
was endowed with a robust common sense, plenty of good
humour and considerable organising powers – produced
a simple practical scheme for universal application. This
greatly strengthened the movement for the critical times
of vilification and persecution which were still to come.

There were regular meetings for worship and for church
business; public meetings for proclaiming the message of
Quakerism and general meetings for leaders from a wider
area. In every meeting a Friend was appointed to keep
a record of the 'sufferings' of their members through
persecution. The same register recorded births, marriages
and deaths.

From 1656 onward northern Friends were holding yearly
meetings for representatives from general meetings across
the north and similar meetings soon sprang up in the
south.

Ten years later Fox was touring the length and breadth

of England organising a system of church government so resilient that it has lasted to our present time. All over the country groups of 'particular' meetings gathered monthly and these in turn joined with similar meetings to form quarterly meetings from counties nearby. The former general meetings which had lapsed during the persecutions were revived in December 1668, with regular meetings being held in London until 1904 when the practice began of holding them occasionally in the provinces.

A system of organisation

George Fox set off for America in 1671 and returned in 1673. Soon afterwards he was unjustly imprisoned for fourteen months. During this period a situation arose which was to cause grave anxiety to the movement. There had always been some dissension in the ranks (an inherent Seeker syndrome) about the setting up of any kind of organisation for the Society of Friends. It was believed by some that the exercising of any group authority, however enlightened, would involve the sacrifice of a fundamental Quaker principle. Many, however, besides George Fox thought otherwise. They sensed the dangers of an individualistic anarchy.

Dissensions increased, especially in the Westmorland region. Two Friends, John Strong and John Wilkinson, led the opposition and began disseminating their views more widely. This all led to a meeting at Drawell, near Sedbergh in 1676 where there was a reconciliation between representative leaders across the country.

This was followed by a period of internal peace for the Quakers, but the lull was to prove only transitory, and in many parts of Britain the 'Wilkinson/Strong' controversy led to open hostility towards Fox and eventually to a separation – though not of a long duration. Most of the Quakers stood by Fox. The separatists either joined other religious groups or eventually found their way back to the Friends once more. The Quakers were to gain more members than the total Church of England membership in the seventeenth century.

In conclusion

The Quaker story is briefly and selectively retold because the history of the Friends constituted a classic movement of the Holy Spirit from the seventeenth century onwards (followed later by the Pentecostalists), and the issues which confronted them are recurring ones whenever the Spirit begins to light up new ways. Questions soon arise over the authority of the leadership (both in the established Church and the new organisation coming into being) and the authority of the Bible is also questioned.

Many church people today, who feel the issues have already been dealt with by history once and for all, are usually loath to re-examine them all over again. What, then, can we learn about prophecy through the Quaker experience?

In the first place Fox, for one, had revelatory gifting and both prophesied and healed the sick.[9] In the second place we do not see much evidence of others likewise gifted in the movement, though it may well have been there. Neither is there much evidence of teaching about the gifts of the Spirit. In the third place the bitter experiences of the Naylor débâcle brought some good: a greater clarity of vision, an awareness of the danger of any claim to spiritual infallibility and a greater willingness to test individual leadings by a corporate guidance sought in silent waiting upon God. Finally it may be observed that social action seems to have become the focus of prophecy for the Quakers, and brought praiseworthy results. But the social evils being addressed (and there were and still are many) are self-evident. The gift had seemingly lost its supernatural dimension.

20

THE CLASSIC CASE OF
EDWARD IRVING

Our special interest in Irving centres not so much on the
implications of direct communication from God for an
individual or for a movement, but for its application in
a local church setting. We also observe how matters got
out of hand through an apparent misunderstanding by the
leader about his own authority in the church where the
gifts were being manifested.

Before telling his story briefly, however, a few statements about our biblical understanding of the spiritual
gifts are called for. Some of the traditional distaste for
the exercise of spiritual gifts in the Church today may
quite possibly be derived from the sad scandals still in
circulation after the experiences of Irving's London city
church 150 years ago.

There is a mistaken idea in some circles that the exercise
of spiritual gifts marks out the gifted person as highly
mature or super-sanctified. This, of course, is not the
case. Any Christian may receive spiritual gifts at any
stage of his spiritual pilgrimage as and when the Lord
is sovereignly disposed to give them and the recipient
desirous of them.

The gifts are not evidence of spiritual maturity (many
gifted persons in the church at Corinth were clearly
immature). They are not trophies for faithful service
or rewards for successful service. They are tools for
effective service and they are dispensed sovereignly by
God (1 Cor. 12:7).

Too much deference to the gifted

The Rev. Edward Irving's major error lay in his handling of the manifestations of the spiritual gifts in the congregation under his charge. He deferred overmuch to those who were spiritually gifted.

This arose partly out of a genuine humility which led him to yield his authority to those who appeared to be anointed with gifts through the Holy Spirit (gifts which he himself had not received) and partly out of an ignorance which confused individual spiritual gifting with authority for local church leadership. This became very obvious in the authority structure of the new Catholic Apostolic Church which he later founded.

Such an unfortunate mistake could only bring disaster and disillusionment, as it has done in some Pentecostal circles, where the belief is that people are infallible in their exercise of the spiritual gifts. Those who are strangers to the exercise of such gifts often mistakenly assume that this must be the case wherever the gifts are operational.

Infallibility

The fact that one of the spiritual gifts is for the discerning of spirits (1 Cor. 12:10), and the rest of the congregation is told to weigh up the prophecies (1 Cor. 14:29) is proof enough that Paul certainly did not believe that gifting in any way implied infallibility.

The manifestations of spiritual gifts in Edward Irving's church, though they had been sought in prayer and taught in public, caught the Church unawares as to the wider issues involved.

This was not surprising, since no contemporary church had practical experience in this area to share with him and there were no written works to hand nor a positive oral corpus of wisdom available on the subject to draw from.

For example, Bruce Yokum's counsel, written nearly 150 years later, would have been most relevant for Irving's situation: 'It is usually a mistake for prophets to be the ultimate authority in a group. A number of heterodox sects and groups have been led by "prophets" whose "inspired" statements led people astray . . . It is the place of prophets to prophesy, but it is the place of the heads of the community to judge prophecy.'[1]

Wayne Grudem observes, following a sympathetic biblical examination of the issues involved, that 'there is no convincing evidence that the New Testament prophets in their role as prophets ever governed early churches through "charismatic leadership" by means of prophetic declarations about the direction of the church. This theory is based on some people's idea of how the church "must have" or "could have" developed, but it is not supported by the facts of the New Testament itself.'[2]

Beginning of life and ministry

Edward Irving was born at Annan, in Scotland, in 1792. After graduation he became an assistant to the foremost Presbyterian of his time – Thomas Chalmers, at St John's, Glasgow. From there Irving was called to the Caledonian Chapel in London (1822).[3]

The premises soon proved inadequate for the brilliant young preacher who numbered among his congregation some of the nation's leading personalities, such as the writer Thomas Carlyle, the politician Robert Peel and the thinker-poet Samuel Taylor Coleridge.

Prior to the manifestation of the spiritual gifts in his congregation, Irving had achieved some notoriety in theological circles through his series of sermons on the Incarnation – the Humanity of Christ. He believed that Jesus took man's fallen flesh (sinful substance) and was made like his brothers in every way (Heb. 2:17) so that as our High Priest he was not 'unable to sympathise with our weaknesses, but we have one who has been tempted in every way, just as we are – yet was without sin' (Heb. 4:15).

Irving was surprised to find himself roundly condemned as a heretic for his honest, intellectual struggle with the mystery of the Incarnation. His question basically was, how could Jesus be tempted in all points just as we are if the sinless Son of God did not share our fallen human nature? It is an extremely delicate question. In discussing this problem, Irving did not hesitate to express his fundamental belief in the absolute purity and sinlessness of Jesus.

Irving's excommunication by the London Presbytery, which hastily ensued, appears to have been an excessive reaction and possibly explains why notable churchmen today are very slow to condemn any serious theological pronouncements of their fellow Christians, however far they may seem to have moved away from orthodoxy.

Search for spiritual gifts

Irving's congregation continued to support him, and thereby enabled him to carry on his ministry (soon in the new church building in Regent Square built in 1827), despite the judgment of the presbytery.

In the summer of 1828, while on a preaching tour in the West of Scotland, Irving had met a talented young licentiate of the Church of Scotland, Alexander J. Scott, whom he engaged as his missionary assistant at Regent Square to help him in his outreach to the neighbourhood and the London Scots.

The new assistant believed that the spiritual gifts should still be operative in the Church today. He urged Irving to pray for them, which he did. Then came news from Clydeside that a young woman from Fernicary named Mary Campbell, who was known to Sandy Scott, was dying of consumption.

On March 30th, after prayer and fasting, the Holy Spirit came with mighty power upon the ailing woman and she began to speak in tongues.

Soon after she was commanded by a friend 'full of the Holy Spirit' to 'arise and stand upright!' The words were repeated; the friend took her by the hand and the patient arose miraculously healed! The whole affair aroused tremendous interest, with many declaring their belief and others their disbelief.

Rumours of this and other manifestations were soon widespread. This was the first recorded manifestation of the gifts in a reformed church among cultured Christians in Britain since the Reformation. The immediate consequences of this are very significant, though hardly edifying.

Early morning prayer meetings

During the autumn of 1830 prayer meetings were started in various private houses in London 'for the outpouring of the Holy Ghost'. On October 20th, a Miss Fancourt received a healing very similar to that of Mary Campbell. Irving was still busy defending his 'Incarnation' sermons and was not present at any of the meetings, but he wrote a favourable article for the *Morning Watch* on 'The Gifts of the Holy Ghost commonly called supernatural'. By his appeal to Scripture he sought to refute thoroughly those who taught that the gifts of the Spirit had been withdrawn.

On April 30th, 1831 the expectations of those who had been meeting for prayer in London began to be realised when Mrs Cardale 'spoke with great solemnity in a tongue and prophesied', thus becoming the first member of the Regent Square congregation to do so.

Very soon Irving was holding large early morning prayer meetings with over a thousand persons present. Intercession was made daily for a release of the spiritual gifts. In June 1831 Irving published a second article on the gifts in the *Morning Watch*. But Irving displayed an understandable hesitation before allowing the tongues and prophecy manifested in private homes (for which he had prayed with such faith and taught with such fervour) to be exercised publicly in the church. For such dilatoriness he was rebuked by a prophecy at the early morning prayer meeting.

He was accused through prophecy of quenching the Spirit by not allowing the gifts to be exercised in public. 'It belongs to you to open the door – you have the power of the keys – it is you that are restraining and hindering it.'

Permission at last

It was plain that he could stall no longer. 'Next morning I went to church, and after praying, I rose up and said in the midst of them all, "I cannot be party to hindering that which I believe to be the voice of the Holy Ghost from being heard in the church."'

Having read aloud some relevant Scripture passages he boldly declared: 'Now I stand here before you . . . I cannot longer forbid; but do, on the other hand, in the Name of the Lord Jesus Christ, the Head of the Church, permit, at the meeting of the church, that everyone who has received the gift of the Holy Ghost, and is moved by the Holy Ghost, shall have liberty to speak': and he indicated who they were (having heard and tested them in private).

He then gave members of the congregation opportunity to judge for themselves whether the manifestations were from God. This announcement was received with some alarm by his faithful office bearers.

The majority of the elders and deacons who had supported Irving against the London Presbytery six months earlier, over the 'Incarnation' controversy, were very apprehensive about this latest development. Irving urged them to withhold judgment until those who exercised the gifts had been given time to cultivate them, and he himself had given the church more teaching on the subject.

Total confusion

On Sunday October 30th the service was thrown into confusion by outbreaks of speaking in tongues. One unsympathetic witness described predictably how 'the sudden doleful and unintelligible sounds being heard by all the congregation produced the utmost confusion: the act of standing up, the exertion to hear, see and understand, by each and every one, perhaps 1,500 or 2,000 persons, created a noise which may be easily conceived'.

After the service Irving, with the elders and deacons, was interviewing one of the tongue-speakers who, claiming to be speaking in the Spirit, urged her minister not to be ashamed of following his Master in spite of opposition. On hearing this, 'Mr Irving sunk into his chair and groaned in distress.'

A decision was clearly called for one way or the other. By the evening he had resolved that the exercise of the gifts must be allowed to continue during Sunday worship services, though he expressed his sympathy for the faithful who might be a little shocked on hearing 'tongues' for the first time – feelings he admitted he himself had originally shared.

The next Sunday, with some 3,000 present, there were outbursts of 'tongues' again and Irving, with his powerful voice, was able to preserve order. But such interruptions during the Sunday services created a tremendous reaction – improper in some cases, with hissing from the galleries and cries of 'silence', and properly in others later, by complaints lodged with the elders and deacons.

Irving was by now firmly resolved to risk all for the principle of allowing space for what he believed to be of God. He continued his teaching programme in the church on the work of the Holy Spirit. Finally on February 20th, 1832 a deputation of trustees called on him (having first taken legal counsel) for the purpose of warning Irving that they would have him removed from his pastoral charge if he did not restore the worship to what it had been before the manifestations of the gifts in the public services of the church.

Irving requested another week before giving them his

answer. On the intervening Sunday he told the congregation that he anticipated being removed and invited the faithful to leave with him.

On March 2nd the trustees met to consider a graciously written but unrepentant reply from Irving. Their response was to lodge a complaint against him with the same London presbytery who had excommunicated Irving already on the grounds of his supposedly heretical views over the Incarnation – an order which Irving's elders had previously ignored.

Ecclesiastical trial

Finally, following normal ecclesiastical procedure, a trial was fixed for April 26th. It was made clear during this trial that the trustees had not come to the court to question whether Irving's doctrine agreed with Scripture, but simply whether, in allowing unconstitutional practices to develop, he had contravened the contract he had himself entered into with the subscribers to the Regent Square church. The trustees made three charges against Irving:

> That he has suffered, permitted and still allows the public services . . . to be interrupted by persons not being either ministers or licentiates of the Church of Scotland . . . That he has suffered . . . the public services to be interrupted by persons not being either members or seat holders of the said church or ministers or licentiates of the Church of Scotland . . . That he has suffered . . . and publicly encouraged females to speak in the said church and to interrupt and disturb the public worship.

Irving was further accused of failing to test or weigh the prophecies responsibly or adequately. His reticence had been understandable from one point of view. He explained that he had wanted people to gain confidence in the public exercise of the gifts before he began to criticise them too thoroughly. Unfortunately he lost the confidence of the rest of the congregation in the process.

Ejected

As he had by now anticipated, he was being finally expelled from his beloved pulpit. But he was not going alone. Though he was found guilty of breach of contract, a majority still followed him to a new centre in London to form the Catholic Apostolic Church, a new denomination which was to survive him by a little over a century.

Irving now had no recognised ministerial status in the Church of Scotland and was free to be 'ordained' as the 'Angel' (Rev. 2:1) or 'Pastor' of the new congregation at the hands of one of the newly appointed apostles.

Sadly Irving was already a broken man. His end soon followed. We can trace him trailing his tortured frame back to Scotland on a preaching tour. The travelling must have given him plenty of time to reflect upon his London years. He had certainly made mistakes, and his great humility would never allow him to gloss over those. But he had had to pioneer alone, and that not in an out-of-the-way country parish but in the centre of the world's metropolis. He had no existing model church to build on; no minister experienced in the spiritual gifts to call on.

Socially and materially he had so much to lose, but he stepped out in great human weakness because he was convinced that somehow, somewhere, God was behind those spiritual gifts.

The whole affair has been suffused through the years with an aura of tragedy. We look back at the sudden snuffing-out of a gifted preacher and humble servant of tender spirit who briefly shone with such promise in the centre of London. Undoubtedly he had godly aspirations for the restoration of the gifts of the Spirit to the mainline Church of his day. Unfortunately, his brave but incompetent handling of the gifts (through lack of any contemporary model) has probably contributed more profoundly, in creating a built-in resistance in the 'collective unconscious' of our clergy, than most of them would ever recognise when confronted with gifts of the Spirit in the Church today.

21

REVELATION AND MYSTICISM

A spiritual discipline

Anyone who aspires to prophesy (and this is twice strongly encouraged by Paul (1 Cor. 14:1 and 39) needs to have a spiritual discipline for his life and there are many helpful rules for this within the mystical tradition.

Twenty years ago William Johnston began his introduction to a newly edited reprint of *The Cloud of Unknowing* with this comment:

> Recent times have witnessed a revival of interest in Western mysticism. It is as though the West, long exposed to Zen and Yoga and the spiritual systems of the East, now searches for its own tradition and its own spiritual heritage . . . interest in Christian mysticism is part of widespread craving for meditation, for contemplation, for depth – a desire to get behind the changing phenomena and the future shock and the global village into a deeper reality that lies at the centre of things. Mysticism is no longer irrelevant; it is the air we breathe.[1]

The interest in Christian mysticism continues unabated.

Because so many mystics claim to have received revelations from God, serious aspirants in the prophetic ministry are bound to have their attention drawn to this whole area sooner or later. Prophets need training and there is little likelihood at the moment of their getting any positive and practical direction for ministering in the prophetic from our theological or Bible training colleges, good as such institutions are.

Extraordinary graces

In a chapter entitled 'Extraordinary Graces' Garrigou-Lagrange, a Catholic writer on spirituality, speaks of 'charisms, private revelations, visions, interior words, divine touches' as being 'in order' for the Christian.[2] This kind of writing (and there is much of it) is bound to concentrate the minds of those who want to train themselves in such gifts, even though many Catholic writers would make a distinction between the gifting of the mystic and the gifting of the charismatic.

Since all gifts come from God, (Jas. 1:17) however, our prophets are not likely to be too concerned about such fine definitions. Certainly some of the disciplines advocated in some mystical traditions could greatly benefit our prophets, provided they had good spiritual directors to guide them.

Some might have expected this chapter to come sooner. There has been hesitance in introducing it on various counts.

In the first place mysticism seems to have originated with the non-Christian philosopher Plotinus in the third century and it is not based on the New Testament nor, seemingly, on the practice of the early Church. Nevertheless Plotinus does appear to have had a beneficial influence on St Augustine for one, who is a hero of both Catholics and Protestants for his teaching on grace.

In the second place it is hardly possible to do justice to such a vast subject in one small chapter. And there are so many ramifications of which Protestants are, in my view, rightfully wary, such as speculative mysticism in the East, speculative mysticism in the West, nature mysticism and even some so-called Christian devotional mysticism.

In the third place one would not personally recommend the path of Christian mysticism for any who had not already found peace with God, who did not know that they had passed from death unto life, and did not have the Spirit of God bearing witness with their own spirits that they were the children of God (Rom. 8:16). Those who are inclined to take this path also need a good understanding of Scripture and the Cross of Christ. The variety of theology in mysticism can be confusing and needs careful watching.

As Catholic theologians would themselves readily admit, many writers and 'saints' had only a limited knowledge of theology and their teachings frequently clashed with Catholic theologians. Sometimes it is the mystics who were at fault; sometimes the theologians. Sometimes they were simply saying the same thing from different points of view. This could explain the apparent contradictions between such a notable spiritual writer as St John of the Cross, who defined contemplation as a non-activity, and the theologian Thomas Aquinas, who described it as the highest possible activity. The suspension of all human activity seems to the soul like non-activity. St John of the Cross was writing from an experimental point of view, Thomas Aquinas as a theologian.

The great desire of Baron Friedrich Von Hugel, a major promoter of mysticism at the turn of the twentieth century, was that spiritual theology and spiritual writing should complement, not contradict one another.

John Wesley wrote to his brother Charles on November 23rd, 1736 saying: 'I think the rock on which I had the nearest made shipwreck of the faith was the writings of the mystics: under which term I comprehend all, and only those, who slight any of the means of grace.'[3]

Like so many others before and since, Wesley had found the whole area made even more confusing by the differences among the Christian divines (particularly the mystics) as to whether the pursuit of holiness lay more in bodily austerity (after the Jesuits and Jansenists) or in the inward temper (after the Carmelites and Quietists).

However, there seems to be evidence of a satisfactory development of Christian spirituality among those promoting the practice of Christian mysticism,[4] and it has been seen to promote a life of dedicated service to others. We have the examples of the Society of Jesus (the Jesuits) and the Society of Friends (the Quakers). And mysticism clearly creates a spiritual environment for enhancing the reception of revelation from God. There is also a massive reserve of mystic tradition within the Church to learn from besides many 'lives' of the mystics to inspire us. 'The purpose of reading what the saints – be they Protestant or Roman Catholics – have experienced', writes the evangelical Peter Toon, 'is not to discourage us by making us think that we cannot attain their heights. Rather it is to show us just what is possible by the guidance and assistance of the Holy Spirit in the enjoying and the glorifying of God in our souls and in our lives.'[5]

An example of how the experience of others can benefit us is illustrated by the case of Augustine. As a young man, this future Bishop of Hippo was first told the story of St Antony, the Egyptian monk, by a visitor from the imperial court in Milan. Excitedly he related to the unconverted Augustine the account of two state officials who had come across St Antony's biography and were so impressed that they immediately abandoned their posts in order to serve God alone. After the visitor had left Augustine wrote: 'I stood naked in my own sight . . . There I was, going mad on my way to sanity.'

He became frantic, tortured by the thoughts of his mistresses, and fleeing to the end of his garden, he threw himself down under a fig tree in desperation. As he lay there he heard what seemed to be a child's voice from one of the other houses saying, 'Take and read! Take and read!' over and over again. He rose and went back to his house for a copy of St Paul's epistles which he had been reading. What he then read (from Romans 13:13–14) led him to Christ. 'Let us behave decently, as in the daytime, not in orgies and drunkenness, not in sexual immorality and debauchery, not in dissension and jealousy. Rather, clothe yourselves with the Lord Jesus Christ, and do not think about how to gratify the desires of the sinful nature.' A new Augustine was born 'in that instant'.[6]

What is mysticism?

Perhaps no word in the English language has been used more loosely than mysticism. Sometimes it is used to mean symbolism or allegory; sometimes theosophy or the occult; sometimes merely the mental state of the dreamer, the fey personality, or vague and fantastic ideas about God and the world. One definition is 'shutting the eyes to all external things'. Another is 'experimental knowledge of God'. Dean Inge gives a whole appendix to definitions of mysticism in his Bampton Lectures (1899), published in a book entitled *Christian Mysticism*.[7] According to Oliver Davies we shall not go far wrong if we take the meaning of this difficult word simply as 'an experience of God'.[8]

Function and focus of mysticism

The historical function of mysticism is as an independent active principle in the Church for the recovery of the spirit of reformation and revival. Every active principle must find for itself appropriate instruments, and mysticism has developed a speculative and practical system of its own. Goethe puts it simply: mysticism is 'the scholastic of the heart, the dialectic of the feelings'.

Even though we make a clear distinction between Christian mysticism and other mysticisms, there remains a suspicion from some quarters concerning the focus of theology in our traditional Christian mysticism. Whereas for many the focus is on the glory of the Cross, for the mystic the focus so often appears to have been on the glory of the Incarnation – the Word becoming flesh and dwelling among us (John 1:14). But it was the mystic Henry de Suso who struck the balance so admirably when he wrote, 'No cross, No crown.'

The same emphasis is seen in England's first female writer and notable Norfolk mystic, Julian of Norwich, who made the Cross the central object of her devotions. Maybe the Incarnation has been overemphasised at the expense of the Cross in some quarters; equally the atonement may have been overemphasised at the expense of the Incarnation in others. Paul says he was resolved 'to know nothing . . . except Jesus Christ' (the Word incarnate) 'and him crucified' (the Cross – 1 Cor. 2:2). One truth is not right and the other wrong – both are true and must be given their rightful emphasis in theology and worship.

Occupational hazards

There are certain dangers in mysticism as there are in any 'ism'. It was Joseph Fletcher, author of *Situation Ethics*, who playfully remarked that mysticism begins in 'mist' and ends in 'schism'.

1 There is the possible danger that mysticism may itself become a kind of religion. This it must never be. It is a means to an end – a means by which the vision of new light, new love and new life may refresh the individual mystic and through the individual the whole Body of Christ.

2 The mystical sense of Scripture itself must never be mistaken for an encounter with the One who speaks through Scripture – the word of God is to bring us to the God of the word.

3 A subtle danger in practice is that of giving higher value to particular personal visions and revelations than to the Bible itself, as St John of the Cross has warned.[9] We saw that this was the mistake with some of the so-called prophets of Zwichau (see chapter 17).

4 The allegorical interpretation of the Bible. There are many helpful and blessed ideas which may be presented through the allegorising of Scripture, a practice which has always been popular among Christian mystics and

promoted by Origen, Ambrose and even Augustine of Hippo. For an extreme example, both Ambrose and Origen could take the thirty-third chapter of the book of Numbers, which lists the wanderings of the children of Israel on leaving Egypt, and describe their various 'mansions' (the places where they rested) as the ever-upward stages on the mystical road to God. Both interpreted the 'mansion' called Terah as the ecstasy of amazement!

Even Erasmus (c. 1466–1536), the leading Christian humanist of the Renaissance, was happy to follow Origen in seeing 'the concubines of Solomon as so many virtues and the Canaanites to be exterminated by the Israelites as so many vices'.[10]

Some mystical writers have been able to find a relevant text in the Bible for almost any conceivable subject.

There is admittedly some biblical precedent for finding allegories in the Bible (see John 3:14, Gal. 4:21–31, 1 Cor. 9:9f, 1 Pet. 3:18–22). Allegorical interpretation suggests other meanings, supposedly deeper meanings, in place of the obvious one. A good rule to remember, when reading the Bible, is that 'the main thing is the plain thing and the plain thing is the main thing'.

Although we have biblical examples of allegory it is in fact unwise to develop this mode of interpretation lest we get back to where the Church was before the Reformation, where often the plain meaning of Scripture was totally obscured by fanciful interpretations. The situation can soon arise where one blessed but rather wild allegory is being used to back up another blessed but equally wild allegory and this is then presented as biblical doctrine.

The principle of allegorising Scripture was not apparently seriously questioned until the sixteenth century, when the Reformers made it their task to get back to the text and rediscover what it actually said.

We need to keep our sights clearly fixed on the Reformers' goal in that respect. It is a dangerous focus if ever mystics are allowed to bypass the uniqueness of Christ, both in his incarnation and his finished work on the Cross. He can never be other than the only way to the Father (John 14:6, Acts 4:12, 1 Tim. 2:15, 1 John 2:22,23, 1 John 5:12, 2 John v.9).

John Wimber, who heads the international Christian Vineyard Fellowships from California, recently rebuked certain prophets connected with his movement for seeking 'to use types and allegories to establish doctrine'. 'This', writes George Mallone, 'is a healthy correction, but should not be viewed as a call to eliminate [entirely] the use of the allegorical.'[11] It is a timely warning to would-be prophets.

5 A mistaken doctrine of the body: mystics have tended to regard the body as a despicable pollutant and, borrowing from Plato, a prison for the soul.

The body is a vessel of God's creation which should be sanctified and honoured (1 Thess. 4:4, 1 Pet. 3:7). It is the carnal desire of the flesh which needs to be put to death daily for its allegiance to the world and the devil.

6 A lack of commitment to social action. The discipline of looking not at the seen but at the unseen makes it easy to overlook the more practical aspects and responsibilities of life, such as the poor begging at the gate, the widow and the prisoner. Obviously Mary had chosen 'the better part' by sitting at the feet of Jesus when he was visiting and simply enjoying his presence but as James so rightly stresses (summarising Jesus' plain teaching in Matthew 25), 'Religion that God our Father accepts as pure and faultless is this: to look after orphans and widows in their distress and to keep oneself from being polluted by the world' (Jas 1:27).

7 The abolition of the individual soul. In the teaching of those such as Plotinus (205–70), ecstasy is supposed to come through the abolition of the individual soul and the fusion into the One. As such it is an anticipation of the final release of the soul from the body at death, when it is absorbed into the One for ever. This is nothing like

the teaching of Christ and it reveals where Plotinus' philosophy and mysticism have corrupted his theology and robbed it of the truth of the gospel of Jesus Christ.

Some propositions

Christian mysticism rests on the following propositions:

1 The soul (as well as the body) can see and perceive. We have a spiritual faculty for the discernment of truth, which, in its proper sphere, is as real as our rational mind and our five physical senses.

2 In order to know God (in the sense of having a relationship with him) man needs to be a partaker of the divine nature.

3 The knowledge of God brings a commitment to holiness of life. 'Be holy; without holiness no one will see the Lord' (Heb. 12:14). Jesus put it even more simply. 'Blessed are the pure in heart, for they will see God' (Matt. 5:8). Sensuality and selfishness will seriously blur or distort our perception of 'the things that come from the Spirit of God' (1 Cor. 2:14). 'The purest mirror in the world is the highest of created things – the human soul unclouded by sin.'[12]

4 The fourth proposition is what Paul terms that most excellent way – love (1 Cor. 13:1). One aspect of love is fundamental; love 'is not self-seeking' (1 Cor. 13:5). Our souls may yearn for the courts of the Lord and our hearts cry out for the living God (Ps. 84:2) but our motive must be higher than simply our need. We must seek him because he desires our presence.

Thomas à Kempis once wrote: 'It is better to be with Christ in hell than without him in heaven.' He erased the words before the ink was dry, knowing that the theology was misleading, but it reveals how in his heart he longed to be with Christ whatever the cost to himself. The true mystic makes love his chief end, both in his service of God and his service of others. 'It was revealed to them [the prophets of old] that *they were not serving themselves but you*, when they spoke of the things that have now been told you' (1 Pet. 1:12).

The rule of Dionysius

The rule of the mystics has been derived traditionally from the teachings of Dionysius the Areopagite who became a Christian following Paul's speech on the Areopagus in Athens (Acts 17:34), though it is more widely believed today that the mystic Dionysius was in fact a Syrian monk of the early sixth century, the actual time when the writings of Dionysius first appeared in circulation.

His extant writings consist of some four books – *Divine Names*, *Mystical Theology*, *Celestial Hierarchy* and *Ecclesiastical Hierarchy*. In *Mystical Theology* he expounds what has become known as his 'apophatic' theory whereby the soul follows a path of systematic negation, passing upward beyond anything it can perceive or know into the darkness where God is. There it experiences 'complete speechlessness' and becomes 'united in its highest part in passivity with Him who is completely unknowable'; it knows by not knowing in a manner that transcends knowledge.

'This', writes Dionysius in his *Mystical Theology*, 'is the Divine Darkness', 'the cloud of unknowing'. Elsewhere we learn that 'the Divine Darkness is the light unapproachable' (cf. Exod. 20:21) – 'a deep and dazzling darkness'. For the individual this is the realisation that his life is 'hidden with Christ in God' (Col. 3:3).

Medieval mysticism in the West began to see a change of emphasis. This reaches its climax in the writings of St Teresa of Avila, where we see a move from the objective participation in the mystery of Christ, with no particular interest in subjective phenomena, which we could find in the Fathers, to an attention to subjective mystical experiences (reflecting the cultural shift in the West towards more interest in the individual and individual feelings). For Dionysius (in some books on spirituality

today his name is modernised to Denys), there are three
rungs on the *scala perfectionis* to be climbed step by step.
They are

1 the purgative life,
2 the illuminative life,

while the third, really the goal rather than the final step, is

3 union or the state of perfect contemplation.

There are many ways of understanding these stages. A
prominent North American Catholic charismatic, Stephen
Clark, explains in his book *Baptized in the Spirit*[13] that
Catholic writers have traditionally described spiritual
growth in these terms. In the purgative stage a person is
purified of habitual sins. In the illuminative stage a person
grows in Christlike qualities and gets to know Jesus, and at
the unitive stage a person begins to experience the work of
the Holy Spirit within him.

There are many different understandings, variations,
additions, subtractions and often unbalanced teachings
that have been introduced along the way and need to
be watched, as indeed with all Christian traditions.

The search for the Christ within (Col. 1:27) and the
Kingdom of God within (Luke 17:21), which some have
seen as an encouragement to 'sink into the depths of our
own souls in order to find God', must be balanced with
seeking those things which come from above (Col. 3:1),
otherwise the exercise can easily become the search for
anti-Christs, so deceitful is the human heart.

The search for Christ in others (Matt. 25:40) must not
deflect our mindset from the things that are above (Col.
3:2). The search for Christ in nature (Col. 2:9) must not
distract our search for the Christ of Scripture (John 5:39).
The search for the Christ in creation (Col. 1:16) must
not deflect our focus from the Christ over all creation
(Col. 1:15).

This all needs underlining because one of the occupa-
tional hazards for the mystic is pantheism. John Tauler
neatly clarified the orthodox view on that subject long

ago: 'God is all but all is not God.' We cannot go as far as Meister Eckhart, who hardly differs from the monistic experiences of the Buddhist or Hindu 'where the soul is oned with nature but moves no further, for God and the soul are one'.[14]

Joyce Huggett gives some gentle and wise advice on this subject in *Listening to God* where she says:

> And the fear of pantheism, which keeps many Christians from hearing God speak through nature, does not trouble me either. I am clear in my mind that when I claim to hear God speak through the lips of a tulip, he speaks, not because he is the tulip, but because, as the creator of the tulip, he is giving expression to facets of himself through its design, its texture, its shape, its size and the streaks of red which he paints on the yellow petals with one stroke of his brush.[15]

In the course of our thinking about this kind of mysticism it is only right to say that not all have found such fulfilment in the contemplation of nature. To many 'the loving wisdom of God has appeared absent from nature. For Tennyson nature seemed "red in tooth and claw" and after the death of his brother at sea, Wordsworth turned from natural to revealed and traditional religion.'[16]

Having our focus well and truly upon Christ, ecstasies, voices and visions may incidentally be vouchsafed, though these are neither a guaranteed fruit of mysticism nor are mystical exercises the only means for receiving such revelations from God.

Visions

According to Dean Inge, visions played a much more important part in the life of the early Church than many ecclesiastical historians are willing to admit. Tertullian once stated quite simply that 'The majority, almost, of men learn from visions.'[17]

Aspirants are cautioned never to seek to induce visions artificially. It has long been known that this could be done with drugs. Aldous Huxley, in *The Doors of Perception*, suggested that mescalin might induce a state similar to that experienced by Christian nature mystics,[18] and David Aune sees a hint of this in the Apocrypha, 2 Esdras 14:39–41, which could refer to the use of hallucinogens. But Huxley spoke of 'escape', which he regularly and mistakenly equated with mysticism, overlooking or ignorant of the real objective which was a loving engagement with God and his creation.

As a rule visions were regarded as special rewards bestowed by the goodness of God on the struggling saint, and especially on the beginner, to refresh and strengthen him in his hour of need.[19] But clearly the temptation to feel pride in one's visions is there and needs to be resisted. Paul spells out his own experience of this: 'To keep me from becoming conceited because of these surpassingly great revelations, there was given me a thorn in my flesh, a messenger of Satan, to torment me' (2 Cor. 12:7). He also describes the tragic state of unspiritually minded people: 'Such a person goes into great detail about what he has seen, and his unspiritual mind puffs him up with idle notions. He has lost connection with the Head' (Col. 2:18–19).

Visions were commonplace among the seers but all visions, like prophecies, need testing (see chapter 9). Richard of St Victor counsels so sensitively and wisely when he says: 'As Christ attested His transfiguration by the presence of Moses and Elijah so visions should not be believed unless they have the authority of Scripture.'

'White ladies'

In his fascinating and widely informative book, *Powers of Darkness: Powers of Light*,[20] John Cornwall, who may be described as a renegade Catholic, reports somewhat racily on his research at the sites of mystical phenomena still venerated in some Catholic circles today. Though cynical at times he is not entirely unsympathetic and having visited Lourdes, Garabandal and Medjugorje (among many others) and personally interviewed witnesses, he writes of his discovery that apparitions of 'beautiful ladies' bathed in 'white light' were by no means the preserve of Christian visionaries even in the West.

In the course of his research he unearthed the findings of a 1954 report in a popular Swiss fortnightly newspaper, the *Schwiezerischer Beobachter*, which had conducted a survey among its readers regarding experiences of the paranormal. Some 1,500 responded. The material was assessed by Aniela Jaffe, a Swiss psychologist and associate of Carl Jung.

A New York psychologist, Martin Ebon, eventually encouraged her to have her findings published. This was done in 1978. In her account she classifies the leading categories of paranormal experiences and one of them was headed: 'Apparitions of the "woman in white"'.

A very significant number of correspondents had witnessed the apparition of a beautiful lady in a white light who conveyed a warning of danger. Invariably the visionaries were girls and boys, and there had been no specifically religious context attached to the experience.

Dr Jaffe quotes a number of stories sent in response to the original survey. They illustrate the kind of thing we have become familiar with if we have followed the well-known recent cases of Garabandal in Spain and Medjugorje in what was formerly Yugoslavia.

She attempts to relate her analysis of these contemporary experiences to a wide range of parallels in what she calls the 'old texts', notably to the *femina alba* – Venus or Aphrodite, the Goddess of Love – but she still asks why the White Lady is so often the bearer of bad tidings. She finds it interesting that not only was Aphrodite the Goddess of Love, but she was also the queen of the underworld or of death – an archetypal figure.

Cornwall, with his wide knowledge of English literature, immediately connects the archetypal figure with Keats' 'La Belle Dame Sans Merci', the loving harbinger of the poet's own fatal disease. He also finds further echoes in the rich materials gathered by Robert Graves in his book *The White Goddess*.

In her conclusion, Aniela Jaffe points out that the White Lady appears invariably to girls at a time when they are first becoming conscious of their femininity. In her view, nature is revealing to them (even though they may not understand this at the time) what they are to become. Apparently these visions may be encountered more than once by the seer.

In the light of these observations Cornwall was left wondering what to make of the evidence of the visions at Medjugorje and Garabandal, or any of the other 230 major sightings of the Virgin Mary recorded throughout the twentieth century.

Work had been done on these apparitions by Michael Carrol in the University of Western Ontario. By putting the details of many hundreds of them into his computer he had been able to discover an empirical pattern. The following were among the most constant features:

1 The Virgin appears to girls at puberty.

2 The favoured seer usually colludes with the local community before announcing the Virgin's identity.

3 The seers are normally working children, who are out looking for lost cattle or sheep at the time of the first phenomenon, which usually occurs as a light.

4 The seer has lost a mother or a mother figure (with Bernadette of Lourdes it was her older sister) in the previous eight weeks.

5 The Virgin imparts secrets and warnings of doom if certain religious formulas are not adhered to.

Some readers may find it strange that I am so ready to quote the findings of psychologists when I have already tried to make it plain that revelations from God are supernatural and therefore not limited to rationalistic norms. I still would claim that revelations from God are supernatural in origin though there may well be some natural understanding.

Just as the revelations need evaluating, so too do the findings of psychologists. Often the psychologist has no true doctrine of man and no true doctrine of God. They can be wrong but they can also be right. Some psychologists have perfectly true and most helpful insights, which it would be utter folly to ignore.

But one of our first tasks is to determine whether these are revelations, or simply the result of a late night pizza or the stressful outworking of some emotional trauma. Of course both the causes may still create the right conditions for God to reveal something, just as, on the other hand, fasting and prayer would do.

Then we need to determine whether these revelations are directly from God to warn or bless mankind, or indirectly through his creation as part of the maturing process of self-awareness. Where such apparitions occur in a Catholic environment they are quickly assumed to be the Blessed Virgin Mary, in a Protestant one a 'White Lady' and in the non-Christian world Aphrodite (or her counterpart). The psychologist just might have a valid explanation here. He or she would probably classify the apparition as an archetypal figure personifying the seer's own unconscious.

I am struggling at this point. I do not want to wound my Catholic friends. I know of their faith in Jesus. But I must apply the same tests to their visions as to mine. I believe we should venerate the Mother of Jesus Christ who herself said 'all generations shall call me blessed' and I must leave plenty of room for the sovereignty of God to do whatever he may want to do. But even the Mother of Jesus, who was and always remained human, must never in any way replace or overshadow Jesus who is, of course, also divine.

I would not deny that the Mother of Jesus could appear to humans as Samuel appeared to Saul (1 Sam. 28:14) and Moses and Elijah to Peter, James and John on the Mount of Christ's Transfiguration (Mark 9:4). But the whole tenor of Scripture seems to make such an appearance most unlikely. Humanity would be far too prone to make too much of it and be led astray into false doctrine as the Church already has been. I cannot believe we should ever actively seek those who have passed on – something wholly forbidden in the Bible. We should never take any initiative to consult with those who have died, pray to them or in any way try to make contact with them. That is out of bounds. Saul had Samuel called up illegally and paid the penalty for his rebellion.

But if our Sovereign Lord God sends one (or two! Mark 9:4) to us unasked, that is 'legal' and should be seen as some kind of blessing. And he does seem to have done this from time to time. I think of C.S. Lewis appearing, a few days after his death, sitting in a chair within a few feet of J.B. Phillips as the latter watched TV, and speaking a few words relevant to some difficult circumstance faced by Phillips on that occasion.[21] But, by my understanding of the Bible, I personally do not think that J.B. Phillips would have had any right to initiate an approach himself to C.S. Lewis, as one of the saints departed.

Neither ecstasy nor mysticism should be an end in themselves – Christ is the goal. But mysticism may be the means for some seers to see, some prophets to hear and some saints simply to know that the Lord is God.

22

PROPHECY AND ECSTASY

Ecstasy has long had tainted associations for the Church. Quoting Clement of Rome, Eusebius comments in his *Historia Ecclesiastica*: 'to deliver utterances in a state of ecstasy is actually one of the criteria by which a false prophet may be detected'. Doubtless false prophets often prophesied in an ecstatic state but not all prophecy associated with ecstasy need be false.

Many of the first Gentile Christians were Greek-speaking and had a cultural background steeped in Greek philosophy. Like Origen (c. 185–254) they 'reflected in their spirituality, as in all else, his attempted domestication of scriptural revelation within current Hellenistic culture'.[1]

Early Christian thinkers also had an oracle orientation since this was the environment of Greece and Persia. Their familiarity with prophecy of all kinds would also give them some familiarity with ecstasy. (It may be appropriate to state here that the word 'ecstasy' in 1 Corinthians 14:2 of the New English Bible is an insertion not found in the original Greek of the New Testament text.)

Towards a definition

Plato once described the ecstatic state of the prophet as he received what he believed was divine revelation: 'There is a madness which is a divine gift and the source of the chiefest blessing granted to man.' What are we to understand by this madness? Madness might be all right for pagans but what about Christians?

Following the Welsh Revival at the beginning of the twentieth century, A.T. Schofield, a Harley Street consultant on strange behaviour, wrote a book called *Christian Sanity*.[2] In his introduction he expressed this caution over what he meant by Christian sanity:

> We must remember that it is not for us to deny the action of the Spirit of God in Almighty power on the hearts and lives of men, nor to lay down any laws for His action.
>
> We thus see how dangerous it is to pronounce any spiritual effects in Christian lives to be sane or insane, according to our preconceived ideas, based solely on human phenomena.
>
> At the same time, while confessing the great difficulty of the task and fully aware of the caution required, we cannot shut our eyes to the crying need there is at the present day to at least attempt it. Everywhere the name of Christ is blasphemed through wild excesses and fanatical outbursts of Christian, or so-called Christian men and women. Such has been the case in all ages of the Church, and the wildest insanities have been permitted under the name of Christ and Christianity.

Lord Penzance, a famous nineteenth-century judge, gave the following finding for a court of law which, though it does not reflect any special sympathy with Christian thought, expressed a commonly held view, in his times, on the subject of sanity:[3]

> It is not assuredly in the region of enthusiasm that we must look for the calm exercise of pure reason and temperate and well-balanced ideas. Still less must we expect that the fervour of fanaticism will follow in the slow steps of philosophy.
>
> It is hardly then by a mere test of reasonableness

that the wild thoughts of religious enthusiasts can be brought to a standard for judgment of their sanity.

But there are surely limits even to so mythical a subject, within which the human mind in a state of health is unreasonable or extravagant; and the common experience of life gives us a sense of those limits sufficient for the formation of judgment in most cases. To draw the exact line – if there be one – which defines such limits may be impossible, but to affirm that some instances surpass it is not so.

Two positions to be avoided

To understand the subject of sanity two positions must be avoided. One is that of branding all beyond our idea of common sense, such as the recognition of the blackness of sin, or the joy of deliverance from it, as insane; the other that of the extremist who holds all absurdities as normal and sane whenever they are done in the name of God.

The standards of sanity are diverse. 'Everyone is more or less mad on one point,' said Rudyard Kipling. In George Bernard Shaw's play *Saint Joan*, Robert (who is the law-abiding conservative) turns to Poulengey and says, 'What! You are as mad as she [Joan] is.' Poulengey answers, 'We want a few mad people now. See where the sane ones have landed us!'[4] 'All the world is mad except for thee and me, and even thee's a little mad' was a common remark once made to raise a smile but which in fact often reflected some home truth about the anomaly of a satisfactory definition.

Madness was considered to be anything strange about the behaviour of one individual which another individual thought he or she would or could never do. The safest standpoint was considered that of strong common sense enlightened by a Christian faith whose judgments were guided by Scripture – bearing in mind that the same Scripture reflected an Eastern rather than a Western culture.

Bear in mind also that even the Eastern onlookers too readily assumed the disciples at Pentecost were full of new wine!

> The early pagans sometimes found the concern of Christians for the poor, the needy, the weak, the backward and the unintelligent to be very odd indeed. Christians could seem, by several different standards, to be acting as madmen. So too could Jesus, Paul and those who followed them. And when judged against the standards of philosophy, God's plan for the redemption of mankind could be made to seem an act of divine lunacy. Both God the Father and God the Son, as Christians conceive them, can be thought of as mad.[5]

In days gone by we used to talk about religious mania. 'As a psychiatrist,' writes Dr John White, 'I have seen many psychotic states which take a religious form.'[6] Tom Butler, the Bishop of Leicester, writing in the *Daily Telegraph* recently (21.4.93) on cults such as that of Jim Jones of Jonestown in Guyana and David Koresh in Waco, Texas, comments: 'It is a sad truth that mystical insight and mad illusion seem to lie close together in the human psyche. The greater religions have always known this, and so have their checks and balances through worship, prayer and pastoral care. Ordinary worshippers can get in touch with the reality of God without destroying themselves in the process.'

Lunacy out of fashion
Today we hardly use the words 'lunacy' or 'insanity' or even 'madness' to describe the condition of inmates of what used to be called asylums. The word 'lunatic' is an obsolete word for insanity[7] and the term 'insanity' in popular terminology has 'regrettably been so brutalized by irresponsible writers over the years that its only remaining

technical meaning is a forensic one, in its use as a legal designation for the state of an individual judged to be legally irresponsible or incompetent'.[8]

Psychologists talk in terms of psychosis and neurosis, and using these definitions as a frame of reference for sanity it is still difficult to determine the point of transition from sanity to insanity. As these are described we may see similar traits in ourselves to a greater or lesser degree, perhaps a lesser degree over longer periods and a greater degree at some crisis period.

The kind of insanity traditionally associated with ecstasy was of a very different ilk.

Socrates, who believed the Greek words for prophecy and madness were related, divided the notion of divine madness into four kinds:

1 Prophecy
2 Healing
3 Artistic inspiration
4 Love

The Father of Theology

Philo (Judaeus) of Alexandria (c. 20 BC–c. AD 50), the 'Father of Theology', was the first to use the word 'ecstasy' in describing the state of a Jewish prophet when receiving revelation. Philo was a contemporary of Christ. This ascetic Jewish thinker came from a priestly family in Egypt. His theology was a blend of Old Testament monotheism and Greek philosophy.

He described Abraham's 'deep sleep' (from the Hebrew word *tardemah*, Gen. 15:12) as 'ecstasy'; Daniel experienced a similar 'deep sleep' (Dan. 10:9). Job also links 'deep sleep' with God speaking (Job 33:15). Isaiah also seems to be telling the prophets and the seers that they should expect a similar experience (Isa. 29:10).

Philo believed this 'ecstasy' could take the following forms:

1 Madness which produces mental delusion

2 Amazement at sudden or unexpected events

3 Passivity of mind

4 Divine possession or frenzy

Some modern definitions

The *Concise Oxford Dictionary* has the following definition of ecstasy, from the Greek *existemi* – to put a person out of his senses:

1 Exalted state of feeling, rapture (especially of delight)

2 Morbid state of nerves in which the mind is occupied by one idea

3 Trance

4 Poetic frenzy

Chambers Dictionary takes its definition from the Greek *histanai* – to make to stand:

1 State of being beside oneself

2 Excessive joy

3 Poetic frenzy

4 Any exalted feeling

The *New International Dictionary of the Christian Church* defines it as follows:[9] 'The supernatural state of being beyond reason and self-control as when obsessed by emotion or overpowering feeling such as joy or rapture'.

The *Oxford Dictionary of the Christian Church* reads:[10]

The term has come to be applied to several preter- or supernatural states which, however, are in no way related to each other . . . Mystic ecstasy in the Christian sense is one of the normal stages of the mystic life.

The chief characteristic of the ecstatic state is the alienation of the senses, caused by the violence of the Divine action on the soul. The body, unable to bear the strain, becomes usually immovable, and sight, hearing etc., cease to function.

In contrast to the pathological 'case', the mystic remembers what has taken place during the ecstasy, which is usually an intuitive knowledge of some mystery of religion accompanied by a distinct consciousness of the divine presence.

A Dictionary of Christian Spirituality defines it as:[11]

A sense of being taken out of oneself, caught up, like Paul, into the third heaven and united with some higher power.

The word is often used to describe the raptures of sexual intercourse, which, as in Donne's poem 'The Ecstasy', is not simply a 'transport of delight', but enables the lovers to penetrate the mystery of love itself.

Such union is the climax of contemplation more than of physical or mental activity.

As part of prayer

While praying, Teresa of Avila in Spain (1515–82) experienced ecstasy which was sometimes accompanied by levitation. She places 'Ecstasy' between the 'Prayer of Union' and 'Mystic Marriage' in *The Interior Castle*, her most important book on prayer.[12]

In Praise of Folly

Desiderius Erasmus[13] of Rotterdam in Holland (c. 1466–1536) dedicated his book *In Praise of Folly* to his English friend Thomas More. In it the following range of distinctions (though not entirely without some overlapping) may be discerned:

1 Ecstasy of amazement (Gen. 15:12, Dan. 8:17, Acts 10:45). This could be regarded almost as being stunned – the kind of sensation which follows a loud explosion nearby, fear in the proximity of violence or death or the after-effect of a physical blow to the head or body.

2 Ecstasy of rapture

a) 'Out of the body' (Ezek. 8:3, 2 Cor. 12:2)

b) Love (Ps. 31, 2 Cor. 5:13,14)

c) 'a kind of Christian joy' ('transports of delight')

d) Erotic love. One of the commonest Greek words used for worship in the New Testament is *proskunein* (John 4:24) which may be understood literally as 'coming towards – to kiss'. Such love is expressed throughout the Song of Solomon and picked up by Christian mystics. The very serviceable German name for this kind of mysticism is 'Brautmystic' (which we may translate as 'bride mysticism' or 'nuptial mysticism'). 'This name derives from the preference among such visionaries and mystics for speaking of Christ as a Bridegroom and the human soul as his bride.'[14] One of its principal practitioners was St Bernard of Clairvaux, who in the twelfth century, wrote a commentary on the Song of Songs.

St Bonaventura coined a phrase which enshrined a notion he took over from St Bernard and which has become a standard expression in this particular mystical tradition: 'The soul (anima), like the "anima" of all lovers, is not where it animates (animat) but where it loves (amat).'[15]

3 Ecstasy of insanity

a) Medically insane (sometimes demonisation – Mark 5:2 – but not always). This category has also been associated with poets, seers and lovers

b) Madness (Holy Spirit possession – 1 Sam. 10:10)

c) Drunkenness (Acts 2:13, Eph. 5:18)

d) Foolishness (Mark 3:20–1, 1 Cor. 1:25)

Two categories

In his book *Prophecy in Ancient Israel* the German theologian J. Lindblom has simply reduced ecstasy to two categories:

1 'Absorption' ecstasy, in which the prophet's personality is fused together with God.

2 'Concentration' ecstasy, in which the soul meditates

so deeply upon a single object that normal consciousness is obscured.

It was this latter which Lindblom applied to the state of mind necessary for receiving revelation from God.

Catholic, Orthodox and Protestant

Thinking in the massive mystical tradition of the Catholic and Orthodox Churches has roamed broadly over definitions of ecstasy. But the 'ecstatic' experience was not limited only to these two Churches. There were plenty of examples from among the Protestants. David Brainerd, a pioneer missionary to the North American Indians and saintly young friend of Jonathan Edwards, entered a typical experience of what Catholics would term 'unitive or contemplative prayer': 'God enabled me to pray with as much spirituality and sweetness as I have done for some time; my mind seemed to be unclothed of sense and imagination, and was in a measure let into the immaterial world of spirits.'[16]

It shows that the field is wide and the manifestations varied. For some this may lead to the despair of ever understanding the meaning and purpose of 'ecstasy'. Others may find it stretches their belief beyond its limits to maintain that God could be associated with these experiences at all, let alone desire them for man.

While certain distinctions and definitions need questioning, others need qualifying. Every genuine manifestation of the power of God has its counterfeits. These may be 'related in some degree to that unfortunate tendency of late medieval mysticism – the tendency to attract emotional and idiosyncratic characters and expect violent psycho-physical phenomena as signs of divine favour'.[17]

Out of order

Under normal circumstances dramatic or seemingly violent manifestation of ecstasy in the course of prophesying would be clearly ruled out of order in a meeting of the church. Paul requires the one prophesying to stand, presumably to demonstrate that the spirit of the prophet is subject to the control of the prophet (1 Cor. 14:32).

There seems to be room, however, for such experiences when the saint is alone with God, as would usually be the case (St Teresa of Avila would certainly be an exception) when receiving revelation through a dream, vision, voice, trance, a visitation from some supernatural being or an out-of-the-body experience.

Where such experiences were genuinely God-given, the soul would not be unconscious but blessed with a holy awareness of the encounter and a clear recollection of it whenever it was the purpose of God to communicate some revelation. Of course God may have other purposes such as a healing (either emotional or physical), a deliverance or simply a blessing when he chooses to overwhelm someone ecstatically. It may also be a commissioning to a new task or ministry with the accompanying gifting for the work.[18]

Counterfeit experiences
Where there are counterfeit experiences from the devil the subject may be completely taken over and afterwards remember nothing – neither what the spirit may have spoken through the person him/herself nor what s/he may have been driven to do.

It is not difficult to understand how many genuine visitations of divine ecstasy may have been too hastily dismissed as sickness, madness or demonisation. But such superficial evaluation would at best amount to throwing the baby out with the bathwater; at worst it would be blasphemy against the Holy Spirit of God.

It has been observed that some Christian mystics, such as the fourteenth-century recluse Julian of Norwich, had almost no access to Scripture, yet her 'showings' or revelations reflected an accurate and profound knowledge of God and of salvation which many today lack despite their knowledge of the Scriptures.

On the other hand several of the greatest mystics (such as Teresa of Avila, John of the Cross and the unknown author of *The Cloud of Unknowing*, to name just three) were alarmed at the readiness with which beginners in contemplative prayer claimed divine revelation as the source of their voices, dreams, visions and ecstatic bodily states.

The genuine mystic would always be aware of how easy it was to be deceived by a sinful heart or the subtlety of Satan.[19]

Dangerous trends

In tracing the development of ideas about ecstasy in the field of Christian mysticism it must never be overlooked that 'ecstasy is a Greek word for a Greek set of ideas; its roots are in Greek philosophy and in Greek pragmatism'.[20] The word has been adopted to describe biblical states of spiritual experience. It is, of course, accepted that any student of mysticism, who seeks to classify these experiences in any way, has little option but to use the most appropriate word available.

We should in no way be bound to these Greek ideas, but in so far as considerable thinking has been given to the subject of spiritual experience such as is found in the Bible (especially when both the Old Testament Septuagint and the original New Testament documents come to us in Greek), it would be foolish to overlook any research which may have been influenced by a Greek mindset; as foolish as it would be to overvalue it in seeking a true understanding of the meanings of ecstasy.

Conclusion

While many of the prophets quite plainly experienced physical states of ecstasy (Jer. 4:19 and 23:9, Ezek. 1:28, 2:22, 3:1–2, 3:26–7 and 8:3, Hos. 9:7b), which may have given the distinct impression at times of some kind of temporary insanity, it is evident that divine communication was never limited to that particular mode alone.

Nor do we think that those who are on record as having been in an ecstatic state (possibly exhibiting that kind of temporary insanity) necessarily experienced similar phenomena every time God wanted to reveal his word to them.

The writer to the Hebrews was careful to say, 'In the past God spoke to our forefathers through the prophets at many times and in various ways' (Heb. 1:1). That word 'various' is worth underlining.

23

RELIGIOUS EXPERIENCE
VALIDATED

Anyone who embarks on the prophetic ministry will soon discover the need for care and discernment in the area of feelings and religious experience. Some can truly discern God's voice and see God's hand in the context of strong emotion. Some are moved to speak the message of God, like Jeremiah, with trembling bones, tears and lamentations. Emotional experiences such as joyful ecstasy or heaviness of heart are appropriate and valid under many circumstances. There is joy in heaven over the sinner who repents and Jesus himself wept over Jerusalem and experienced great heaviness of heart at Gethsemane.

This is not to overlook the potential for the misuse or abuse of emotion in religious experience. Nor is it to suggest that all revelation must be accompanied by emotion.

Although usually regarded in psychology as characteristic of depression it is claimed that one can recognise beauty intellectually while being unable to appreciate it emotionally. In the same way it may also be possible to recognise truth intellectually while still being unable to appreciate it emotionally. Jonathan Edwards, as we shall see below, doubted that such intellectual recognition would bring about much beneficial change of mind or life-style.

All human beings are basically religious, but it must not be assumed that every religious experience is Christian, nor that every spiritual experience emanates from the Kingdom of God.

All experience of God through Jesus Christ is a religious and spiritual experience, but not all religious and spiritual experience is of the God revealed to us in Jesus Christ.

Feelings and revelation

Jonathan Edwards was possibly the first to make a serious study of the place of feelings in Christian spiritual experience after his major encounter with the problem following George Whitefield's evangelistic preaching in New England in the 1740s.

In a most useful book, still relevant for today, called *The Religious Affections*, he seeks to evaluate the proper place of emotion in a climate of strong opposition from local churches to the powerful feelings manifested in the revival (and a general suspicion of anything of the kind in religion), while he accepts that there may also be some abuse of the emotions.

He writes:

> I am bold to assert, that there never was any considerable change wrought in the mind or conversation of any one person, by anything of a religious nature that ever he read, heard, or saw, who had not his affections moved.
>
> Never was a natural man engaged earnestly to seek his salvation; never were any such brought to cry after wisdom and lift up their voice for understanding, and to wrestle with God in prayer for mercy; and never was one humbled and brought to the foot of God, from anything that he ever heard or imagined of his own unworthiness and deserving of God's displeasure; nor was ever one induced to fly for refuge unto Christ, while his heart remained unaffected.
>
> Nor was any saint awakened out of a cold lifeless frame, or recovered from a declining state in religion, and brought back from a lamentable departure from God, without having his heart affected.[1]

Today, after years of careful research into our emotions, it is clear that while careless giving way to emotional impulses can be harmful and destructive, many of us are sick, and some of us will ultimately die because of repressed or over-controlled emotions.

Even as far back as 1740 Edwards believed that teachers were in great error if they were 'for discarding all religious affections, as having nothing solid or substantial in them'.[2] Well aware that heat and light must go together, he urged that we need more than mere knowledge.

We also need 'holy affections', by which he means emotions within God's will. 'The Holy Scriptures everywhere place religion very much in the affections; such as fear, hope, love, hatred, desire, joy, sorrow, gratitude, compassion and zeal.'[3]

It is significant that three books affecting recent Christian spirituality have positively emphasised the word 'joy' in their titles – *Joy Unspeakable* by Martin Lloyd Jones; *The Joy of Listening to God*, Joyce Huggett's book published recently in the USA, and finally *Surprised by Joy* by C.S. Lewis, which retells his journey from atheism to Christianity and describes the reality of a deeply emotional experience of conversion.

Lewis writes:

> How far the story matters to anyone but myself depends on the degree to which others have experienced what I call 'joy' . . . I have been emboldened to write of it because I notice that a man seldom mentions what he had supposed to be his most idiosyncratic sensations without receiving from at least one (often more) of those present the reply, 'What! Have *you* felt that too? I always thought I was the only one.'[4]

In the book he describes three childhood 'raptures' which had a profound effect upon his life and his life's work. One just happened while he was standing beside a flowering currant bush on a summer's day. Without warning a feeling arose within him 'from a depth not of years but of centuries', accompanying the earlier childhood memories of a miniature model garden that his older brother had made in a tin lid some years before.

He speaks of an 'enormous bliss' of Eden (quoting Milton). It was a sensation of desire – but for what? 'And before I knew what I desired, the desire itself was gone, the whole glimpse withdrawn, the world turned commonplace again.'[5] He wrote that it had taken only a moment of time, but in a certain sense everything else that had ever happened to him was insignificant by comparison.

His second 'rapture' came through reading *Squirrel Nutkin*, one of Beatrix Potter's many books, which he had loved as a child. While he found the rest of her books entertaining *Squirrel Nutkin* gave him 'the shock . . . it was the Idea of Autumn . . . he became enamoured of a season'. He would often return to the book to recapture that desire.

In that experience also 'there was the same surprise and the same sense of incalculable importance. It was something quite different from ordinary life and even from ordinary pleasure; something, as they would now say, "in another dimension".'[6]

Lewis's third rapture came through poetry. He liked the story and vigorous rhythms of Longfellow's 'Saga of King Olaf'. 'But then, and quite different from such pleasures, and like a voice from far more distant regions, there came a moment when I idly turned the pages of the book and found the unrhymed translation of Tegner's Drapa.' He read:

> I heard a voice that cried,
> Balder the beautified
> Is dead, is dead –

The young Lewis knew nothing of Balder but was instantly

uplifted into huge regions of northern sky. 'I desired something with almost sickening intensity, something never to be described (except that it is cold, spacious, severe, pale and remote).'

As in his other 'experiences' he found himself 'at that very moment, falling out of that desire and wishing I were back in it'.[7]

These three ecstatic episodes were in a sense the central story of Lewis' life. He saw them as fleeting but exquisite raptures of Joy which were utterly desirable: 'I doubt whether anyone who has tasted it would ever . . . exchange [that Joy] for all the pleasures in the world.'[8]

Although these experiences started Lewis on a search which led him eventually to be 'surprised by joy', there seems something else which is significant. There is a universal here for spiritual awakening which is also meaningful for the prophet of the Lord. There is also a universal here for the creative impulses (a muse) which move the poet, the writer, the artist and the composer of music. It would seem that a level of consciousness was opened up to the child which surprised Lewis. It is quite possible that both the prophetic insight into reality and the creative imagery by which he communicated his message were equally awakened by those experiences.

We British have been brought up to be so wary of feelings (almost ashamed of them as far as our faith is concerned) that most of us rarely refer to what is, in fact, a common denominator in all true Christian spirituality.

Of course such testimony meets the greatest hostility from those who assume they are Christian but have actually had no conversion experience to speak of. Jesus told his disciples that there was great joy in heaven over one sinner who repented – more than over ninety and nine who needed no repentance (Luke 15:7).

If there can be such joy in heaven, should we not expect some in the Church? And can we expect it for the Church and not for the individuals who make up the

Church? Certainly we can expect this in a church engaged in evangelism.

Emotions essential to spiritual life

Jonathan Edwards insists that affections are essential to spiritual life. A hard heart is an unaffected heart – a heart not moved by divine truth. Edwards' pastoral heart compelled him to conclude that nothing of religious significance ever took place in a human heart if it was not deeply affected by such godly emotions.[9]

John White observes:

> Emotion comes from seeing, from understanding. I experience fear when I realise I might die during the operation the surgeon has suggested to me. The depth of my fear measures the clarity with which I see. My fears will be healthy if what I 'see' truly corresponds with reality, for emotion is a test of my grasp of reality.
>
> Emotions do not save me – except in the sense that they may startle and shake me into acting in the light of truth. When the Holy Spirit awakens people, he seems to cause them to perceive truth more vividly.[10]

Expression of the soul's movements

Edwards claimed that feelings expressed the soul's movements. Without them a radical change of direction was not likely to follow. This explained why some people were never changed by the Word of God. 'They hear . . . commands . . . warnings . . . and sweet invitations of the gospel. Yet they remain as before . . . because they are not *affected* [moved] by what they hear.'[11] Feelings affect our perception of truth and they also affect our wills.

It is as great a folly to ignore feelings with regard to our spiritual well-being as it would be when considering our physical health. A medical doctor has written: 'It is likely that there is not a bodily ailment which is not connected in some way with our hidden fears, our unexpressed griefs and our inability to rejoice without restraints.'[12] How much then might we also suffer spiritual trauma if we ignore our emotions?

Experience and Scripture

We have all had experiences which seemed to conflict with what we thought Scripture was saying. This is the time to go back to Scripture to see whether in fact we had understood both the Scripture and the experience correctly in the first place. 'We cannot always believe our eyes, our ears or our "spiritual experiences",' says psychiatrist John White, and it is very necessary for any who are 'eager to prophesy' to understand that.

But neither can we always trust our own or anyone else's 'exegesis' – our interpretation of Scripture.

> It is therefore helpful to have both exegesis and experience each in its proper place.
>
> There are twin perils here. The peril of re-interpreting Scripture in the light of experience, and the danger of forcing experience to conform to an incorrect notion of Scriptural truth (that is denying reality in some way). All of us incline in one of these directions or the other.[13]

And there is still another point that needs to be made. All of us have experience, whether we experience the supernatural or what we believe to be the complete absence of the supernatural. And all of us are inclined to interpret Scripture according to the experiences we have had, whether they be positive or negative, present or absent. To deny this tendency is to deny our very humanity.

The late Martin Lloyd Jones' comment on this is apposite:

> Fanaticism . . . is a terrible danger . . . It arises from

a divorce between Scripture and experience, where we put experience above Scripture claiming things that are not sanctioned by Scripture, or are perhaps even prohibited by it.

But there is a second danger and it is equally important that we should bear it in mind. The second is the exact opposite of the first, as these things generally go from one violent extreme to the other. How difficult it always is to maintain a balance! The second danger, then, is that of being satisfied with something very much less than what is offered in the Scripture, and the danger of interpreting the Scripture by our experiences and reducing its teaching to the level of what we know and experience; and I would say that this second danger is the greater danger of the two at this present time.[14]

Evaluation of experience

The possibility of seeming imbalanced here is exemplified in the following quote:

> The church has relied on authority and doctrine, on theological understanding about experience, instead of trusting the experiences themselves. But this new generation, both young and old, are not satisfied with authority; they want experiences of God and the Holy Spirit to verify the theology and the dogma. And this . . . is exactly what the modern church and modern theology are short on, even hostile to.
>
> Here may be one of the most important answers to our question: why is the church declining in numbers and influence, and even in its power to deal with the social implications of the faith it confesses? Because of this lack of experience of the divine, a gulf has become fixed between the religious strivings of men and the church's ministry to the modern world.[15]

The need for experience of God is essential, and the

evaluation of the religious experience of revelation, and the place of Christ 'the Word', still remains an open challenge to Christian theologians. First we need to define what kind of religious and/or spiritual experience we are talking about. Secondly we must ask whether the recipient of God-given revelation needs to be redeemed in order to receive and relay a word from God.

Christian experience

In response to the first challenge we may learn much from the work of the German theologian Friedrich Daniel Ernst Schleiermacher (1768–1834). He was regarded as the foremost theological thinker after Kant. Karl Barth said of him, 'He did not found a school, but an era.'

It was almost a century after his death, however, before his influence began to be felt in the English-speaking world. This was after his most important work, *The Christian Faith*, had been translated into English. 'Only now', writes Colin Brown, 'are we in the English-speaking world beginning to appreciate Schleiermacher's real significance for better or for worse.'[16]

Reared in a pastor's family among the Herrnhuter Brethren, Schleiermacher reacted against the deep pietistic devotion and missionary spirit of his home; a spirit which positively affected so many other Christian minds in the eighteenth century. The influence of the Herrnhuter Brethren extended via the Moravians to Lutheran Pietists and English Methodists, but was always belittled in academic circles for its emphasis on a personal experience of Jesus Christ.

After study at Halle (then a centre of radical thought in Germany) and Berlin, Schleiermacher became an accepted member of a brilliant circle of Romantic writers and poets. The group had rebelled against the rationalistic views of the Enlightenment, and stressed the role of mystery, imagination and feeling.

It was at this period that Schleiermacher published his

celebrated *On Religion: Speeches to its Cultured Despisers* (1799). He played a foremost role in the founding of the University of Berlin in 1810 and dominated its theological faculty. During the same period he pastored the fashionable Trinity Church of Berlin.

In later life Schleiermacher described himself once again as a pietist, but a pietist of a higher order. In his approach to biblical criticism, of which he was a pioneer in Germany, he sought to steer a middle way between secular philosophy and orthodox Christianity by taking Christian experience as his starting point.

Schleiermacher saw the essence of religion as being experience, and the essence of experience as the believer's sense of absolute dependence. Schleiermacher thought he was saving Christianity from the attack of reason as he learnedly described the feelings of dependence and union with ultimate reality which humans experience from time to time, and he argued that these experiences had a higher authority than reason.

The problem with this line of argument is, however, that vague experience (vague, not in terms of emotional sensation but in terms of theological definition) belongs to all religions and even to those who claim to have no religion at all to articulate.

Feelings of dependence

All religions have feelings of dependence, a taste for and sensation of union with the Infinite, the Ultimate, the Absolute, or as some call it 'the World Soul'. Plotinus (205–270), philosopher and mystic, was one whose teaching approximated to this.

Danger of illusion

But we are in grave danger of degrading or eroding our personality in some way should we ever become dependent upon our sense of oneness with the World Soul. If God is merely a 'World Soul', or a 'Life Principle of the Universe', then to merge with this 'Principle' as our ultimate objective in life must in the end lead to despair – because it amounts to idolatry which is the shortest path to illusion.

God is supremely personal, as he has revealed himself to be through Christ and the Holy Scriptures, and he wants us to be supremely personal, and to know and to love him. Seeking to merge with an impersonal 'World Soul' can lead only to personality suicide.

Those who know the God revealed to us in Christ and the Bible can deny neither their own significance as persons, nor the distinctive personality of the God whom they serve in Christ Jesus.[17]

Servants but not necessarily sons

With regard to the second question, as to whether a recipient of divine revelation must of necessity be included among the redeemed of the Lord at the time of reception, I have to say I do not believe this to be the case.

Although the revelation may lead to the individual's conversion, as with Abraham, Moses and others ('Abraham rejoiced to see my day – he saw it and was glad' – John 8:56; Moses 'regarded disgrace for the sake of Christ as of greater value than the treasures of Egypt, because he was looking ahead to his reward' – Heb. 11:26; also, nearer to our own times, we have the example of C.S.Lewis), not all who have had divine revelation have necessarily or demonstrably come to faith themselves.

We need to remind ourselves of a number of biblical examples which show that folk outside the Old and New Covenants also received messages through revelations from God:

1 Abimelech (Gen. 20:3)
2 Laban (Gen. 31:24)
3 Pharaoh's butler and baker (Gen. 40:5)
4 Pharaoh (Gen. 41:7, 15–26)
5 Midianite soldier (Judg. 7:13, 14)
6 Nebuchadnezzar (Dan. 2:1, 4, 36)

7 Wise men (Matt. 2:12)
8 Pilate's wife (Matt. 27:19)

It is also possible to experience being used as God's voice (as nature is used sovereignly by God – Ps. 19:1–4) or as God's servant (for the blessing of God's people) without necessarily enjoying the experience of God's sonship.

We recall God's anointing upon Cyrus his servant (Isa. 45:1) who overthrew the Babylonian Empire in 539 BC and sent the first party of Jews back to Palestine to rebuild their Temple – a magnificent service to the People of God, yet Cyrus never appears to have had a place within the Covenant of God.

Experience for experience's sake

Once it is appreciated that feelings must have their full and proper place in the experience of any Christian, there are still other dangers which need watching. Experience can so easily become an end in itself. Our experience is to help us to know, to appreciate, to acknowledge and to worship God. We live by faith and not by our feelings – though our feelings may be affected and our traumatised emotions may find healing, we are in fact saved by faith alone (Eph. 2:8–9). If our focus is on the experience and not on God we are in trouble or soon will be, as the following episode illustrates:

In his book *Surprised by Joy* C.S. Lewis tells of his foolishness as a boy in setting himself a particular standard for private prayer. He allowed no part of his prayers to God to pass muster unless it was accompanied by an experience of what he called a 'realisation' – a certain vividness of the imagination and the affections.

It became a nightly task to produce by sheer will-power a phenomenon which will-power could never produce, which was so ill-defined that he could never with any absolute confidence know whether it had occurred, and even when it did occur it was of very mediocre spiritual value. He had no one to show him that it was wrong to use one's prayers to extort from God something God may not have wished to give.

Night after night he sought 'to pump up realisations', not understanding that though sometimes these 'mystical favours'[18] are granted by a sovereign God to those in the process of waiting on him, yet they are in no way guaranteed. He had no one to counsel him. 'If only someone had read to me old Walter Hilton's warning that we must never in prayer strive to extort "by maistry" what God does not give!' he lamented. On reflection he realised that it had been this ludicrous burden of false expectations in prayer which led to the breakdown of his boyhood faith.[19]

Lewis reflects upon this breakdown later in his book.

> I had destroyed my religious life by a vicious subjectivism which made 'realisations' the aim of prayer; turning away from God to seek states of mind and trying to produce those states of mind by 'maistry' . . . And there lies the deadly error . . . Only when your whole attention and desire are fixed on something else . . . does the 'thrill' arise. It is a by-product.
>
> Its very existence presupposes that you desire not it but something other and outer. If by any perverse askesis or the use of any drug it could be produced from within, it would at once be seen to be of no value. For take away the object, and what, after all, would be left? – a whirl of images, a fluttering sensation in the diaphragm, a momentary abstraction. And who could want that?
>
> This, I say, is the first and deadly error, which appears on every level of life and is equally deadly on all, turning religion into self-caressing luxury and love into auto-eroticism. And the second error is, having thus falsely made a state of mind your aim, to attempt to produce it.[20]

Conclusion

Experiences of God are part and parcel of the Christian life. These may vary in manner, intensity and frequency according to our individual personalities, variable predicaments and particular circumstances. All of us, and especially those called to a prophetic ministry, must be open to all kinds of experience in our walk with God.

We must not manipulate these or demand them. God is forever Sovereign. He will speak in any way he pleases, be it through a peal of thunder (John 12:28, 29) or a gentle whisper (1 Kgs 19:12), for any purpose he pleases, to any person he pleases – and even, if need be, through an ass! (Num. 22:29–31).

24

WHAT ABOUT SECOND SIGHT?

The gift of 'second sight'
Contrary to what is frequently taught in certain Christian circles, we believe that clairvoyance is a neutral God-given faculty. It is a good gift – 'Every good and perfect gift is from above, coming down from the Father of the heavenly lights' (Jas 1:17) – but, like clairaudience, it has been readily exploited by the devil. The latter never gives any gifts to anyone but all too often usurps, for his own ends, the gifts that God has given to us.

J. Stafford Wright, an Old Testament Bible scholar and late principal of an Evangelical theological seminary, once wrote, 'The laws of telepathy are part of his [God's] creation',[1] so, we believe, are the laws of clairvoyance and clairaudience. In spite of Stafford Wright's courageous lead many Christians today are still ignorant of any positive teaching on the subject and are rightly fearful of deception. Besides this it is very perplexing not really knowing what one is meant to do, if, without in any way seeking it, one 'sees' something in the future – perhaps a disaster or a death.

Stafford Wright had no problem believing in the integrity of the writings of Old Testament prophets nor in the fact that some writers, such as Isaiah, were predicting, centuries before they happened, events which were later literally fulfilled.

He knew that other secular 'prophets' (see chapter 25) had accurately forecast future events, so why should God's people not be able to make similar predictions through the inspiration of the Holy Spirit? Some of the ready biblical examples are the Blessings by Jacob in Genesis 49 and by Moses in Deuteronomy 33, the forecast of exile and return in Leviticus 26, the naming of Josiah in 1 Kings 13:2, three centuries before his time, and the Book of Daniel.

'At the risk of becoming obscurantist,' he continues, 'I would also include the second part of the Book of Isaiah' (chapters 40–55). 'In those fifteen chapters the change of atmosphere is so marked that many critics have attributed the whole section to at least one later author writing after most of the events had occurred! The writer appears to have had the Babylonian exile in mind and even named Cyrus as the deliverer in ch.44:28 and 45:1.'[2]

Such things were nowhere near happening at the time of writing and if the author was Isaiah the son of Amoz who lived in the last part of the eighth century BC, as was the traditional view, then Isaiah was receiving some very accurate visions of the future. We believe this ability to predict so precisely is brought by the Holy Spirit through the God-given gift of second sight.

Instead of recognising that here is a gift of God in operation, and that a warning has been given by God that needs heeding, church leaders too readily dismiss such things as impossible or as being of the devil and therefore needing to be renounced. As we have said repeatedly in this book, revelations are not necessarily of something inevitable. God so often changes his mind when man changes his attitude. The Church needs to learn how to handle these things positively.

What is more, these ignorant judgments and sweeping statements about extra sensory perception of any kind have been passed down from one generation to another in our churches, and members in our congregations who have revelatory gifts have been made to feel guilty and unclean and the rest of the congregation very wary.

We accept that second sight is a gift that the enemy of souls is only too ready to exploit. But let us beware of refusing a gift of God. It is too easy for the Church to make innocent people feel uncomfortable about having such gifts. But it is not as bad as it was. In the sixteenth and early seventeenth centuries anyone who admitted to having this gift would have been in danger of being accused of witchcraft and burned at the stake.[3]

Towards the end of the seventeenth century John Aubrey carried out an investigation of second sight in Scotland. He included his findings in his *Miscellanies* in 1696.[4] He obtained much of his information by means of a questionnaire which he circulated, and in it were included two questions that are of special interest to us here. He wanted to verify:

1 'If the Second Sight be a thing that is troublesome and uneasy to those that have it, and as such would gladly be rid of?'

2 'If there be any person, or persons, truly godly, who may justly be presumed to be such, [who] have been known to have had this gift or faculty?'

He learned that the gift was certainly troublesome to at least one person, and that most people who had it would like to be free of it. It was clear that many possessors of the gift were mainly virtuous but scarcely godly.

One reply of special interest was from a minister in Inverness. He agreed that the gift was troublesome, but said that godly people frequently had it, though they regarded it as something sinful and proceeding from the devil. (We believe it very understandable that they would feel this way if that was what the Church had traditionally taught.) Sometimes, he said, public prayer had been made for their deliverance, and this had been effective! Very few people who had the gift would want to own up to having it still after having it confirmed as diabolical in such a public way. Such a gift of God could not in any case be cast out since the gifts and calling of God are irrevocable (Rom. 11:29).

Other Christian ministers have possessed the gift. There was a famous seer, the Rev. John Morrison, the minister at Petty in Inverness-shire from 1759 until 1774 who received prophecies about coming events including the imminent deaths of certain members of his parish.

Dr Kurt Koch provides an evaluation of the positive significance of second sight for Christians. He refers to the work of the German Dr Karl Schmeïng who developed what he called his 'eidetic' theory.[4]

Summary of eidetic theory

This eidetic capability is inborn in man. By means of this capability objects once registered can be seen again, as 'after-images' or 'intuitive images', in an external optic appearance before us after the light source is cut off or the object removed. This kind of eidetic vision is a form of perception generally found in childhood, which normally disappears with the onset of puberty.

This eidetic tendency may be retained to an advanced age in some persons; in artists, highly sensitive people, or in cases of late maturity due to inheritance or environment. Many clairvoyant phenomena can thus be explained on the eidetic basis as aftervisions.

The explanation of prevision is more difficult. Schmeïng thinks that people with eidetic gifts have a subconscious intuition, a teleological depth-vision. On the basis of this ability they would then be able, by means of a 'mental snapshot', to see as present before them the end of the development – through a combination of the data.

Those who have previsions usually have (1) a highly developed logical faculty for thinking, and (2) empathy. In this explanation of 'aftervision' and 'prevision'

Schmeïng insists that they are purely subjective experiences, excluding all metaphysical and metapsychical presuppositions.

Evaluation of the eidetic theory

After this brief introductory sketch, Dr Koch positively evaluates Schmeïng's theory. First he establishes that theology has no need to fear the eidetic theory in regard to biblical prophecy.

Anti-Christian and atheistic critics will, he concedes, adopt the position that it is now even easier for them to bring biblical prophecy and the religious visions of the Bible down to a rationalistic common denominator. In this way critics will attempt to reduce every religious vision to a natural, subjective occurrence, and think they have thereby demonstrated a delusion.

'This assault will in no way trouble theology,' Dr Koch believes. 'God has the power, and the habit, of making use of man's spirit, soul and body in His revelations to man. Is the Creator not permitted to use natural ordinances which He himself has created? He can make use of eidetic capabilities, too, in order to get through to man. Schmeïng has by means of his researches unwittingly come upon a further mode of revelation.'

We would question whether the giving of a new name to an old phenomenon is sufficient to call it 'a further mode'. The mode is probably as old as the creation of man. It is the name and the discussion on the subject which is novel. It remains for others to recast and further develop Schmeïng's work in a theological form.

The Greeks recognised that young virgins were especially gifted with second sight and would engage them to provide oracles. At Delphi two prophetesses were fully employed by the crowds seeking predictions and a third prophetess was usually at hand to help when there was an overflow. Plutarch described these young girls as of ordinary birth, with no prior training, no technical skill and no previously demonstrated talents that enabled them to prophesy. However, a willingness to act as intermediaries between the gods and the paying enquirers enhanced their 'art'. Where this was fully entered into Plutarch discerned that a form of possession would overwhelm the girls. He attributed this to the gods, while we would regard it as spirit-possession. The spirits transmitted their messages through the extra-sensory susceptibilities which are often present in pre-pubescent girls (more pronounced in some than others). Sometimes there was a notable change of voice when the spirit of the gods possessed them and this could be accompanied by hysterical behaviour and falling to the ground.

The case of a slave girl who earned money for her owners through prophecy is found in Acts 16:16. In that situation Paul eventually cast out the spirit. Like the girls at Delphi she had the potential for receiving spiritual messages which was natural and neutral. This was somehow easy for both the enemy of souls and her owners to exploit and she had clearly allowed a spirit to possess her and to dominate her gift. Once that spirit was cast out, the slave girl was much reduced in effectiveness and no longer useful to her owners who became angry with Paul because of their resulting loss of earnings.

The gift of second sight is found more frequently among adults in certain races. I have noticed in some of my friends in America that often those who have a more highly developed prophetic gift are Jewish or part Jewish, or Amerindian or part Amerindian. Some have traces from both races as their forefathers had intermarried. This is not to imply their forebears were either demonised or Holy Spirit filled. The gift itself is God-given but neutral.

The Irish, the Welsh and the Scots are said to possess this gift more commonly than the English. It is obviously possible for cultures to 'desensitise' themselves of such fine gifting – especially when it is 'ridiculed away' because it seems irrational.

Those who have lived among the Skolt Laplanders say that their powers of telepathy and prevision are highly developed and they are said to use telepathy to make appointments to meet one another across those wild frozen wastes.

John Sandford, who has written wisely and widely on the prophetic ministry, was descended (on his maternal side) from a long line of Osaga Indians, very devout and mystical, among whom were those who could charm snakes and had various 'mystical' powers. Both he and his parents were also involved in Rosicrucianism and other occult activity. After conversion to Christ John Sandford was exorcised of an evil spirit.[6]

He would probably say that he needed to renounce a gift which he had inherited and we would certainly respect his views, but our reading from his continuing prophetic ministry is that God accepted that the devil's part in it was renounced and the gift was truly cleansed through the blood of Jesus.

The gift itself, like all gifts, came originally from God and is now used very effectively, being rededicated to the service of God. We know of others from a similar background who are being used in a similar way today.

Seeing through touch
Before closing this chapter we must mention psychometry.[7] This term has been commonly applied to a certain faculty made more familiar by a Professor Buchanan in the middle of the nineteenth century.[8]

This gift is a neutral gift from God which can be used creatively to the glory of God or for the devil. A person with this gift or faculty can take some object, and after handling it, can disclose facts about the people who have handled the object, or who have been closely connected with it. The facts that are revealed contain the past, present or future of the person concerned.

One book to read on this subject, originally published

in French in 1922, was written by Dr Eugene Osty. It was translated and published in English under the title *Normal Faculties in Man: An Experimental Study*.[9] We mention the gift of psychometry here because it may have relevance in those cases where a godly 'prophet' has sometimes been known to put the flat of his hands to those of the person over whom he is prophesying.

25

DO NON-CHRISTIANS RECEIVE REVELATION FROM GOD?

We need to remind ourselves that even pagans have received messages through dreams by God's mercy and grace and have often been selected by God to be his instruments (e.g. Pharaoh's daughter – Exod. 2:5) for some holy purpose.

However, where revelation was concerned the relationship was scarcely more than that of a servant; not of a son or of a daughter (e.g. Belshazzar – Dan. 5:2).

For the purposes of this discussion anyone outside the covenants of God (unredeemed man) is pagan. We do not mean this offensively. S/he may seem a good pagan or a bad pagan but is still pagan. By this we cannot say that such people have no knowledge of God. The Jews even recognised some Gentiles as God-fearers.

It would seem clear from Scripture that all people have some knowledge of God, however much it might have been distorted by social custom and personal sin (Acts 14:17, 17:23; Rom. 1:19–22, 2:1–16).

Clearly there are times when God openly allows unbelievers to be used by him. The classic cases are those of Nebuchadnezzar whom God calls his 'servant' (Jer. 43:10) to bring judgment upon Israel, and Cyrus whom God calls 'his anointed' (Isa. 45:1) and whom God chose to be his instrument in the liberation of the Jews. It is also possible that Cyrus was influenced[1] by Zoroaster who himself believed he had divine revelations.

There are other biblical examples of non-believers

(Dan. 4:34–7) and God-fearers (Acts 10:2) praying to God. We know in the latter case that those prayers were heard (Acts 10:4). There is plenty of evidence to show that God is constantly speaking to men and women, young and old, right across the world.

Those who have been missionary evangelists in third world countries will have been almost surprised to have met people who readily recognised the truth of the gospel the first time they heard it. The inner light (John 1:9) had been beamed on to the truth and when the name of Jesus Christ was proclaimed they were the first to come to faith in him.

God prepares his people. John Bunyan tells in his book *Grace Abounding to the Chief of Sinners* of how often 'even in my childhood He did scare and affright me with fearful dreams, and did terrify me with dreadful visions; for often, after I had spent this and that other day in sin, I have in my bed been greatly afflicted, while asleep, with the apprehensions of devils and wicked spirits'.[2]

On one of our visits to Israel we were privileged to minister to a number of Messianic Jews – believers in Jesus – many of whom were able to tell us of powerful dreams, visions and voices. God spoke to them long before they came to Christ.

However, he will never allow his holy name to be used without divine consent, as demonstrated by the case of the seven sons of Sceva (a Jewish chief priest). They were practising exorcism in Jesus' name (without apparently trusting him as Messiah) and got badly beaten up by the demon (Acts 19:14–16).

Divine revelation to a heathen priest

Kurt Koch wrote up some of his own findings on the Revival in Indonesia in the 1960s in a book of that title.[3] In one place he relates the case of a heathen priest called Shem, formerly a sun-worshipper on the island of Soe who had somehow, through a process of direct revelation in hieroglyphics, had given to him the story of the creation.

When Shem later came into contact with the Bible he discovered that this account agreed with what was recorded in the first chapters there. Furthermore it was revealed to him that he would one day be visited by people who would tell him more about this faith. About a year later some Christians arrived at his village and he was healed of his leprosy although this did not lead to his immediate conversion to Christ, which did not take place for another twelve months. At that point he joined up with other believers who were meeting for worship in Soe.

He also started some meetings of his own for his former heathen followers. There seems to be a similarity here with some of the phenomena of the mid-nineteenth-century revival in Ulster.[4]

Pagans healing in the name of Jesus

Peter Wagner reported an interesting case from India which he wrote up in *Pastoral Renewal*,[5] under the heading 'A Third Wave':

Suba Roa was the headmaster of a governmental school in India, a member of one of the middle castes and a wealthy man. He hated missionaries and laughed at baptism. He thought of the church as an assembly of low castes (which in India it was).

His near neighbour and close friend fell ill. He was sick for two years and was gradually wasting away. He went to many doctors but to no avail. One night, while Suba Roa was asleep, the Lord appeared to him and said, 'If you will go and lay your hand on that man's head and pray in my name, I will heal him.'

Suba Roa woke up and laughed; he thought it was a funny dream and went back to sleep.

The next night the Lord Jesus stood by his side and said, 'If you go and lay your hand on that man's head and pray for him to be healed, I will heal him.' Suba Roa woke up. He did not laugh this time, and he did not go back to sleep; but he did not lay his hands on the sick man either. He thought, 'That's impossible!'

The third night the Lord Jesus appeared to him again. This time he got up at once and went to his neighbour. He laid his hand on the man's head and prayed for him, and in the morning the man said, 'I feel much better. Do it again.' The man was healed. Suba Roa became a believer.

According to Genesis 1:26, man was made in the image of God. It should not surprise us to learn that this would have included psychic gifts. But these gifts were greatly dulled through the Fall.

The German Abbot Wiesinger conjectures that 'all parapsychic faculties are relics of Paradise gifts, gifts belonging to the "spiritual" body of unfallen man'.

For the average Christian the word 'psyche' is still tainted by association with the occult and we should beware in the case of some 'psychic gifting', because where the Church may have no use for it and no idea how to handle it, the devil will be only too glad to take over such gifting for his own evil purposes.

The Greek word 'psyche' is actually a wholesome New Testament word meaning soul. We must redeem this word with biblical teaching and get it back into Christian parlance, since prophecy has consistently been regarded by serious Bible academics and theologians as a 'psychic' gift.[6]

Judith Tydings writes:

It would seem that some people are particularly sensitive and possess one or more psychic endowments . . . It seems logical that if such persons were to be completely committed to the Lord these 'powers' would also be at the service of the Lord and the Body

. . . It should be obvious then that the phenomena surrounding the Saints are varied in value and varied as to their causes.

Some phenomena are manifestations of psychic endowments, influenced by the grace of God; others are manifestations of charisms, yet others the visible consequences of the 'overflow' effects from the sanctifying work of God in the heart.[7]

According to some psychologists, the 'psyche' is the whole personality, including the ego and the unconscious. In older times clergy used to refer to their parishes as having so many 'souls'. They regarded people, quite properly, as souls.

There has been interesting discussion about whether we are souls or have souls. Some think the soul is in the body and others think the body is in the soul – this could account for the auras which are often seen round people.

The word 'psychic' is used as an adjective to describe the inner energy or activity of the 'psyche'.[8] The 'psychic' centre in each of us seems to have a vital role to play in the area of revelation from God. The 'psyche', which may be viewed as a kind of TV receptor, can be used for portraying pornography or propagating the gospel.

We can tune in our 'receptor' gift to the Lord or the devil, according to what spirit we are in. But again, because the Lord is sovereign, we suppose he could 'crash in' on to any screen at any time should he so desire; just as he did when he visibly flashed a message of doom on the wall before King Belshazzar when he was surrounded by his pagan drinking friends (Dan. 5:4,5) or audibly 'thundered' his voice from heaven (John 12:28) for the benefit of everyone round about.

26

FORBIDDEN FRUIT FOR PROPHETS

I have dealt with this subject in two other books, *Come, Holy Spirit* and *Some Said It Thundered* and in this chapter the material is repeated and amplified because it would be irresponsible, with a subject such as prophecy and in a book such as this, not to set out clearly my own position, which I believe to be a biblical one. For the latter part of this chapter I have adapted material from the late Canon Stafford Wright, principal of my theological college (now Trinity College, Bristol), to whose wisdom and godly scholarship I am greatly indebted.

Definition of the occult
The word simply means 'kept secret' – something hidden. There are many hidden things, secrets which belong to the Lord, which mankind is not permitted to know unless the Lord chooses to reveal them (Deut. 29:29).

Since mankind in his search for power has often sought illicit access to some of this hidden 'inside information', this has become known as occultism.

Satanic misuse and counterfeit of God's holy and supernatural power manifests itself in three areas – miracles, communication and knowledge of the future.

Scriptures which warn against the occult
Exod. 22:18, Lev. 19:26, Deut. 18:10–22 and 32:17, 2 Kgs 21:6, 1 Chr. 10:13, Ps. 106: 36–7, Isa. 8: 11–22, Acts 16:16–18 and 19:1, 1 Cor. 8:4 and 10:20, Rev. 16: 12–21

and 18:23 and 21:8 and 22:15.

Why the occult is forbidden

The Bible is addressing here those who turn in rebellion from the Lord God Almighty. Although the case may not be quite so damaging for the person who has never known the Lord and has turned to the occult in his genuine search for the truth, it is nevertheless a very dangerous place to be and the need for deliverance is urgent.

1 It places a person under the control of a power which is not of God – a power which is hostile to the Lord (1 Cor. 10:19–21).

2 The lust for certain knowledge which was forbidden to mankind was the cause of humanity's fall – occultism is an attempt to bypass God's specifically stated boundaries (Gen. 3:3–5).

3 The desire to dominate and control in occultism is opposed to God's will (Exod. 8:7–9; Isa. 47:12–15; Mic. 6:8).

4 It creates a dangerous, destructive and corruptive personality (Mark 3:27 and 5:1–20).

5 It is rank disobedience to God; this is rebellion and arrogance (1 Sam. 15:23).

There is a very high risk, therefore, for those who continue to prostitute God's gifts for the devil's purposes in occultism. We list the progressive dangers as follows:

1 Desensitisation of the soul – hardness of heart.

2 Deception – both the prophet and those who hear the prophecy are deceived. There may be an element of truth (Deut. 13:1–3 and Acts 16:16–18) but remember that fishermen often bait their hooks with real worms!

3 Occultism deliberately creates confusion about spiritual reality – darkness is reality, but it still leaves one unable to see.

4 Destruction – through occultism the soul is ultimately lost and destroyed. Should someone with any gift be found to have deliberately put this to the service of the devil

(New Agers, occultists, etc.) s/he will need to repent and rededicate the gift to the Lord.

It would be good for the *church leader to pray for* anyone who has repented and done this, that both the gifted and the gift should be cleansed through the blood of Jesus and the thoughts of the heart cleansed by the inspiration of the Holy Spirit.

We need a healthy understanding concerning the gift of prophecy because, with the rise of the New Age movement (actually a resurgence of Old Age movements) there will be an increasing number of false prophets about.

Christian concern

It is perfectly natural for Bible-loving Christians to be concerned on finding that some of their brothers in Christ are wanting to introduce the revelatory gifts of the Spirit into the worship and ministry of the church. This is especially likely to be the case where those particular members are perceived to be the lunatic fringe and are not well integrated or committed to the local Body of Christ.

But there are two other reasons why such endeavours will encounter stout opposition in the church.

1) The total unfamiliarity that many Christians have with anything of the kind. In spite of the fact that Paul writes to the Corinthians (1 Cor. 12:1) that he would not have them ignorant about the gifts of the Spirit, there are many Bible-loving Christians who are in truth very ignorant. More than that, they are very fearful.

The fact that their church leaders either address the issue of the gifts of the Spirit negatively or simply ignore the subject completely in their teaching and practice actually creates this fear. Never having been exposed to such manifestations in a wholesome environment, the laity remain suspicious.

2) The possibility of an occultist ploy! Such experiences or manifestations of the supernatural seem 'spooky'. There

is genuine fear and suspicion that this could be an 'apparently' biblical and innocent disguise for introducing something occult into the worship and ministry of the church.

On guard

It is always right to be on guard about such things. Men and women have a latent tendency when out of a true relationship with the Lord, to seek help from the occult. The tragic end of King Saul in this matter is common knowledge and is referred to later in the chapter.

Natural 'fallen' man tends to revert to natural religion, which is animism. This is simply a primitive man-made religion which takes its name from the Latin word *anima*, meaning breath, spirit or soul. Animist practice includes spirit worship (the invisible spirits to be found in the earth, air, fire, water, rocks, trees, mountains, and in animal life), necrolatry (worship of the dead) and naturism (worshipping the personification of such major 'powers' as the sun, the moon and the stars).

A common background

'It is not only the religion of wild and savage tribes before contact with civilisation who engage in animistic practices. Animism has frequently provided a spiritual dimension to the religious philosophies of Hinduism, Buddhism, Shintoism, and Confucianism.'[1]

It is also fundamental to the folklore of Christendom in Europe as well as the mythology of Egypt, Babylonia, Assyria, Greece, Rome and Scandinavia. In the Americas, before the conquests by Spain and Portugal, we find animism in a highly developed form as the religion of the Aztecs of Mexico, the Incas of Peru or the Araucanians of Chile. The evidence for animism in folk Catholicism in Latin America is also common knowledge.[2]

The 'Red' Indians of North America and Canada also had a developed system of animistic beliefs and practice. It is not so long ago that a number of churches across Britain were expressing concern at the language employed in the liturgical material supplied for the Women's World Day of Prayer which had been put together for the occasion by some Christian 'Red' Indians.

While we are in no position to challenge the integrity of the Christian faith in those who prepared the material, we do know that the language used caused real concern to some of the women using it while others refused to use it at all.

Prophecy in occultism – the case of Nostradamus

Michel de Notredame was a French-born (1503) Hebrew Christian (Roman Catholic) who was brought up a protégé of Catharine de' Medici. Whether he was ever more than a Christian in name seems doubtful. Legends about his prophetic powers abounded.

One legend held that around 1538 when he was in Italy he saw a young monk who had been a swineherd pass by in the street. Immediately Nostradamus knelt down and called him 'Your Holiness'. The monk was Felice Peretti who became Pope Sextus V in 1585, long after Nostradamus' death.

He made some very accurate prophecies. He seems, however, to have been a classic example of someone gifted who, wanting to enhance that gift but having no wise and godly counsellor, turned, either in ignorance or rebellion, to the occult practice of divination.[3]

He finally stumbled on a book called *De Mysteriis Egyptorum* written by the fourth-century Neoplatonist Iamblichus, published in 1547 at Lyons. By his confession his secret practice of what he learned there through the midnight hours actually evoked a great fear within him.

He was already trained as a medical doctor, and appears to have been a very competent and courageous one though his unorthodox remedies were suspect. His life soon became filled with tragedy (which may well be related to his spiritual rebellion) and he lost his beautiful young wife and two children in the Black Plague.

Soon afterwards he quarrelled with his brilliant medical partner and the practice was divided. His wife's family tried to sue him for the return of her dowry and finally he was accused of heresy by the Church. He fled for his life, fearing the Inquisition.

He became famous, however, for his book known as the *Centuries*, of which several editions were published between 1555 and his death in 1566. This book consists of sets of four-line verses, written in French, Latin and doggerel, and in these verses Nostradamus claimed to foretell up to the year AD 2000.

The most accessible book for studying him is *Nostradamus*, a biography by James Laver.[4] Some of the predictions are so startling that, as J. Stafford Wright comments: 'the casual reader may wonder whether there is something "fishy" about their publication, and whether they were really touched up after the event'.

This was Stafford Wright's own first impression,[5] so he consulted an edition dated 1605 in the British Museum Reading Room and found that the verses really do stand as they are quoted.

> The quatrains of Nostradamus usually appear to be obscure and nonsensical. Nostradamus claims that he deliberately made them obscure, because otherwise the civil and ecclesiastical leaders of the day would be likely to condemn his predictions, when they found many things in them that did not suit their own ideas. As a result one gathers the impression of a great deal of dross, amongst which gold may be found from time to time.

Nostradamus, who died in 1566, undoubtedly foresaw the French Revolution in 1789. A striking example of this comes from quatrain IX, 34:

> *Le part solus mary sera mitre:*
> *Retour: Conflict passera le thuille*
> *Par cinq cens: un trahyr sera tittre*
> *Narbon: et Saulce par coutaux d'huille.*

This has been translated by Laver as follows:[6]

> The husband alone will be mitred. Return.
> A conflict will pass over the tiles by five hundred;
> a traitor will be titled Narbonne;
> and from Saulce we have oil in quarts.

'We may disagree with small details of this translation, and the 1605 edition has slight differences of punctuation; but the main words are not in dispute,' writes Stafford Wright.[7] He continues:

> The first two lines could refer to the mob who invaded the Tuileries and compelled Louis XVI to wear the red cap of liberty, which was not unlike a mitre. This may not sound very convincing.
>   But when we come to the two names, we are bound to take notice. The Comte de Narbonne was Louis XVI's War Minister, who was intriguing with the revolutionaries, and so was justly named 'a traitor'. The other man was actually named Sauce. He was the Procureur of Varennes, who arrested Louis XVI on his attempted flight: he was by trade a grocer and chandler.

Carlyle in his *French Revolution* describes the incident 'Alas, alas! Sieur Sausse, Procureur of the Township, Tallow-chandler also, and Grocer, is there, with official grocer-politeness.'

The gloomy predictions of Nostradamus, full of 'divers calamities, weepings and mournings' and 'civil sedition and mutination of the lowest against the highest', were translated into English and published in 1559. The book was soon dismissed by Archbishop Parker as a 'fantastical hotch-potch' and the government took legal action against the booksellers who sold it.[8]

The preachers of God's Word thundered against the circulation of these prophecies and it was right for the Church to sound clear warnings. Time was to reveal that some of the prophecies of Nostradamus would seemingly come to pass. If there were cause to fear such prophecies the Christian Church has the power and authority to revoke them in the name of Jesus Christ.

Increased awareness of the occult

Today there is an increased awareness of the rise of occult practice in the West with its witchcraft, satanism and magic. It is not, therefore, surprising to find among some Christians real fear and suspicion of prophecy and other gifts of the Spirit as they are being revived in the life of the Church. There is a natural suspicion that they could be a cover for some kind of occult take-over.

In any situation where someone believes that s/he has a message from a supernatural source (a hotline to God) which s/he makes known to the community there is always the potential for counterfeit. False prophets were the bane of Israel, as they have been of the Church down the ages.[9]

Scripture examined

We need to examine Scripture to see what sources man was permitted to communicate with and what not.[10] The Bible, as we have seen, is emphatically opposed to man's attempting any communication at all with the spirits of the dead (Deut. 18:11) or the elemental spirits of the universe (Col. 2:8).

To simplify our understanding of the occult practice reported in the Old Testament, there are two particular Hebrew words we need to know – *ob* and *yiddeoni*. Following J. Stafford Wright we take the liberty of forming the plurals for these two unfamiliar Hebrew words by simply adding an 's'.

1 *ob* – In the King James Authorised Version of the Bible this word is always translated as 'familiar spirit' but it can also imply the medium (Lev. 20:27) who is communicating with this familiar or controlling spirit. The precise meaning of *ob* is uncertain, but a similar word in Arabic means 'to return'.

2 *yiddeoni* – In the King James Authorised Version this word was always translated as 'wizard'. *Yiddeoni* is connected with the Hebrew word 'to know'.

Communicating spirits

Both words appear to involve a communicating spirit. The main references are quoted below.

'Do not turn to *obs* (mediums) or seek out *yiddeonis* (spiritists), for you will be defiled by them. I am the Lord your God' (Lev. 19:31).

'I will set my face [says the Lord] against the person who turns to *obs* (mediums) and *yiddeonis* (spiritists) to prostitute himself by following them, and I will cut him off from his people' (Lev. 20:6).

'A man or woman who is an *ob* (medium) or *yiddeoni* (spiritist) among you must be put to death' (Lev. 20:27, cf. Exod. 22:18).

'Let no one be found among you . . . who is an *ob* (medium) or *yiddeoni* (spiritist) or who consults the dead (necromancer)' (Deut. 18:11 – this is part of a more comprehensive list of occult practices to be found among the Canaanite inhabitants who were being driven out of the promised land).

'The nations you will dispossess listen to those who practise sorcery or divination. But as for you, the Lord your God has not permitted you to do so' (Deut. 18:14).

Backsliding monarchs

Saul had expelled the *obs* (mediums) and the *yiddeonis* (spiritists) from the land (1 Sam. 28:3). Then in his rebellion and desolation he sought out an *ob* (medium).

'Find me a woman who is a medium (*ob*), so that I may go and enquire of her.' They replied, 'There is one (an *ob*) in Endor.' Saul ordered her to 'consult an *ob* (controlling spirit) and bring up for me the one I name' (1 Sam. 28:7–8). This was his crowning act of rebellion against God.

'Saul died because he was unfaithful to the Lord; he did not keep the word of the Lord, and even consulted an *ob* (medium) for guidance, and did not enquire of the Lord. So the Lord put him to death' (1 Chr. 10:13–14).

Saul was not the only king who led God's people astray. Among the list of King Manasseh's sins it is recorded that he used an *ob* and *yiddeonis* (2 Kgs 21:6, 2 Chr. 33:6).

Josiah gets rid of mediums

The reforming king Josiah 'got rid of the *obs* (mediums) and *yiddeonis* (spiritists)' (2 Kgs 23:24).

Isaiah is relentless in driving home God's law on this detestable practice: 'When men tell you to consult *obs* (mediums) and *yiddeonis* (spiritists), who whisper (high pitch) and mutter (low pitch), should not a people enquire of their God? Why consult the dead on behalf of the living? To the law and to the testimony!' (Isa. 8:19–20).

'Brought low, you will speak from the ground; your speech will mumble out of the dust. Your voice will come ghostlike (literally, 'shall be as an *ob*') from the earth; out of the dust your speech will whisper' (literally, 'chirp', as in Isaiah 8:19) (Isa. 29:4).

Spiritist mediums

Stafford Wright[11] has suggested that since in the Bible the word *ob* is sometimes used by itself, whereas *yiddeonis* is always linked with an *ob*, it would be reasonable to suppose that the *ob* is the main control spirit and the *yiddeonis* are the spirits called up by the control spirit or *ob*.

The Hebrew, however, does not only imply that an *ob* is a control spirit, but may also be a man or a woman (Lev. 20:27). A person who has a controlling spirit can become a medium. Most modern-day mediums appear to have one or two controlling spirits in tow. Mediums open themselves up to being channels for communication with spirits. The punishment for mediums in the Old Testament was death.

Although the New Testament does modify some of the social and food regulations of the Old Testament, it never withdraws the ban on contact with spirits. Instead the New Testament encourages Christians to build up a relationship with God the Father through Jesus Christ.

It is then a perfectly proper concern for the Church today to beware lest in fostering the exercise of the gifts of revelation we should overlook the clear warnings given concerning all the pagan and occult practices plainly forbidden in the Bible.

Detestable practices

The operation of the proper revelatory gifts of the Spirit, which are holy and supernatural in origin, should be positively encouraged but there are a number of abominable pagan practices from the occult which are to be strictly rejected.

Solemn warnings were repeatedly given to God's chosen people who were about to enter the promised land (Deut. 19:9–13). They were to beware of the forbidden practices employed by the Canaanite inhabitants who were being driven out precisely because of such abominations as are listed below:

1 Februation. This is the terribly cruel practice of passing offspring of either sex through fire (as sacrifices to heathen gods – Deut. 12:31 – supposedly to placate

their pagan god for obtaining some favour or averting some calamity).

2 Divination (see below for amplification).

3 Sorcery. The securing of a desired answer by tampering or introducing secret influences (magic) to operate in one's favour.

4 Soothsaying. This is especially linked with divination. Both are arts for unlawfully obtaining knowledge of the future. There is an alternative translation for Numbers 23:23 which is very pertinent: 'There is no omen in Jacob and no divination in Israel. At the appropriate time in Jacob and Israel God gives the revelation.' Whenever it is the right time God will speak to his people by the prophets. The verse makes a clear distinction showing the legitimate means for obtaining information from God.

5 The practice of witchcraft.

6 Spell-casting – which effected what amounted to curses. Ezekiel refers to certain women who made use of magic wristbands and veils to put death curses on people and to give assurance of personal safety to others (Ezek. 13:17–23).

7 Mediumistic practices working with a control spirit (already referred to).

8 Spiritism (also already referred to).

9 Necromancy – consulting the dead – a comprehensive term which included all forms of spiritism and superstition.

Immorality and idolatry

These detestable practices – they were associated with gross immorality (Lev. 20) and idolatry (Lev. 26) – were a constant temptation to the people of Israel when they fell into backsliding and only served to prove that the warnings were indeed all too necessary.

Manasseh, King of Judah, is on record as leading Israel into doing more evil than the nations who had been driven out by the Lord (2 Kgs 21:6, 9).

Divination

This was the most prevalent of occult activities in ancient heathendom. There are numerous references to this in the Old Testament (e.g. Gen. 44:5, Lev. 19:31, Deut. 18:10–12, 1 Chr. 10:13, Isa. 44:25, Jer. 29:8b, Ezek. 21:21, Hos. 4:12, Mic. 3:6f and Zech. 10:2).

Though sometimes in common parlance the word is used more casually for things, like guessing, which are not necessarily contrary to the Lord's will, the divination which is forbidden is linked with the art of soothsaying, i.e. the unveiling of hidden (occult) and forbidden knowledge from the past, present and future. Divination has appeared in every epoch of human history. From the Old Testament we learn of Canaanite charmers, wizards (a male medium, literally, 'one who knows'), augurs, necromancers, etc.

In nearly every part of the world where Christian missionaries have pioneered there has been opposition from heathen practitioners of divination, who have used it to resist the gospel.

Schwendimann's basic catalogue

To help identify some methods of divination in today's society we include Schwendimann's catalogue with some of our own additions below.

Arithmancy (from numbers)
Coffee-grout reading
Horoscopy (star divination)
Geomancy (dot reading)
Cartomancy (card reading)
Crystallomancy (crystal-gazing)
Capromancy (smoke reading)
Dice reading
Liver reading
Lead pouring
Pyromancy (fire reading)
Selenomancy (moon divination)

Sun divination
Sleep reading
Tephromancy (ash reading)
Tea leaves
Pendulums
White of egg in drinking glass
Bird formation in flight

Solemn warnings

The Old Testament solemnly pronounces the death penalty upon those who fall into such heathen rites of divination (Exod. 22:18, Lev. 20:6, 27, Deut. 17:5).

Any Christian believer today who seeks to be open to revelations from the Spirit of the Lord God Almighty, through Jesus Christ, certainly needs to beware of such practices. They are the arts of witchcraft which is equated with rebellion against the Lord (1 Sam. 15:23). Such practices lead to moral defilement, abominations in the land and ultimately to destruction. Remember Balaam! (Num. 24:1–2, 2 Pet. 2:15 and Jude v.11).

CONCLUSION

Our hope is that this material may go a little way towards helping churches where the Holy Spirit is beginning to move in this manner.

We have observed and evaluated some of the spiritual gifting which is edifying the contemporary Church. We have kept to the fore the mistakes, both of those who have misused the spiritual gifts in the past, and of those in authority who have responded with deadening over-reaction. It is our prayer that the contents of this book may prove a small contribution to the growing corpus of wisdom available to God's people on the subject of prophecy, as they seek to move forward in this gift for the edification of the Church, which today is to be found generally weak, comfortless and discouraged. According to Paul, the gift of prophecy is given to strengthen, comfort and encourage (1 Cor. 14:3) – exactly what is needed to turn the whole situation around. There is nothing so upbuilding in faith, hope and love as a prophetic word from the Lord.

We end on the challenging note of C.M. Robeck Jr:[1] 'The renewal of interest in the gift of prophecy speaks well for the church at the end of the twentieth century . . . Insofar as Christians listen for the voice of God, discern what is that voice, and act upon it, this "charisma" will be of profit to the whole church as it faces the challenge of the new millennium.'

APPENDIX

REVELATION AND THE
HUMAN BRAIN

To help us in our understanding of prophecy we offer a
conjecture. We have no authority to teach this in any sense
as an article of faith. We are merely suggesting a possible
and plausible location in the physical human brain for the
operations of the gifts of the Spirit.

The human brain
In layman's language the brain is a double organ consisting
of two similar-looking hemispheres joined together by
several bundles of nerve fibres (the corpus callosum).
These two hemispheres are physiologically identical, but
develop very distinct, though complementary, functions.

For almost a century it has been known that human
powers of speech reside primarily in the left hemisphere
of the brain. (To avoid complications here we overlook the
fact that 5 per cent of the population, indeed one-third of
all left-handed people, have their powers of speech located
in the right side and their powers of non-verbal thinking in
the left side of the brain.)

It appears that the billions of neurons in the two
hemispheres are not fully organised until about the fifth
year of life. Prior to that time the left hemisphere could
be removed (following an accident, for example) and
the right hemisphere would then develop speech abilities
and so on.

Fundamental differences in hemispheres

At the California Institute of Technology in the 1960s
Dr Roger Sperry (with his students Michael Gazzaniga
and Jesse Levy) found that each half of the brain has
its own separate train of conscious thought and its own
memory stores. The two sides of the brain also think in
fundamentally different ways.

Nevertheless the two halves of the brain have a kind
of partnership, in which the left hemisphere usually han-
dles language and one-step-at-a-time logical thinking pro-
cesses, while the right side copes with things difficult to put
into words by using picture images. The right hemisphere
can recognise a face in a crowd or put together the pieces of
a jigsaw, something which would normally baffle the left.

Hemisphere specialisations

Left hemisphere abilities	*Right hemisphere abilities*
Speech	Tone, facial expression and body language
Reading	Facial recognition
Writing	Understanding of metaphor
Abstract categorising	Spatial and holistic perception
Musical ability	Musical sense
Verbal memory consolidation	Form memory consolidation
Detail in drawing	Proper form in drawing
Left–right discrimination	Ability to find a way
	Dreams/visions

Each hemisphere of the brain is capable of inhibiting
the other if it feels more strongly that it can solve the
presenting problem. The working relationship between
the left and right hemispheres is developed in much the
same way as any partnership develops. A slight advantage
for one hemisphere is magnified with time as its partner
recognises that it is out of its depth and yields to the other
to tackle the particular task in hand.

Two memory banks

A memory can actually exist in the right hemisphere which affects behaviour (much of our emotional behaviour is under the control of the right hemisphere of the brain), yet this same memory can be unknown and unavailable to the left hemisphere which is the locus of verbal consciousness.

A person can have a different set of childhood memories, one in the left and one in the right hemisphere of the same brain. For example, a father may approach his child to punish him or her for some misdemeanour. The father says: 'I am going to punish you because I love you and this beating is for your own good.' The child hears this in the left hemisphere of the brain and it is stored away in the memory bank accordingly. But in the right hemisphere is recorded what the child has seen in the father's face and heard in the father's voice: a message of anger and hatred.

In our ministry of inner healing we are trying to help the counsellee to get fully in touch with the emotion, which will take him back to the original trauma, which can then be dealt with appropriately. It is not possible for the troubled person to fully verbalise such hurts because they are stored in the right hemisphere of the brain which does not express itself so much in words. The message was never sent to the memory bank in that way in the first place.

But the Holy Spirit, who searches all things (1 Cor. 2:10), can help the sufferer to feel the buried emotion, track the original trauma and guide the counsellee into how to bring healing to it.

Bad habits in the brain

Ideally each hemisphere does what it is best equipped to do, but bad habits may easily develop if the wrong hemisphere prevails and prevents a person's true abilities from being expressed. One of the benefits of having two kinds of thinking – one visual and one verbal – is that they can work together in any task. The nerve connection between the hemispheres makes it possible for them to exchange information, though only very little from the right hemisphere can be verbalised.

Indulging the left hemisphere

Modern educational theory has been dominated by what is essentially a left-hemisphere verbal concept. This has become the hemisphere of the brain which is most highly prized and encouraged – one could even say 'self-appointed' since the left hemisphere decided it to its own advantage. Any partnership where one partner is silent and unseen is bound to develop in a lopsided manner. Since the left hemisphere is the talking part of the brain it has been easy for it to talk down the other side; to assume that it alone can think and has memories of any significance and requires training. As the left hemisphere is strongly attracted to logic and the deductive approach in the discovery of knowledge through reasoning, the right hemisphere of the brain has been unengaged. The non-verbal side of knowledge has tended to be ignored and undervalued in most parts of our Western culture, to our great loss.

Right hemisphere atrophy

A right hemisphere can become virtually atrophied, making the owner of it shamed and inept, not just in sports, art and dance, but in the truly creative side of intellectual or spiritual pursuits. Intuitive judgments are not arrived at step by step, but in a flash. As with any ability, intuitive judgment can be developed or disallowed. Abilities will be developed according to the amount they are used and trusted. Most creative breakthroughs are the result of an 'intuitive leap' which is then analysed in logical terms by observing the result almost as an outsider.

This is borne out by the testimony of the late developer (in the disciplines of the left hemisphere) but brilliant mathematician Albert Einstein, who said: 'The words or the language, as they are written or spoken, do not seem to play any role in my mechanism of thought.' Aristotle said much the same in his discourse (in *De Anima*) when he wrote: 'It is impossible to think without a mental picture.'

Archimedes made a famous intuitive leap to discover the principle that bears his name. His protector had asked him his opinion about the gift of a gold crown which he suspected had been adulterated with silver. Archimedes knew that he could tell whether the gold crown was pure by its weight if only he could measure its volume – something which seemed impossible to do without melting it down. Then, one day, as he was getting into his bath, the water level rose before his eyes, as he had noticed many, many times before. But this time Archimedes saw that the rising water was the solution to his problem. The volume of water being displaced was equal to the volume of his body being immersed. So excited was he by his discovery that he ran through the streets crying, 'Eureka!' ('I have found it!') – a word which has brought him almost more fame than the discovery itself.

Where do the gifts come in?
Freud talks of dreams as 'the royal road to the unconscious'. We all dream several times a night. According to scientific testing, dreaming occurs primarily in the right hemisphere of the brain. Certainly the content of many dreams has the characteristic of right hemisphere activity. Dreams are often non-verbal, emotional, image-full and lacking in both logic and time-sequence. Most people who claim they do not dream probably have difficulties in transferring the right hemisphere images to their verbal consciousness. It seems reasonable to postulate that the right hemisphere is the operations room of the gifts of the Holy Spirit.

Glossolalia or speaking in tongues – right hemisphere speech

Rock, blues and jazz musicians have a term called 'soul' which represents the complete elimination of intellectualism in favour of feeling. Too much intellectual training tends to destroy the quality of 'soul'.

Associate New Testament Professor, Russell P. Spittler, at Fuller Theological Seminary, California, says that his interest in such an hypothesis (as the right hemisphere location for tongues) was first triggered by Professor F.F. Bruce's definition of 'glossolalia' in his study on 1 Corinthians. Spittler believes that glossolalia is a form of right hemisphere speech. He suggests that speaking in tongues has its own transrational kind of meaning – not irrational but supra-rational; deeply personal, interior, existential, non-cognitive but nevertheless meaningful. 'Twice in my own experience at least,' he writes, 'glossolalia came as a response to beauty in nature.'[1]

The mind of a child

Jesus expressly states that the Kingdom of God belongs to little children (Mark 10:14). Children are plainly included in God's Kingdom. Jesus also said that only those who are willing to change and become as little children can enter the Kingdom of God (Matt. 18:3).

Until about the age of five the unsophisticated child innocently trusts the dictates of either hemisphere of the brain. Then the commitment of the left hemisphere to verbalising commences as his teachers concentrate on developing the functions of that particular hemisphere.

On one occasion Jesus reminded his critics of the Scripture which says, 'From the lips of children and infants you have ordained praise' (Ps. 8:2, Matt. 21:16). The Greek here for children is *nepios*, which means non-speakers (literally 'without the power of speech' and metaphorically 'to the unsophisticated in mind and trustful in disposition').[2] Does this not suggest to us that the right hemisphere is the broadcasting centre of the brain for praise? In other words, the intuitive and emotional part of man, which receives spatial, holistic, creative and mystical concepts, is the studio for expressing his praise.

Some right hemisphere feelings and revelations are also communicated via the corpus callosum to the left hemisphere to be verbalised and transmitted as adequately as possible from there. The seventh-century Northumbrian Saint Cuthbert received a prophetic message from a three-year-old child (when Cuthbert himself was only eight). The child called the boy 'a priest and a bishop'. This was prophetic insight.[3] This is what Cuthbert came to be.

But much truth and feeling is impossible to communicate in words. However, while it may not be verbalised, it may be vocalised and expressed in 'tongues' – like the meaningful gurgles of a non-speaking infant.

Further, when the Seventy-two reported back from their first mission (Luke 10) they said, 'Lord, even the demons submit to us in your name.' Jesus responded by praise to God the Father 'Because you have hidden these things from the wise and learned, and *revealed them to little children*. Yes, Father, for this was your good pleasure.' Why did he speak of these grown men as little children? Was he in fact commending them for trusting the non-verbal but intuitive side of their brains to discern the presence of demons and to exercise the gift of 'works of power' (miracles) in casting them out? Hidden things (revelation from God) had been perceived by those who allowed the right side of the brain to be increasingly operative. As a result of their training with Jesus the disciples were willing to be childlike towards God. They adopted the mind of a non-rationalising child which allowed the impulses from the right hemisphere to be trusted and acted upon.

When Christians begin to allow impulses from the right hemisphere equal rights with the insistences of the left they are on the way to developing a fuller means of spiritual communication with God the Father – the safeguard being that the mind is renewed by the Holy Spirit and dedicated to Christ, proving 'what is that good, and acceptable, and perfect, will of God' (Rom. 12:2 KJV).

Without such an open approach, inevitably many parts of the right hemisphere (which give spiritual perception to the child and the childlike) will simply atrophy through disuse – to the spiritual detriment of the Church. If this hypothesis is capable of further substantiation, it could contribute to a reconciliation through a new understanding within the Church – so many of whose leaders have been selected on the basis of knowledge filtered through a highly developed left hemisphere of the brain.[4]

NOTES

Details of publisher and place of publication, where known, may be found in the Bibliography.

INTRODUCTION

1 Charles Dickens, *A Tale of Two Cities*, p. 1.
2 J.E.C. Welldon, *The Revelation of the Holy Spirit*, p. 296.

1 IS THERE A BIBLICAL CASE FOR PROPHECY TODAY?

1 David Pawson, *Renewal*, Oct. 1990.
2 K. McDonnell and G.T. Montague, *Christian Initiation and Baptism in the Holy Spirit*, p. 79.

2 WHAT DO WE MEAN BY PROPHECY AND PROPHETS?

1 J.I. Packer, *Keep in Step with the Spirit*, p. 217.
2 John Godwin quoted by Geoffrey F. Nuttall in *The Holy Spirit in Puritan Faith and Experience*, p. 75.
3 James Houston introducing Os Guinness in *The Mind on Fire – Blaise Pascal*, p. 21.
4 Kenneth Slack, *Martin Luther King*.
5 David Edwards, *Church Times* review of Diana Collins' book *Partners in Protest*, Oct. 2, 1992.
6 D.W. Hardy and D.F. Ford, *Jubilate*: *Theology of Praise*, p. 137.
7 David Pytches, *Some Said It Thundered*.
8 C.M. Robeck Jr, article in *Dictionary of Pentecostal and Charismatic Movements*, ed. Stanley M. Burgess and Garry B. McGee, p. 728.

9   This is a view of Bishop Graham Dow expressed personally to the author.

10 Max Turner, *Spiritual Gifts Then and Now*, pp. 7–64, especially p. 9.

11 Ibid., p. 16.

12 Graham Houston, *Prophecy Now*, p. 38.

13 Ibid., p. 57.

14 Roger Beckwith, *The Old Testament Canon of the New Testament Church*, p. 370.

15 Ibid.

16 Ibid., p. 371.

17 Josephus, *The Jewish Wars*, p. 221.

18 Ibid., pp. 221–2.

19 Wayne Grudem, *The Gift of Prophecy in 1 Corinthians*, pp. 54–113.

20 Roger Beckwith suggests that the report mistakes Simon the Just for Simon Kantharas who became High Priest in AD 41, op. cit., p. 375.

21 David Aune, *Prophecy in Early Christianity and the Ancient Mediterranean World*, p. 147.

22 It would be most misleading to suggest that my old college friend, the Rev. Dr Beckwith, would endorse the line being taken by the author here. His learned study is cited because it provides useful examples gathered into one book which is clearly referenced.

23 Beckwith, op. cit., pp. 369–76.

24 Houston, op. cit., pp. 67, 47.

25 John Stott, *The Message of Thessalonians*, p. 128.

26 Thomas Aquinas, *Summa Theologica*, 2.2, p.7 quoted by R. Faricy in 'The Writings of Thomas Aquinas', *Theological Renewal* 19 (1981), pp. 16–21. Cf. Houston, op. cit., p. 19.

27 John Stott, *The Contemporary Christian*, p. 104.

28 Michael Green, *To Corinth with Love*, p. 75.

29 David Pawson, 'Prophecy and Scripture', *Renewal*, Oct. 1990.

30 Ibid.

31 Paul Cain at the Beulah Word and Spirit Conference, Wembley, Oct. 1992.
32 Green, op. cit.
33 William K. Kay, *Prophecy*, p. 55.
34 John and Paula Sandford, *The Elijah Task*, p. 24.

3 WHAT KIND OF A PERSON IS A PROPHET?

1 Julian of Norwich, *Revelations of Divine Love*, ed. Halcyon Backhouse and Rhona Pipe, p. xx.
2 J. I. Packer, *A Passion for Holiness*, p. 211.
3 John Paul Jackson, *Streams of Shiloh*.

4 HOW CAN WE LEARN TO BE PROPHETS?

1 Carlo Carretto, *The Desert in the City*, p.15.
2 Donald S. Whitney, *Spiritual Disciplines for the Christian Life*, p. 176.
3 John Wimber, *Power Evangelism*, p.195.
4 Joyce Huggett, *Listening to God*.
5 Klaus Bockmuehl, *Listening to the God who Speaks*.
6 Huggett, op. cit., p. 221.
7 Sergius Bolshakoff, *The Russian Mystics*.
8 Barry Kissell, *Walking on Water*, pp. 110–15.
9 James Ryle, *A Hippo in the Garden*, ch. 3, pp. 46–68.
10 John and Paula Sandford, *The Elijah Task*, p. 223.
11 Huggett, op. cit., pp. 142–3.
12 David Hay, *Exploring Inner Space*, p. 190.
13 David Pytches, *Some Said It Thundered*, p. 124.
14 David Parker, from a seminar talk given at St Andrew's Church, Chorleywood, Herts, in October 1992.
15 John and Paula Sandford, op. cit., p. 62.
16 Ibid., p. 63.
17 John Paul Jackson, *Streams from Shiloh*.

5 HOW IS PROPHETIC GIFTING INITIATED?

1 John and Paula Sandford, *The Elijah Task*, p. 49.
2 John L. Nickalls (ed.), *Journal of George Fox*, ch. 17.

3 Ibid., pp. 20–1.
4 Marcel Driot, *Fathers of the Desert*, p. 25.
5 Robert Cruden, *Concordance*, p. 475.
6 John Rea, *The Holy Spirit in the Bible*, p. 222.

6 HOW IS PROPHECY RECEIVED FROM GOD?
1 Cyprian, *Epistle*, 16:4 and 7.
2 Cyprian, *Epistle*, 11:1–4.
3 Clifford Hill, *Prophecy Past and Present*, pp. 36–9.
4 W.R. Inge, *Christian Mysticism*, p. 219.
5 Agnes Sanford, *Sealed Orders*, p. 29.
6 John A. Sanford, *God's Forgotten Language*, p. 121.
7 Iain Murray (ed.), *George Whitefield's Journals*, p. 66.
8 John Finney, *Finding Faith Today – How Does It Happen?*, p. 49.
9 Joyce Huggett, *Listening to God*, p. 94.
10 Magazine of the Africa Inland Mission International.
11 John White, *When the Spirit Comes with Power*, pp. 199–200.
12 Catherine Marshall, *Something More*, pp. 188–94.
13 David Pytches, *Some Said It Thundered*, p. 86.
14 Ibid., p. 69.
15 Ibid., pp. 75–6.
16 J. Cameron Peddie, *The Forgotten Talent*, pp. 37, 38.
17 Agnes Sanford, op.cit., pp. 281–3.
18 Kallistos Ware, *The Orthodox Way*, p. 54.
19 John and Christine Huggett, *It Hurts to Heal*, p. 58.
20 Rosemary Attlee, *William's Story*, p. 283.
21 E.J. Young, *My Servants the Prophets*, p. 56.
22 Bill Hamon, *Prophets and the Prophetic Movement*, pp. 70–5.
23 Inge, op. cit., p. 221.
24 M.J. Cartledge, 'Prophecy in the Contemporary Church: A Theological Examination', M.Phil. thesis, 1989, Library of London Bible College.
25 Francie Lygo – a report about her in *HTB in Focus*, Oct. 11, 1992.

26 David Aune, *Prophecy in Early Christianity and the Ancient Mediterranean World*, p. 86.
27 Ibid.

7 HOW IS PROPHECY ANALYSED?
 1 Wayne Grudem, *The Gift of Prophecy in 1 Corinthians*, pp. 129–30; also Graham Houston, *Prophecy Now*, p. 97.
 2 David Pytches, *Some Said It Thundered*, p. 127.
 3 Wayne Grudem, *The Gift of Prophecy*, pp. 94–102.

8 HOW IS PROPHECY RELAYED?
 1 John and Christine Huggett, *It Hurts to Heal*, p. 57.
 2 Bill Hamon, *Prophets and Personal Prophecy*, p. 118.
 3 Ibid., p. 42.
 4 George Canty, *The Practice of Pentecost*, p. 135.
 5 George Mallone, *Arming for Spiritual Warfare*, ch. 9.

9 HOW IS PROPHECY EVALUATED?
 1 Peter Masters, *The Healing Epidemic*.
 2 John Stott, *The Message of Thessalonians* – his comments on 1 Thess. 5:19 are very helpful here.
 3 David Pytches, *Come, Holy Spirit*, pp. 79–86.
 4 Bruce Yocum, *Prophecy*, p. 116.
 5 Ibid., p. 115.

10 HOW IS PROPHECY MANAGED IN THE LOCAL CHURCH?
 1 C.M. Robeck Jr, article in *Dictionary of Pentecostal and Charismatic Movements*, ed. Stanley M. Burgess and Garry B. McGee, p. 736.
 2 Gordon Strachan, *The Pentecostal Theology of Edward Irving*.
 3 James Ryle, *The Hippo in the Garden*.
 4 J. I. Packer, *Knowing God*, p. 263
 5 Ronald Knox, *Enthusiasm*.

11 PRACTICALITIES FOR PUBLIC WORSHIP
1 J. Moltmann, *The Church in the Power of the Spirit*, p. 292.

12 WHAT ABOUT CHURCH ORDER?
1 *The Canons of the Church of England*, promulgated by the Convocations of Canterbury and York in 1964 and 1969, p. xii.
2 *Certain Sermons or Homilies appointed to be read in Churches*, pp. 109–22.
3 C.S. Lewis, *Surprised by Joy*, p. 139.
4 Martin Lloyd Jones, *The Sovereign Spirit: Discerning His Gifts*, 1985, p. 56.
5 George Bernard Shaw, *Saint Joan*.
6 Michael Green, *To Corinth with Love*, p. 75.

13 TOWARDS A BETTER THEOLOGY
1 Colin Brown, *Philosophy and the Christian Faith*, p. 16.
2 Robert G. Clouse, *The New International Dictionary of the Christian Church*, ed. J. D. Douglas, p. 68.
3 Colin Brown, article in *The History of Christianity*, ed. Tim Dowley, p. 287.
4 Roland Bainton, *Erasmus of Christendom*, p 191.
5 J.H. Merle D'Aubigné, *History of the Reformation of the Sixteenth Century*, p. 584.
6 John Flavel, *Works*, vol. III, p. 482.
7 Richard Holloway, *Evangelical Anglicanism*, eds R.T. France and A.E. McGrath, p. 180.
8 Morton Kelsey, *Healing and Christianity*, pp. 219–20.
9 Richard Sibbes, *Works*, vol. V, p. 129.
10 Morton Kelsey, *Encounter with God*, p. 30.
11 Brown, op. cit., p. 181.
12 Anthony Thistleton, article in *The History of Christianity*, ed. Tim Dowley, p. 600.
13 Brown, op. cit., p. 187, citing *Kerygma and Myth: a Theological Debate*, Eng. trans. R.H. Fuller, ed.

H.W. Bartsch, and Bultmann himself in *Jesus Christ and Mythology*.

14 R.E. Davies, *I Will Pour Out My Spirit – A History and Theology of Revivals and Evangelical Awakenings*, ch. 4, pp. 55–62.

15 J. Moltmann, *The Spirit of Life*, p. 17.

16 Karl Barth, *Evangelical Theology: an Introduction*, p. 58.

17 Karl Rahner, *Visions and Prophecies*, p. 21.

18 Brown, op. cit., p. 139.

19 David Barrett, *World Christian Encyclopedia*, and figures from the Lausanne Statistical Task Force, 1990.

20 Daniel W. Hardy and David F. Ford, *Jubilee – Theology of Praise*, p. 67.

21 David Wilkerson, *The Cross and the Switchblade*.

22 Morton Kelsey, *Encounter with God*, p. 37.

23 Arnold Bittlinger, *Gifts and Graces*, see Preface by Michael Harper.

24 Mark Stibbe, 'The Renewal of Theology and the Theology of Renewal', article in *Anglicans for Renewal*, vol. 51, Winter 1992.

25 Ibid.

26 Morton Kelsey, *Transcend*, p. 17.

27 Stibbe, op. cit.

28 Ibid.

14 PROPHECY IN THE EARLY CHURCH

1 Robert Brow, *Religion: Origins and Ideas*, pp. 55–8.

2 Stephen Neill, *A History of Christian Missions*, pp. 94–6.

3 F.L. Cross (ed.), *The Oxford Dictionary of the Christian Church*, p. 1490.

4 Henry Chadwick, *The Early Church*, p. 63.

5 F.F. Bruce, *The Canon of Scripture*, p. 145.

6 Chadwick, op. cit., pp. 43, 81.

7 Eusebius, *Ecclesiastical History*, Bk I.

8 Ibid., Bk V.

9 K. McDonell and G.T. Montague, *Christian Initiation and Baptism in the Holy Spirit*, pp. 332–3.
10 The Didache, 15: 1–2.
11 Yves Congar, *I Believe in the Holy Spirit*, Vol. I, p. 65.
12 John Wesley, *Journal* – Wed., Aug. 15, 1750.

15 PROPHECY DURING THE DARK AGES
 1 J. Moltmann, *The Church in the Power of the Spirit*, p. 318.
 2 Ibid., p. 320.
 3 Ibid.
 4 Bishop Novatian, *Treatise Concerning the Trinity*, ch. 39.
 5 A. Cleveland Coxe, *Ante-Nicene Fathers*, 5:641.
 6 Benedicta Ward (ed.), *The Lives of the Desert Fathers*, trans. N. Russell.
 7 Irina Gorainov, *The Message of Saint Seraphim*, p. 7. Iulia de Beausobre, *Flame in the Snow*, p. 139.

16 THE FRENCH PROPHETS
 1 B.L. Bresson, *Studies in Ecstasy*, p. 41.
 2 J. Hastings, *Encyclopedia of Religion and Ethics*, Vol. VII, p. 480.
 3 J. M'Clintock and J. Strong, *Encyclopedia of Biblical, Theological and Ecclesiastical Literature*, Vol. IV, pp. 396–7.
 4 Ronald Knox, *Enthusiasm*, p. 366.
 5 Rufus M. Jones, *Spiritual Reformers of the Sixteenth and Seventeenth Centuries*, p. 117.
 6 James Houston, *The Mind on Fire – Blaise Pascal*, see Introduction by Os Guinness, p. 27.

17 THE GERMAN PROPHETS
 1 E.H. Broadbent, *The Pilgrim Church*, p. 103.
 2 J.H. Merle D'Aubigné, *The History of the Reformation of the Sixteenth Century*, p. 579.

3 F.L. Cross (ed.), *The Oxford Dictionary of the Christian Church*, p. 727.
4 R.E. Davies, *I Will Pour Out My Spirit*, p. 61.
5 Cf. chapter 14.
6 Leonard Verduin, *The Reformers and their Stepchildren*, p. 6.
7 Roland Bainton, *Here I Stand*, p. 209.

18 THE RANTERS
1 J.C. Davis, *Fear, Myth and History; The Ranters and the Historians*.
2 John L. Nickalls, *Journal of George Fox*, pp. 195, 212, 232, 279, 525–6, 622.
3 John Bunyan, *Grace Abounding to the Chief of Sinners*, 3rd edn, 1672–4. See the penultimate section, 'A Brief Account of the Author's call to the work of the ministry'.
4 Christopher Hill, *A Turbulent, Seditious, and Factious People – John Bunyan and his Church*, p. 342.
5 Robert Barclay, *The Anarchy of the Ranters*, quoted in Ronald Knox, *Enthusiasm*, p. 172.
6 John Strype, *Life of Cranmer*, 1848–54, vol. ii, ch. 33.
7 Robert Barclay, *An Apology for the True Christian Divinity etc.*, 8th edn, pp. 25–32.
8 Keith Thomas, *Religion and Decline in Magic*, p. 322.
9 Ibid., p. 447.
10 Ibid., p. 470.
11 John Cavalier, *A Collection of Prophetical Warnings of the Eternal Spirit*.
12 Charles Tyler, *The Camisards*, p. 99.
13 J. Sutherland, *The Background for Queen Anne*, 1939, pp. 235–6.
14 Thomas, op. cit., pp. 133–78 for more about Ranter activity.
15 Hill, op. cit., pp. 80–1.
16 Keith Thomas, op. cit., p. 203.

19 THE QUAKERS

1 John L. Nickalls, *Journal of George Fox*, 1975.
2 Ibid., p. 21.
3 Ibid., p. 27.
4 Ibid., p. 33.
5 Ibid., p. 34.
6 Ibid., Introduction, pp. xxxiii-xxxiv.
7 Christopher Hill, *A Turbulent, Seditious, and Factious People – John Bunyan and his Church*, p. 83.
8 Charles Evans, *Friends of the Seventeenth Century*, p. 39.
9 Nickalls, op. cit., pp. 171–2.

20 THE CLASSIC CASE OF EDWARD IRVING

1 Bruce Yokum, *Prophecy*, p. 86.
2 Wayne Grudem, *The Gift of Prophecy*, p. 188.
3 Gordon Strachan, *The Pentecostal Theology of Edward Irving*. This work is the main source for the facts in this chapter.

21 REVELATION AND MYSTICISM

1 William Johnston (intro.), *The Cloud of Unknowing*, p. 7.
2 Garrigou-Lagrange, O.P., *The Three Ages of the Spiritual Life*, 2 vols.
3 Robert G. Tuttle, *John Wesley – His Life and Theology*, p. 140.
4 W.R.Inge, *Christian Mysticism*, Lecture II, p. 39.
5 Peter Toon, *Meditating as a Christian*, p. 150.
6 *The Confessions of Saint Augustine*, p.141; David Bentley-Taylor, *Augustine: Wayward Genius*, pp. 39–40.
7 Inge, op. cit., pp. 335–48.
8 Oliver Davies, *God Within*, p. 1.
9 John of the Cross, *Ascent*, II, 22.
10 Roland Bainton, *Erasmus of Christendom*, p. 178.
11 George Mallone, *Go Bump in the Night*, pp. 9–10.
12 Inge, op. cit., p. 26.
13 Stephen Clark, *Baptized in the Spirit*.

14 Davies, op. cit., p. 48.
15 Joyce Huggett, *Listening to God*, p. 126.
16 John H. Davies, article in Gordon S. Wakefield (ed.), *A Dictionary of Christian Spirituality*, pp. 274–5.
17 Inge, op. cit., p. 16.
18 Wakefield, op. cit.
19 Adolf Harnack, *History of Dogma*, vol. 1, p. 35.
20 John Cornwall, *Powers of Darkness: Powers of Light*, pp. 180–7.
21 J. B. Phillips, *Ring of Truth*, p. 177.

22 PROPHECY AND ECSTASY
1 Gordon S. Wakefield (ed.), *A Dictionary of Christian Spirituality*, p. 281.
2 A. T. Schofield, *Christian Sanity*, p. 3.
3 Ibid., p. 38.
4 George Bernard Shaw, *Saint Joan*, p. 80.
5 Arthur S. Reber, *Dictionary of Psychology*, p. 410.
6 John White, *When the Spirit Comes with Power*, p. 43.
7 Reber, op. cit., p. 359.
8 Ibid., p. 359.
9 J. D. Douglas (ed.), *The New International Dictionary of the Christian Church*, p. 327.
10 F. L. Cross (ed.), *The Oxford Dictionary of the Christian Church*, p. 437.
11 Wakefield, op. cit., p. 125.
12 Alison Peers, *Complete Works of Saint Teresa of Jesus*, cf. *The Interior Castle*.
13 M. A. Screech, *Erasmus – Ecstasy and The Praise of Folly*.
14 Oliver Davies, *God Within*, p. 2.
15 N. J. Perella, *The Kiss, Sacred and Profane*, pp. 90f.
16 David Brainerd, Journal, Dec. 21, 1742, in Jonathan Edwards, *An Account of the Life of Rev. David Brainerd*, p. 316.
17 A. G. Dickens, *The English Reformation*, p. 36.
18 J. Cameron Peddie, *The Forgotten Father*, p. 38.

19 White, op. cit., p. 54.
20 Screech, op. cit., p. 48.

23 RELIGIOUS EXPERIENCE VALIDATED
1 Jonathan Edwards, *The Religious Affections*, p. 14.
2 Jonathan Edwards, *A Treatise Concerning Religious Affections*, in *The Works of Jonathan Edwards*, p. 243.
3 Ibid., p. 238.
4 C. S. Lewis, *Surprised by Joy*, p. 7.
5 Ibid., pp. 18–19.
6 Ibid., p. 19.
7 Ibid., pp. 19–20.
8 Ibid., p. 204.
9 Edwards, *A Treatise*, op. cit., p. 237.
10 John White, *When the Spirit Comes with Power*, p. 51.
11 Edwards, *A Treatise*, op. cit., p. 237.
12 White, op. cit., p. 50.
13 Ibid., pp. 54–5.
14 Martin Lloyd Jones, *Joy Unspeakable*, p. 18.
15 Morton Kelsey, *Encounter with God*, p. 24.
16 Colin Brown, *Philosophy and the Christian Faith*, p. 108.
17 Robert Brow, *Religion: Origin and Ideas*, ch. 13.
18 Julian of Norwich, *Revelations of Divine Love*, p. xx.
19 Lewis, op. cit., p. 54.
20 Ibid., p. 136.

24 WHAT ABOUT SECOND SIGHT?
1 J. Stafford Wright, *What is Man?*, p. 172.
2 Ibid., p. 53.
3 H. R. Trevor-Roper, *The European Witch-craze of the Sixteenth and Seventeenth Centuries*, p. 12.
4 Wright, op. cit., p. 55.
5 Kurt Koch, *Christian Counselling and Occultism*, p. 208.
6 John and Paula Sandford, *The Elijah Task*, pp. 156–7.

7 Morton Kelsey, *The Christian and the Supernatural*.
8 Wright, op. cit.
9 Eugene Osty, *Normal Faculties in Man: An Experimental Study*.

25 DO NON-CHRISTIANS RECEIVE REVELATION FROM GOD?
1 Robert Brow, *Religion: Origin and Ideas*, p. 27.
2 John Bunyan, *Grace Abounding to the Chief of Sinners*, para. 5.
3 Kurt Koch, *The Revival in Indonesia*.
4 W.M. Wilkinson, *The Revival in its Physical, Psychical, and Religious Aspects*.
5 Peter Wagner, 'A Third Wave', *Pastoral Renewal*, July–Aug. 1983, pp. 1–5.
6 Edward J. Young, *My Servants the Prophets*, p. 176.
7 Judith Tydings, *Gathering a People – Catholic Saints in Charismatic Perspective*, p. 243. See also Abbot Wiesenger, *Occult Phenomena in the Light of Theology*.
8 John A. Sandford, *God's Forgotten Language*, p. 10.

26 FORBIDDEN FRUIT FOR PROPHETS
1 J.N.D. Anderson (ed.), *The World's Religions*, p. 9.
2 W.J. Coleman, SJ, *Latin American Catholicism*.
3 Erika Cheetham, *The Prophecies of Nostradamus*, p. 20.
4 James Laver, *Nostradamus*.
5 J. Stafford Wright, *What is Man?*, p. 52.
6 Laver, op. cit., p. 151.
7 Wright, op. cit., p. 52.
8 J. Bruce and T.T. Perowne (eds), *Correspondence of Matthew Parker*, p. 59.
9 Keith Thomas, *Religion and the Decline of Magic*, provides numerous examples, especially in ch. 13.
10 David Pytches, *Some Said It Thundered*, Appendix. This material was adapted from J. Stafford Wright, *Christianity and the Occult*, and repeated

here to create a complete textbook as far as possible.

11 Wright, *What is Man?* op. cit., p. 53.

CONCLUSION

1 C.M. Robeck Jr, article in *Dictionary of Pentecostal and Charismatic Movements*, p. 740.

APPENDIX: REVELATION AND THE HUMAN BRAIN

1 Russell P. Spittler, *Suggested Areas for Further Research in Pentecostal Studies*, paper presented to the Society for Pentecostal Studies, Nov. 20, 1982.

2 William E. Vine, *Expository Dictionary of Biblical Words*, p. 48.

3 J. F. Webb and D. H. Farmer (trs), *The Age of Bede*, pp. 43–4.

4 Thomas R. Blakeslee, *The Right Brain*. This book has been the main source for this chapter.

BIBLIOGRAPHY

Anderson, J.N.D. (ed.), *The World's Religions*, IVF, 1950.

Aquinas, Thomas, *Summa Theologica*,

Attlee, Rosemary, *William's Story*, Highland, Crowborough, 1987.

Aune, David, *Prophecy in Early Christianity and the Ancient Mediterranean World*, Eerdmans, Grand Rapids, 1983.

Bainton, Roland, *Erasmus of Christendom*, Lion, Oxford, 1988.

Bainton, Roland, *Here I Stand*, Lion, Oxford, 1990.

Barclay, Robert, *The Anarchy of the Ranters*, 1676.

Barclay, Robert, *An Apology for the True Christian Divinity etc.*, 8th edn, Baskerville, 1765.

Barrett, David, *World Christian Encyclopedia*, OUP, Oxford, 1982.

Barth, Karl, *Evangelical Theology: an Introduction*, T. & T. Clark, 1980.

Beckwith, Roger, *The Old Testament Canon of the New Testament Church*, SPCK, London, 1985.

Bentley-Taylor, David, *Augustine: Wayward Genius*, Hodder and Stoughton, London, 1980.

Bittlinger, Arnold, *Gifts and Graces*, Hodder and Stoughton, London, 1967.

Blakeslee, Thomas R., *The Right Brain*, JJB, New York, 1983.

Bockmuehl, Klaus, *Listening to the God who Speaks*, Helmers & Howard, Colorado Springs, 1990.

Bolshakoff, Sergius, *The Russian Mystics*, Mowbray, London, 1977.

Brainerd, David, *Journal*, Dec. 21, 1742, in Jonathan Edwards, *An Account of the Life of Rev. David Brainerd*, Boston, 1749.

Bresson, B. L., *Studies in Ecstasy*, Vantage Press, 1966.

Broadbent, E. H., *The Pilgrim Church*, Pickering and Inglis, Basingstoke, 1974.

Brow, Robert, *Religion: Origins and Ideas*, Tyndale Press, 1966.

Brown, Colin, *Philosophy and the Christian Faith*, Tyndale Press, 1969.

Bruce, F.F., *The Canon of Scripture*, Chapter House, Glasgow, 1988.

Bruce, J. and Perowne, T.T. (eds), *Correspondence of Matthew Parker*, Cambridge, 1853.

Budgen, Victor, *Charismatics and the Word of God*, Evangelical Press, Darlington, 1986.

Bunyan, John, *Grace Abounding to the Chief of Sinners*, 3rd edn, 1672–74.

Bunyan, John, *Grace Abounding to the Chief of Sinners*, SCM Press, London, 1955.

Canty, George, *The Practice of Pentecost*, Marshall Pickering, Basingstoke, 1987.

Carretto, Carlo, *The Desert in the City*, Collins, London 1979.

Carson, D.A., *Showing the Spirit: A Theological Exposition of 1 Corinthians 12–14*, Baker Book House, Grand Rapids, 1987.

Cartledge, M.J., *Prophecy in the Contemporary Church: A Theological Examination*, M. Phil. thesis, 1989, Library of London Bible College.

Cavalier, John, *A Collection of Prophetical Warnings of the Eternal Spirit*, Thomas Whitehead, Bristol, 1709.

Chadwick, Henry, *The Early Church*, Penguin Books, Harmondsworth, 1967.

Cheetham, Erika, *The Prophecies of Nostradamus*, New York, 1981.

Clark, Stephen, *Baptized in the Spirit*, Paulist Press, 1969.

Clouse, Robert G., *The New International Dictionary of the Christian Church*, ed. J.D. Douglas, Zondervan, Grand Rapids, 1974.

Coleman, W.J., SJ, *Latin American Catholicism*, New York, 1958.

Congar, Yves, *I Believe in the Holy Spirit*, vol. I, Geoffrey Chapman, London, 1983.

Cornwell, John, *Powers of Darkness: Powers of Light*, Viking, London, 1991.

Coxe, A. Cleveland, *Ante-Nicene Fathers*, Grand Rapids, 1951.

Cross, F.L. (ed.), *The Oxford Dictionary of the Christian Church*, OUP, Oxford, 1961.

Cruden, Robert, *Concordance*, Lutterworth, Cambridge, 1943.

Davies, Oliver, *God Within*, Darton, Longman and Todd, London, 1988.

Davies, R.E., *I Will Pour Out My Spirit – A History and Theology of Revivals and Evangelical Awakenings*, Monarch, Eastbourne, 1992.

Davis, J.C., *Fear, Myth and History: The Ranters and the Historians*, CUP, Cambridge, 1986.

De Beausobre, Iulia, *Flame in the Snow*, Collins, 1979.

Dickens, A.G., *The English Reformation*, Collins, London, 1974.

Dickens, Charles, *A Tale of Two Cities*, Chapman and Hall, London.

Douglas, J.D. (ed.), *The New International Dictionary of the Christian Church*, Paternoster Press, Exeter, 1974.

Dowley, Tim, *The History of Christianity*, Lion, Oxford, 1977.

Driot, Marcel, *Fathers of the Desert*, St Paul Publications, Slough, 1992.

Edwards, David, *Church Times* review of Diana Collins, *Partners in Protest* (Gollancz, 1992) Oct. 2, 1992.

Edwards, Jonathan, *The Religious Affections*, London, 1898.

Edwards, Jonathan, *A Treatise Concerning Religious Affections*, in *The Works of Jonathan Edwards*, Banner of Truth, Edinburgh, 1974.

Evans, Charles, *Friends of the Seventeenth Century*, Philadelphia, 1885.

Finney, John, *Finding Faith Today – How Does It Happen?*, B & F Bible Society, 1992.

Flavel, John, *Works*, Vol. III, Banner of Truth, Edinburgh, 1982.

Gorainov, Irina, *The Message of Saint Seraphim*, Fairacres Publications, 1987.

Green, Michael, *To Corinth with Love*, Hodder and Stoughton, London, 1982.

Grudem, Wayne, *The Gift of Prophecy*, Kingsway, Eastbourne, 1988.

Hagin, K.E., *Seven Steps for Judging Prophecy*, Kenneth Hagin Ministries, 1982.

Hamon, Bill, *Prophets and Personal Prophecy*, Destiny Image, 1991.

Hamon, Bill, *Prophets and the Prophetic Movement*, Destiny Image, 1990.

Hardy, D.W. and Ford, D.F., *Jubilate: Theology of Praise*, Darton, Longman and Todd, London, 1984.

Harper, Michael, *Prophecy – A Gift for the Body of Christ*, Logos International, 1964.

Hastings, J., *Encyclopedia of Religion and Ethics*, vol. VII, New York, 1914.

Hay, David, *Exploring Inner Space*, Mowbray, London, 1987.

Hill, Christopher, *A Turbulent, Seditious, and Factious People – John Bunyan and his Church*, OUP, Oxford, 1989.

Hill, Clifford, *Prophecy Past and Present*, Highland, Crowborough, 1989.

Hill, David, *New Testament Prophecy*, Marshall, Morgan and Scott, 1979.

Holloway, Richard, *Another Country, Another King*, Collins, London, 1991.

Holloway, Richard, eds R.T. France and A.E. McGrath, *Evangelical Anglicanism*, SPCK, London, 1993.

Houston, Graham, *Prophecy Now*, IVP, Leicester, 1989.

Houston, James, *The Mind on Fire – Blaise Pascal*, Hodder and Stoughton, London, 1989.

Huggett, John and Christine, *It Hurts to Heal*, Kingsway, Eastbourne, 1984.

Huggett, Joyce, *Listening to God*, Hodder and Stoughton, London, 1986.

Inge, W.R., *Christian Mysticism*, Methuen, 1899.

Jackson, John Paul, *Streams of Shiloh*, Quad Cities VCF, 1992.

Johnston, William (intro.), *The Cloud of Unknowing*, Doubleday, London, 1973.

Jones, Rufus M., *Spiritual Reformers of the Sixteenth and Seventeenth Centuries*, Macmillan, 1914.

Josephus, *The Jewish Wars*, Penguin Books, Harmondsworth, 1981.

Kay, William K., *Prophecy*, Lifestream, 1991.

Kelsey, Morton, *Encounter with God*, Minneapolis, Minnesota, 1972.

Kelsey, Morton, *Healing and Christianity*, Harper and Row, 1973.

Kelsey, Morton, *The Christian and the Supernatural*, Minneapolis, Minnesota, 1976.

Kelsey, Morton, *Transcend*, Crossroad, New York, 1981.

Kissell, Barry, *Walking on Water*, Hodder and Stoughton, London, 1986.

Knox, Ronald, *Enthusiasm*, Collins, London, 1987.

Koch, Kurt, *The Revival in Indonesia*, Evangelisation Publishers, c. 1970.

Koch, Kurt, *Christian Counselling and Occultism*, Kregel Publications, Grand Rapids, 1972.

Laver, James, *Nostradamus*, Collins, 1942, reissued by Penguin Books, 1952.

Lewis, C.S., *Surprised by Joy*, Fontana Books, London, 1960.

Lloyd Jones, Martin, *Joy Unspeakable*, Harold Shaw, Wheaton, Illinois, 1985.

Lloyd Jones, Martin, *The Sovereign Spirit: Discerning His Gifts*, Harold Shaw, Wheaton, Illinois, 1985.

Lygo, Francie, a report about her in *HTB in Focus*, Oct. 11, 1992.

McDonell, K. and Montague, G. T., *Christian Initiation and Baptism in the Holy Spirit*, Minnesota, 1991.

M'Clintock, J. and Strong J., *Encyclopedia of Biblical, Theological and Ecclesiastical Literature*, Vol. IV, Harper & Bros, 1873.

MacNutt, Francis, *Overcome by the Spirit*, Eagle, Guildford, 1991.

Mallone, George, *Arming for Spiritual Warfare*, IVP, Leicester, 1991.

Marshall, Catherine, *Something More*, Hodder and Stoughton, London, 1977.

Masters, Peter, *The Healing Epidemic*, The Wakeman Trust, London, 1988.

Merle D'Aubigny, J.H., *History of the Reformation of the Sixteenth Century*, Ward, Lock & Co., London, 1838.

Mitton, Michael, *Sounds of God*, Highland, Guildford, 1993.

Moltmann, J., *The Church in the Power of the Spirit*, SCM Press, London, 1977.

Mother Julian of Norwich, *Revelations of Divine Love*, ed. Halcyon Backhouse and Rhona Pipe, Hodder and Stoughton, London, 1987.

Murray, Iain, *Jonathan Edwards – A New Biography*, Banner of Truth, Edinburgh, 1987.

Murray, Iain (ed.), *George Whitefield's Journals*, Banner of Truth, Edinburgh, 1989.

Nickalls, John L., *Journal of George Fox* (rev. edn based on Thomas Ellwood edn, 1694), 1975.

Nuttall, Geoffrey F., *The Holy Spirit in Puritan Faith and Experience*, Blackwell, Oxford, 1946.

Osty, Eugene, *Normal Faculties in Man: An Experimental Study*, Methuen, 1923.

Packer, J.I., *Knowing God*, Hodder and Stoughton, London, 1973.

Packer, J.I., *Keep in Step with the Spirit*, IVP, Leicester, 1984.

Packer, J.I., *A Passion for Holiness*, Crossway, East Sussex, 1992.

Pain, Timothy, *Prophecy*, Kingsway, Eastbourne, 1986.

Pawson, David, 'Prophecy and Scripture', *Renewal*, Oct. 1990.

Peddie, J. Cameron, *The Forgotten Talent*, Fontana Books, 1966.

Peers, Alison, *Complete Works of Saint Teresa of Jesus*, Burns, Oates and Washbourne Ltd, London, 1951, cf. *The Interior Castle*, 1963.

Perella, N.J., *The Kiss, Sacred and Profane*, California, 1969.

Phillips, J.B., *Ring of Truth*, Hodder and Stoughton, London, 1967.

Pytches, David, *Come, Holy Spirit*, Hodder and Stoughton, London, 1985.

Pytches, David, *Some Said It Thundered*, Hodder and Stoughton, London, 1990.

Rahner, Karl, *Visions and Prophecies*, Herder & Herder, New York, 1963.

Rea, John, *The Holy Spirit in the Bible*, Marshall Pickering, Basingstoke, 1992.

Reber, Arthur S., *Dictionary of Psychology*, Penguin, 1987.

Robeck, C.M., Jr, article in *Dictionary of Pentecostal and Charismatic Movements*, eds Stanley M. Burgess and Garry B. McGee, Zondervan, Grand Rapids.

Ryle, James, *The Hippo in the Garden*, Highland, Guildford, 1992.

Sandford, John and Paula, *The Elijah Task*, Logos International, 1977.

Sanford, Agnes, *Sealed Orders*, Logos International, 1972.

Sanford, John A., *God's Forgotten Language*, 1960.

Schofield, A.T., *Christian Sanity*, Marshall Bros, 1908.

Screech, M.A., *Erasmus – Ecstasy and The Praise of Folly*, Penguin Books, Harmondsworth, 1980.

Shaw, George Bernard, *St Joan*, Penguin Books, Harmondsworth, 1950.

Sibbes, Richard, *Works*, Banner of Truth Trust, Edinburgh, 1977.

Slack, Kenneth, *Martin Luther King*, SCM Press, London, 1970.

Spittler, Russell P., *Suggested Areas for Further Research in Pentecostal Studies*, paper presented to the Society for Pentecostal Studies, Nov. 20, 1982.

Stibbe, Mark, 'The Renewal of Theology and the Theology of Renewal', in *Anglicans for Renewal*, vol. 51, Winter 1992.

Stott, John, *The Message of Thessalonians*, IVP, Leicester, 1991.

Stott, John, *The Contemporary Christian*, IVP, Leicester, 1992.

Strachan, Gordon, *The Pentecostal Theology of Edward Irving*, Darton, Longman and Todd, London, 1973.

Strype, John, *Life of Cranmer*, 1848–54.

Sutherland, J., *The Background for Queen Anne*, 1939.

Thistleton, Anthony, article in *The History of Christianity*, ed. Tim Dowley, Lion, Oxford, 1977.

Thomas, Keith, *Religion and Decline of Magic*, Penguin Books, Harmondsworth, 1985.

Toon, Peter, *Meditating as a Christian*, Collins, London, 1991.

Trevor-Roper, H.R., *The European Witch-craze of the Sixteenth and Seventeenth Centuries*, Penguin Books, Hardmondsworth, 1969.

Turner, Max, *Spiritual Gifts Then and Now*, Vox Evangelica, 1985.

Tuttle, Robert G., *John Wesley – His Life and Theology*, Zondervan, Grand Rapids, 1978.

Tydings, Judith, *Gathering a People – Catholic Saints in Charismatic Perspective*, Logos International, 1977.

Tyler, Charles, *The Camisards*, Simpkin, Marshall, Hamilton, Kent and Co., 1893.

Verduin, Leonard, *The Reformers and their Stepchildren*, Paternoster Press, Exeter, 1964.

Vine, William E., *Expository Dictionary of Biblical Words*, Nelson, 1985.

Wagner, Peter, *Pastoral Renewal* (July-August 1983).

Wakefield, Gordon S. (ed.), *A Dictionary of Christian Spirituality*, SCM Press, London, 1983.

Ward, Benedicta (ed.), *The Lives of the Desert Fathers*, trans. N. Russell, Mowbray, Oxford, 1981.

Ware, Kallistos, *The Orthodox Way*, Mowbray, London, 1979.

Welldon, J.E.C., *The Revelation of the Holy Spirit*, Macmillan, London, 1902.

Wesley, John, *Journal*.

White, John, *When the Spirit Comes with Power*, IVP, USA, 1988.

Whitney, Donald S., *Spiritual Disciplines for the Christian Life*, Scripture Press, 1991.

Wiesinger, Abbot, *Occult Phenomena in the Light of Theology*, London, 1957.

Wilkerson, David, *The Cross and the Switchblade*, Marshall Pickering, Basingstoke, 1974.

Wilkinson, W.M., *The Revival in its Physical, Psychical, and Religious Aspects*, London, 1859.

Wimber, John, *Power Evangelism*, Hodder and Stoughton, London, 1992.

Wright, C.J., 'The Nature of the Gift of Prophecy in the New Testament', Unpublished thesis, index no. 12929/89, London Bible College Library, 1989.

Wright, J. Stafford, *What is Man?*, Paternoster Press, Exeter, 1955.

Yocum, Bruce, *Prophecy*, Word of Life, 1976.

Young, E.J., *My Servants the Prophets*, Eerdmans, Grand Rapids, 1980.